DYNASTY

DYNASTY

Co-Editors
JOE HOPPEL
MIKE NAHRSTEDT
STEVE ZESCH

Statistical Research
CRAIG CARTER

Design
MIKE BRUNER

President and Chief Executive Officer
RICHARD WATERS

Book Publisher
GREGORY WILEY

Editorial Director of Books and Periodicals
RON SMITH

The Sporting News

Published in the United States by THE SPORTING NEWS
Publishing Co., 1212 North Lindbergh Boulevard,
St. Louis, Missouri 63132.

Library of Congress Catalog Card Number: 89-61708

ISBN: 0-89204-313-X
10 9 8 7 6 5 4 3 2 1

First Edition

Table
Of
Contents

Introduction

"Break up the Yankees."

That plaintive cry, emanating from fans and journalists alike, was heard time and again in the late 1930s and early 1940s. After a brief respite, the lament was heard once more in the late '40s. It echoed through the 1950s and re-echoed well into the 1960s.

Everyone outside the Bronx, or so it seemed, had seen enough of the New York Yankees' domination. Seven American League pennants in eight seasons. Then, 14 league championships in a 16-year stretch. And all of this *after* Babe Ruth had completed his tenure in a Yankee uniform.

Clearly, there was an oft-expressed yearning for someone to rise up and knock the Yankees from their lofty perch. In fact, fans throughout the American League flocked to their home ball parks with the hope of seeing the local team take the measure of the vaunted New Yorkers.

Those same Yankee-hating fans went to the park for other reasons, too—ones they seldom wished to acknowledge. The truth is, they wanted to see baseball's greatest practitioners at work. They wanted to see the game played as it was meant to be played. They wanted to see majestic home runs, ringing doubles, fielding wizardry, pitching mastery and all-around heads-up play. Maybe, just maybe, the home club could provide a few of those thrills. The Yankees, though, almost surely could.

Yes, those fans wanted to see the Yankees lose, but most of all they wanted to see the Yankees play. They wanted to see the very best. They wanted to see winners of the highest order.

Winning, of course, tends to breed contempt among ne'er-do-well teams and their fans. But success also brings admiration—albeit grudging approval at times—and if perpetuated to dynastic proportions, it produces a tradition of excellence that sets one franchise or two apart from all the rest in that sport.

The Yankees set themselves apart. So, too, did the the Boston Celtics. The Green Bay Packers. The UCLA Bruins basketball team. The Montreal Canadiens. The Pittsburgh Steelers. The Brooklyn Dodgers. The Notre Dame football squad. The Los Angeles Lakers. The Cleveland Browns. The New York Islanders. And the Oklahoma Sooners football team.

Attaining an occasional championship is heady stuff in itself. But maintaining top-of-the-mountain status over an extended period—thereby creating that magical reign known as a *dynasty*—takes an amalgam of talents and a bit of luck that few teams in any sport have ever realized.

In "Dynasty," The Sporting News explores the manner in which the sports world's perennially successful teams were molded. The special qualities of the men at the controls, the managers and coaches, are conveyed in word and deed, and the consummate skills of the on-field performers are brought to life with recollections of the glory of their times. On the professional level, the deft work of always-a-step-ahead front offices receives in-depth attention.

"Dynasty," which focuses on what we believe are the top 12 athletic teams in history in terms of sustained success, captures the unmistakable aura of superiority. Winning, after all, is more than simply outscoring the opposition. It is sights and sounds and places. Symbols of excellence. An attitude. A feeling.

Indeed, a dynasty is the Yankee pinstripes and the monuments at Yankee Stadium. The parquet floor and championship banners at Boston Garden. Vince Lombardi exhorting his troops. The Wizard of Westwood. The Forum in Montreal. The Steel Curtain. The frenzy that was Ebbets Field. Notre Dame's Johnny Lujack making the quintessential big play. "Showtime," featuring Magic Johnson. The organizational genius of Paul Brown. The fury of a bone-jarring body check, as leveled by a member of the New York Islanders. Oklahoma's fleet Sooners racing back to the line of scrimmage.

The 12 teams in this reflection on greatness proved they could pass virtually any test on the field, on the court or on the ice. Most of all, they proved that their special talents could stand the test of time—the stuff of which dynasties are made.

By 1972, they were venerable old-timers who had thrilled two different generations of Yankee fans with their extraordinary baseball talents: No. 5 Joe DiMaggio and No. 7 Mickey Mantle.

Nearly 30 years separated their yearnings to be Yankees. It was 1921, when the first of 33 American League pennants would be won by the storied franchise, that Tommy Henrich caught the glimmer of New York. The Yankees were then just beginning to rumble forth into dominance.

By the time Bobby Richardson had similar aspirations, it was almost 1950. The Yankees by then had reigned through the majestic era of Joe McCarthy and were embarking on an even grander period under Casey Stengel and Ralph Houk that would leave them without equals.

"I remember when I was coming along, there was no draft involved, so you could sign with any ball club," Richardson said. "And when I was 14 years old playing American Legion baseball, they took our team out to see a film, 'Pride of the Yankees,' the story of Lou Gehrig. Gary Cooper played the part.

"And at that time as a 14-year-old, I thought, 'Man, what a great organization.' Next year at 15, Mayo Smith, who was managing a farm club (the Yankees' Amsterdam, N.Y., team) that had spring training in my hometown of Sumter, S.C., came over to me after a high school game and said, 'When you graduate, I'll see to it that you have a chance to sign with the Yankees.' So all my years in high school and playing ball in American Legion, I was aiming toward the Yankees...I signed with the Yankees right out of high school."

Henrich followed a more roundabout path. A Massillon, Ohio, native, he had signed with the Cleveland Indians in 1934 and played well for three seasons in the minor leagues. When Commissioner Kenesaw Mountain Landis ruled that the Indians had impeded the outfield prospect's advancement to the majors—the commissioner said the Indians had moved him around in the minors to fend off other big-league clubs' interest in the Ohioan—Henrich was declared a free agent. He joined the Yankees in 1937, after they outbid everyone and signed Henrich for $25,000.

"As a young boy 8 years of age, I rooted for nobody but the Yankees because of Babe Ruth," Henrich remembered. "When I got a chance to get away from Cleveland and sign and go over to the New York Yankees, that was, oh, what are the words, a dream come true. When I got there, I said, 'Man alive.'"

Henrich and Richardson are part of a rich sporting mosaic, two of the many pieces that contributed to an unprecedented run of success. From 1936 through 1943, the Yankees won seven pennants and six World Series. Following a wartime respite, they regrouped. Starting in 1949, the Yankees won 14 pennants over the next 16 seasons and added nine Series victories—including a record five straight from 1949 through 1953—to their championship haul.

A declining farm system, the institution of the amateur draft and the sale of the team to the Co-lumbia Broadcasting System helped halt that success after 1964. In the nearly quarter century since then, the Yankees have won just three pennants—in 1977, 1978 and 1981—or about what they used to win in half a decade or less. Oh, the Yankees did rule the American League's East Division five times from 1976 through '81, but this is a franchise that measures its success in league championships and World Series titles.

Even today, as the Yankees evoke their storied past and struggle forward, they are surrounded by a ghostly remnant in Yankee Stadium itself. When the ball park was closed and remodeled after the 1973 season, the seating capacity was cut some 11,000 from 65,000 and reductions were made in the outfield canyons. Since the reopening of the park in 1976, the capacity has been readjusted to 57,545.

"Just that stadium, it doesn't exist anymore," said Jerry Coleman, a Yankee infielder from 1949 through 1957. "Four hundred sixty-one feet to center field; I don't think people realize how big and massive that is. It had that huge triple deck with the facade up there. You'd get days like July 4th when they'd hang the pennants out there. My God, it was like going into a cathedral, really. To people who were trying to make their living in that sport, it's very impressive.

"The difference between New York then and now was there was no second place...Second or third didn't mean a thing. Either you won or you lost; consequently, we were all aware of that.

"It's the biggest media market in the world, the biggest city in our country. And the pinstripes by themselves...It's all there, and it's built on itself even though they don't win (anymore). If you talk to anybody in baseball about *the* most dominant team in this century, it's got to be the New York Yankees."

The 1920s were the foundation for the two towering eras that followed. With six pennants in that decade, along with three Series titles, the Yankee teams led by Ruth helped baseball rise from the muck of the 1919 Black Sox scandal. McCarthy, who became the Yankees' manager in 1931, added another pennant and Series victory in 1932. But by 1936, the Yankees had lost a bit of their brilliance. They had finished second for three successive years and had won just one pennant in the last seven seasons.

The Dynasty To End All Dynasties

By Jack Etkin

Veteran Yankee pitcher Lefty Gomez and New York Giant counterpart Carl Hubbell are the center of media attention before the opening of the 1936 World Series.

The Yankees, despite their winning riff in the Roaring '20s, weren't then statistically elite. In the National League, whose 1876 beginnings gave it 25 more years of history than the American League, the Chicago Cubs had won 14 pennants and the New York Giants 13. Even in the American League, the Philadelphia Athletics with nine flags had won two more times than the Yankees going into the 1936 season.

New York returned to the top spot in '36, and the emphatic nature of the Yankees' triumph was noted by John Foster in the Spalding Official Baseball Guide. "Their progress was that of the slow but certain motion of the irresistible avalanche," Foster wrote, "and they crushed the entire league before them as they moved steadily onward to indisputable victory." On May 10, the Yankees moved into first place. For good. They clinched the pennant on September 9, the earliest date in league history to that point, and coasted home 102-51, 19½ games ahead of the second-place Detroit Tigers. That was a league record margin; the 1927 Yankees had won the pennant by 19 games. And in 1936, the Yankees set a major league mark with 182 home runs.

First baseman Lou Gehrig led the majors with 49 homers while hitting .354 and driving in 152 runs. He also paced the majors with 167 runs scored and 130 walks and was named the American League's Most Valuable Player.

Among Yankee regulars, only second baseman Tony Lazzeri and shortstop Frank Crosetti failed to hit .300, which were trifling statistical transgressions considering their other offensive contributions. Lazzeri batted .287 with 14 homers and 109 runs batted in and set an A.L. record for RBIs in one game with 11 against Philadelphia on May 24. His spree against the Athletics included three homers, two of which were grand slams. Crosetti hit one point higher than his double-play partner and homered 15 times with 78 RBIs.

Third baseman Red Rolfe batted .319 with 10 homers and 70 RBIs. Catcher Bill Dickey hit a career-high .362 but without sacrificing power: 22 homers and 107 RBIs.

Outfielder George Selkirk had a .308 season, embellished by 18 homers and 107 RBIs, and Jake Powell, acquired in mid-June from Washington for Ben Chapman, went .306, 7, 48, with the Yankees.

**The rookie, Joe DiMaggio (second from right), and the veteran, Lou Gehrig (right), pose
with fellow New Yorkers Mel Ott (left) and Joe Moore during the 1936 World Series.**

Powell initially played center field for the Yankees, with Selkirk and a kid named Joe DiMaggio alternating between right and left field. By August, DiMaggio had been moved to center, flanked by Powell in left and Selkirk in right.

The Yankees had bought DiMaggio for $25,000 from the San Francisco Seals of the Pacific Coast League, and the 21-year-old DiMaggio drove to New York's 1936 spring camp in St. Petersburg, Fla., with Lazzeri and Crosetti, both of whom also lived in San Francisco.

"The three of us were riding in Tony's car," Crosetti recalled. "About the end of the first day, Tony said, 'Let's let the dago kid drive a while.' He said, 'I don't know how to drive.' I said, 'Let's throw the bum out.'"

There was more needling when DiMaggio reached the Yankees' clubhouse. Pitcher Red Ruffing, who would go 20-12 that year, the first of his four successive 20-victory seasons, greeted the rookie with: "So you're the great DiMaggio. I've heard all about you. You hit .400 on the Coast, and you'll probably hit .800 here because we don't play night games and throw in a nice, shiny white ball anytime

one gets the least bit soiled."

DiMaggio, who in fact had batted .398 in the PCL in 1935 and put together a 61-game batting streak as an 18-year-old Coast Leaguer two seasons earlier, injured his ankle while sliding early in the Yankees' exhibition schedule. During treatment under a diathermy lamp, he suffered a badly burned foot. The Yankees opened the season without him, and it wasn't until May 3 that DiMaggio was able to make his official big-league debut.

On a rainy Sunday afternoon at Yankee Stadium, DiMaggio broke into the majors with two singles and a triple as the Yankees pounded the St. Louis Browns, 14-5. That beginning would end in a .323 season, the first of DiMaggio's 13 with the Yankees, and a Series victory. In addition to his impressive batting average, the rookie sensation clubbed 29 home runs and knocked in 125 runs.

In the first Subway Series since 1923 and the Yankees' first fall classic without Ruth, the Yanks beat the Giants in six games. After falling to Carl Hubbell in Game 1 and thereby ending a Series winning streak of 12 games (four-game sweeps in 1927, 1928 and 1932), the resourceful Yankees pounded out 17

The Yankees' Iron Horse with Manager Joe McCarthy on Lou Gehrig Day in 1939.

Dynasty Data
Yearly Record
1936-1943

Year	W	L	Pct.	GA(+)/GB	Place	Manager
1936	102	51	.667	+19½	1st	J. McCarthy
1937	102	52	.662	+13	1st	J. McCarthy
1938	99	53	.651	+ 9½	1st	J. McCarthy
1939	106	45	.702	+17	1st	J. McCarthy
1940	88	66	.571	2	3rd	J. McCarthy
1941	101	53	.656	+17	1st	J. McCarthy
1942	103	51	.669	+ 9	1st	J. McCarthy
1943	98	56	.636	+13½	1st	J. McCarthy

1949-1964

Year	W	L	Pct.	GA(+)/GB	Place	Manager
1949	97	57	.630	+ 1	1st	C. Stengel
1950	98	56	.636	+ 3	1st	C. Stengel
1951	98	56	.636	+ 5	1st	C. Stengel
1952	95	59	.617	+ 2	1st	C. Stengel
1953	99	52	.656	+ 8½	1st	C. Stengel
1954	103	51	.669	8	2nd	C. Stengel
1955	96	58	.623	+ 3	1st	C. Stengel
1956	97	57	.630	+ 9	1st	C. Stengel
1957	98	56	.636	+ 8	1st	C. Stengel
1958	92	62	.597	+10	1st	C. Stengel
1959	79	75	.513	15	3rd	C. Stengel
1960	97	57	.630	+ 8	1st	C. Stengel
1961	109	53	.673	+ 8	1st	R. Houk
1962	96	66	.593	+ 5	1st	R. Houk
1963	104	57	.646	+10½	1st	R. Houk
1964	99	63	.611	+ 1	1st	Y. Berra
Total	2356	1362	.634			
Under McCarthy	799	427	.652			
Under Stengel	1149	696	.623			
Under Houk	309	176	.637			

Additional Data

Best Record—1939 (106-45).

Worst Record—1948 (84-70).

Longest Winning Streak—18 games from May 27 through June 14 (second game), 1953.

Longest Losing Streak—9 games from June 21 (second game) through July 1, 1953.

Best Record vs. One Opponent, Season—19-3 vs. St. Louis, 1939; Baltimore, 1955; Kansas City, 1957.

Worst Record vs. One Opponent, Season—8-14 vs. Detroit, 1940 and 1959.

hits, enabling Lefty Gomez to cruise to an 18-4 victory in Game 2. The following day, the Yankees were held to four hits by Freddie Fitzsimmons but still won, 2-1. They finished the Giants and capped their season with a seven-run ninth inning that sealed Game 6, 13-5.

That outburst was something of a prelude for the 1937 season. The Yankees again coasted, this time taking the measure of the runner-up Tigers by 13 games while compiling a 102-52 record. Gehrig had what was to be his last monstrous season. DiMaggio, meanwhile, exceeded him in most statistical categories.

In the American League batting race, Gehrig at .351 and DiMaggio at .346 finished second and third, respectively, behind the Tigers' Charlie Gehringer, .371.

DiMaggio led the majors with 46 homers, while Gehrig's 37 ranked third. With 167 RBIs, DiMaggio finished second behind Detroit's Hank Greenberg, 183, and just ahead of Gehrig, 159.

Gomez, 21-11, and Ruffing, 20-7, were one-two in the league in victories, and Gomez led it with an earned-run average of 2.33, 194 strikeouts and six shutouts. It was the fourth and final 20-victory season for Gomez, who finally wound down with the

Yankees in 1942 before finishing his big-league career with Washington in 1943.

Only Gomez could kid the rather private DiMaggio. But then no one was immune to Gomez's humor, which was just as often self-effacing.

Toward the end of his Yankee days, Gomez, who compiled a 189-102 major league record in 14 seasons, got a message of sorts from McCarthy. "Lefty, I don't think you're throwing as hard as you used to," the manager told him.

"You're wrong, Joe," Gomez replied. "I'm throwing twice as hard, but the ball isn't going as fast."

Years after his retirement, Gomez could mirthfully harken back to his playing days. In the summer of 1969, he and his wife were watching man's first walk on the moon. "They were talking back and forth, picking up pieces of the moon's surface," Gomez said. "Then they saw a strange white rock, something they couldn't identify.

"I said to my wife, 'I know what that is. It's a ball Jimmie Foxx hit off me.' "

The Giants did no such damage in the 1937 Series. Although Mel Ott did hit a two-run homer against Gomez in Game 5, Lefty pitched two complete-game victories and allowed just three runs as the Yankees rolled to the title in five games.

As the 1940s unfolded, the Yankees boasted a slugging outfield of (left to right) Charlie Keller, DiMaggio and Tommy Henrich.

Just as Henrich joined the Yankees in 1937 and saw considerable outfield service, other important newcomers came aboard the following two seasons. Joe Gordon replaced Lazzeri at second base in 1938 and outfielder Charlie Keller came up in 1939. The Yankees won going away in both seasons.

The 1938 club went 99-53, good enough to finish 9½ games ahead of Boston. Gehrig faltered to .295, his first sub-.300 season since he became a regular in 1925, hit 29 homers (his lowest total in a decade) and drove in 114 runs (his worst production since 1926). Today, those figures win arbitration hearings.

"People say, 'What do you remember about Lou Gehrig?' " Henrich said. "I say, 'I saw the tail end of him, and boy what I saw was tremendous.' Geemineez, if I saw the last of Gehrig, I wonder what the heck he was like."

Gordon gave the Yankees 25 home runs and 97 RBIs in '38, Henrich chipped in with figures of 22 and 91 and Dickey finished with a .313 average, 27 homers and 115 RBIs. Meanwhile, DiMaggio was booed at the outset of the season after holding out.

DiMaggio had made $8,500 as a rookie and $15,000 in 1937. Seeking $40,000, DiMaggio was offered $25,000 by the Yankees. He stayed in San Francisco rather than report to spring training. Finally, with the Yankees back from Florida and about to begin the season, DiMaggio capitulated and signed for $25,000. When he made his first appearance of the season, it was April 30, and the Yankees had won only six of 12 games.

Form ultimately prevailed. DiMaggio hit .324 with 32 homers and 140 runs batted in. The Yankees took over first place for good on July 13 and swept the Cubs in four games in the World Series. There was a disquieting footnote as the Yankees became the first team to win three successive Series; Gehrig, with 10 homers and 34 RBIs in 30 previous games over six Series, had just four singles against the Cubs and didn't drive in a run.

The Yankees became the first American League team to win four straight pennants in 1939, and McCarthy became the first manager to win four consecutive Series when the Yanks swept four games from the Cincinnati Reds. But it was a bittersweet year for the New Yorkers.

They took over first place for good on the 11th of May, a month in which they won 24 of 28 games. By July 4, the Yankees had the comfort of an 11½-game lead. Their 106-45 finish put them 17 games ahead of the Red Sox.

New Yankee Manager Casey Stengel holds a "hot stove" conference with his players as the team opens its 1949 spring training camp in St. Petersburg, Fla.

DiMaggio won the first of his three MVP awards —the others came in 1941 and 1947—by leading the majors with a career-high average of .381. He was second in the league with 126 RBIs and fourth with 30 homers.

Rolfe hit .329, Keller batted .334 and Dickey finished at .302 with 24 homers and 105 RBIs. Gordon buttressed his .284 average with 28 homers and 111 RBIs, while Selkirk contributed a .306 mark, 21 homers and 101 RBIs. Only Ruffing, 21-7, won more than 13 games, but rookie Atley Donald went 13-3 after starting the season with 12 straight victories and Monte Pearson was 12-5, Gomez 12-8 and Bump Hadley 12-6.

The year began badly when Yankees President Colonel Jacob Ruppert died on January 13, 1939. Spring training brought more bad news. It was apparent that something was gravely wrong with the 35-year-old Gehrig.

"What we saw in '39 was unbelievable," Henrich said. "Golly sakes. There's no doubt about it; it hit him over the end of '38 before he got to '39 spring training.

"It slowed down his reflexes and everything else at home plate. He couldn't move. He was in danger at home plate. Pitch him inside, and he couldn't get out of the way of the ball in spring training. And he

couldn't move; he couldn't run worth a darn. We can't believe that. Sooner or later he's going to come out of it. No, he never did."

"In spring training that year," recalled Babe Dahlgren, who soon was to replace Gehrig, "he hit a ball that normally would be a three-base hit. It was against the Dodgers. . .The ball went to the wall and everybody thought it would be a triple. We watched the throw in. Simultaneously everybody on the bench went, 'Where's Lou?'

"Well, gee, we looked back to second. We thought he was pulling up at third standing up; he slid into second head-first. The shortstop took the throw in, and they damn near got him. Everybody went, 'Geez.' All you could hear is, 'What happened?' "

Gehrig opened the season at first base and played the first eight games, extending to 2,130 his streak of consecutive games that had begun on June 1, 1925. On April 30 against Washington, he fielded a routine grounder and flipped to pitcher Johnny Murphy covering first base.

"Murph, Gordon and Dickey all gathered around me," Gehrig said, "and patted me on the back. 'Great stop,' they all said together, and then I knew I was washed up. They meant to be kind, but if I was getting wholesale congratulations for making

Winning pitcher Allie Reynolds (left), DiMaggio (center) and Jerry Coleman enjoy hero status after the Yanks' 10-inning victory over Philadelphia in Game 2 of the 1950 Series.

an ordinary stop, I knew it was time to fold."

The Yankees were off on May 1 and opened a series in Detroit on May 2. It was a game that would be remembered for far more than the fact the Yankees mauled the Tigers. Gehrig took himself out of the lineup, forever as it turned out, and Dahlgren replaced him at first base.

"Art Fletcher came up to me," Dahlgren said. "He was the coach. The clubhouse was very quiet. There were rumors going around that Lou was going to take himself out, but rumors, you hear a lot of them.

"So anyhow, old Art came up to me. I was fooling around with the lacing on my glove. And he said, 'You're playing first today, Babe. Good luck.'

"I said, 'You've got to be kidding.'

"He said, 'You're playing first,' and walked away."

Gehrig came onto the field and posed with Dahlgren at first base. Just before the start of the game, Gehrig assumed a ceremonial role and carried the Yankees' lineup to home plate.

"He came back to the bench with his head down," Dahlgren remembered. "They did announce that his record was going to be broken that day, and he wasn't going to play. He came back to the bench and went to the far end. I was sitting on

the far end. He leaned over to take a drink of water, and it was a long drink. He didn't come up.

"Johnny Murphy was sitting next to me. He threw a nice fresh towel over Lou's head. And Lou really appreciated it. He didn't say thanks or anything, didn't even know where it came from. But he wiped his tears. He was crying.

"Well, we won that game, 22-2. I had a home run and a double that day. At the start of the game, I said to Lou, 'Look, why don't you change your mind and keep the streak going? If you don't feel like finishing the game, I'll come in.' He said, 'No, get in there and knock in some runs.'

"The seventh inning I went to him before I went out on the field and said, 'Lou, keep the record going.' He was a boyhood favorite of mine. I had his drawing in my high school binder; I had Babe Ruth on the front and Lou Gehrig on the back. I never dreamed that someday I'd be about 2,000 miles from home in San Francisco and taking his place. So I went to him in the seventh inning, the eighth inning and the ninth inning. He said, 'You're doing fine, Babe.' That was it. The record was over."

Gehrig voiced his own assessment of what was wrong—and illness was never mentioned.

"My so-called collapse was my own fault," he said. "I forgot to look at the calendar. I spent the

Yankee Stadium, all spruced up (above) for Game 1 of 1961 World Series, was never
lacking for atmosphere. Among its many appealing features were its irregular dimensions
and the three monuments (below) that occupied a choice position in center field.

off-season riding in a car and sitting in a boat. I rode to get a newspaper, two blocks away. I should have been jogging, and should have come into training camp with my legs fit for the task.

"I always looked forward to the opening game as a big tonic. But this year, for some reason, the bell failed to rouse me...."

The reason soon became apparent. The following month, Gehrig underwent a week of examination at the Mayo Clinic in Rochester, Minn. On June 21, it was announced that he was suffering from amyotrophic lateral sclerosis, an incurable sickness that forever more would be known as Lou Gehrig's disease, and his playing career was over.

The Yankees made it official with a Lou Gehrig Day on July 4 at Yankee Stadium. Ruth, whose playing career had ended after a stint with the Boston Braves in 1935, returned and was photographed in a memorable embrace with Gehrig.

"McCarthy came out late (onto the field)," Dahlgren said. "I was standing right along the third-base line. When McCarthy came out, he came up behind me and said, 'Watch Lou. If he starts to fall, try to get him. Don't let him hit the ground.'

"So I glued my eyes on him all through his speech. His rear end looked like he had a motor inside of him. Just bouncing around. His nerves. He was telling the crowd that he was the luckiest guy in the world and to see he couldn't control this nerve, this, whatever it was, geez, that was frustrating.

"You wanted to help the guy. And you wanted to tell him to sit down and rest a minute. You didn't know what to do. You were dumbfounded. From May 2 to July 4 was two months, and, gosh, to be told to see that he don't fall down."

Playing an entire season without Gehrig for the first time since 1922, the Yankees came up short in 1940. They went 88-66 and finished third, two games behind the pennant-winning Tigers and one behind the Indians. DiMaggio did hit .352 to win his second successive batting title and added 31 homers and 133 RBIs. It was a prelude to his 1941 heroics.

On May 15 of that season, he went 1 for 4, a first-inning single, against Edgar Smith of the Chicago White Sox. It was the start of a 56-game hitting streak, a major league record, that lasted until July 17. During the streak, DiMaggio hit .408 (91 for 223) with 16 doubles, four triples, 15 homers, 55 RBIs and 56 runs scored.

He surpassed Willie Keeler, who had hit in 44 straight games for the National League's Baltimore Orioles in 1897, and George Sisler, whose 41-game streak in 1922 with the St. Louis Browns had set an A.L. record.

DiMaggio's streak ended before a night-game record crowd of 67,468 in Cleveland against Al Smith and Jim Bagby Jr., thanks largely to outstanding fielding plays by third baseman Ken Keltner in the first and seventh innings. In his other two at-bats, DiMaggio walked in the fourth and hit a hard grounder off Bagby in the eighth that shortstop Lou Boudreau managed to stop and turn into a double play.

As if to signify that he was up to any challenge, DiMaggio immediately ran off another hitting streak of 16 games that ended August 3.

"You've got to understand DiMaggio," Henrich said. "I don't think he knew what the heck pressure was. He knew what was going on, but he was so doggone tough he would match anything that ever came along. I don't give a doggone, DiMaggio's the toughest guy I ever saw in my life on a ball field. Absolutely."

DiMaggio finished the 1941 season at .357 with 30 homers and 125 RBIs (tops in the majors). He won the MVP balloting with 291 points, 37 more than Ted Williams, who hit .406 that year with 37 homers and 120 RBIs.

Meanwhile, during DiMaggio's streak, the Yankees reeled off a 14-game winning streak. Their 25-4 July helped clinch the pennant on September 4, which nearly a half-century later still stands as the earliest clinching date in big-league history. New York coasted home, 101-53; second-place Boston was 17 games behind. There was, however, a sad note during DiMaggio's rampage. Lou Gehrig died on June 2, 17 days before his 38th birthday.

Having regained the top rung of the American League, the Yankees also made it a triumphant return to the Series by beating the Brooklyn Dodgers in five games. The turning point came in the ninth inning of Game 4, with two men out for the Yankees, no one on base and the Dodgers ahead, 4-3, and apparently about to even the Series.

Catcher Mickey Owen couldn't stop a low curve from Hugh Casey that Henrich swung at and missed for strike three. Henrich made it to first base. DiMaggio followed with a single, and Keller hit a two-run double to put the Yankees in front, 5-4. After Dickey walked, Gordon's two-run double solidified the final score of 7-4. Henrich homered the next afternoon as Ernie Bonham threw a four-hitter to beat the Dodgers, 3-1, and end the Series.

Bonham went 21-5 in 1942, finishing second in the league in victories and ERA—2.27. Right behind him at 2.38 was Spud Chandler, who was 16-5. They

Yankees vs. A.L.

1936-43 and 1949-64

Opponent	W	L	Pct.
Washington*	52	20	.722
Philadelphia-Kansas City†	361	150	.706
St. Louis-Baltimore‡	344	168	.672
Washington§-Minnesota x	339	170	.667
Los Angeles y	46	26	.639
Chicago	314	197	.614
Cleveland	312	199	.611
Boston	302	206	.594
Detroit	286	226	.559

*Second franchise.
†213-94 (.694) vs. Philadelphia; 148-56 (.725) vs. Kansas City.
‡193-71 (.731) vs. St. Louis; 151-97 (.609) vs. Baltimore.
§First franchise.
x293-145 (.669) vs. Washington; 46-25 (.648) vs. Minnesota.
yNow known as California Angels.

Another changing of the guard took place in 1951 when Mantle (right) arrived on the New York scene to replace soon-to-be-retired center fielder DiMaggio.

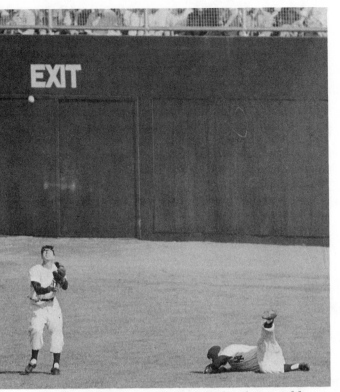

The first of numerous knee injuries that would plague Mantle throughout his career occurred when he stumbled in Game 2 of the 1951 Series.

One of the Yankees' 1951 Series heroes was Gil McDougald, who is shown crossing the plate after hitting the Giants with a grand slam in Game 5.

were the pitching cornerstones on a club that went 103-51 and beat the Red Sox by nine games.

DiMaggio fell slightly from his 1941 heights, hitting .305 with 21 homers and 114 RBIs. But Gordon won the MVP award by batting .322, which was fourth in the league, connecting for 18 homers and driving in 103 runs. Gordon also finished fourth in RBIs, and sandwiched between him and DiMaggio was Keller, who knocked in 108 runs while slugging 26 homers and averaging .292.

After prevailing in their last eight Series appearances, the Yankees fell to the St. Louis Cardinals in five games. Winning the opener by a 7-4 score only served to put the Yankees on notice. They carried a 7-0 lead into the bottom of the ninth, as the Cardinals didn't get a hit against the 37-year-old Ruffing until there were two out in the eighth. With two away in the ninth and two men on base (a hit and a walk), the Cardinals struck for four runs on five consecutive hits. Two of the hits came against Chandler, who had to bail out Ruffing. The Cardinals, who had won 43 of their last 51 regular-season games to go 106-48 and pass the Dodgers, won the next four games.

The Yankees did get revenge in 1943, beating the Cardinals in five games. Henrich had gone into the service during the 1942 season, and in '43 DiMaggio, Ruffing, shortstop Phil Rizzuto and first baseman Buddy Hassett were lost to the war effort.

Still, the Yankees were talented enough to go 98-56 and finish 13½ games ahead of the Washington Senators. Chandler became the third straight Yan-

kee to win the MVP award on the strength of a 20-4 season. He tied for the league lead in victories and complete games, 20, and was the leader in ERA, 1.64, and winning percentage, .833. To this day, Chandler is the only Yankee pitcher ever to be named the MVP.

"I had good control," explained Chandler, who walked just 54 batters in 253 innings in 1943, "and I developed five pitches—fastball, curve, forkball, screwball and slider. When you have a variety of pitches, it's hard for a batter to guess what he's going to get. And they all look for something."

The rest of the American League was seeking relief from the Yankee domination. It arrived because of World War II. The 1943 team was the last champion for McCarthy, who managed the Yankees into the 1946 season before taking over the Red Sox in 1948. He left a regal legacy in New York.

The Yankees had a .652 winning percentage (799-427) while winning seven pennants and six Series in the eight seasons from '36 through '43. They averaged 99.9 victories in that span and never won a pennant by fewer than nine games.

"We were not overconfident; we were confident," Henrich said. "That's the best thing of playing with a ball club run by Joe McCarthy. We thought of him as the real master. And it's the best feeling I ever had being on an athletic team—being on a team managed by Joe McCarthy."

"He didn't rant and do all that," said Chandler, reflecting on McCarthy's style. "He talked in a very sober voice. But he was a good analyst. He knew the

The 1953 Yankees' starting rotation was rock solid with (left to right) Vic Raschi, Reynolds, young Whitey Ford and Ed Lopat.

game. He was a very calm manager and confident and had confidence in his players."

The Yankees, winners of only one pennant in a five-season stretch that began in 1944, weren't sure just what to expect when Stengel was hired to replace Bucky Harris as manager after the 1948 season. In '48, New York had finished third, 2½ games behind the Indians, who won the pennant in a one-game playoff with the Red Sox. Stengel had managed the Dodgers and Boston Braves, never finishing higher than fifth in nine seasons and five times finishing seventh.

He also had the reputation for being a comic rather than a strategist. Yet because of his long association with Yankees General Manager George Weiss, Stengel, despite his niche in the second division, found himself in pinstripes.

"I'm probably the only guy on that club who knew that he was a good ball player at one time," Henrich said. "I remember Stengel in '21, '22 and '23 with the New York Giants. But the other guys, all they know is he was a clown with Brooklyn, and he was a clown with the Boston Braves.

"So we take him as he is. And he was bearing down with us. There weren't any jokes per day, I guarantee you that, because Casey was serious. He knew that this was his chance. Casey the clown didn't exist with the New York Yankees in '49. He didn't have any opportunity to show that."

Not with the injuries he had to contend with. DiMaggio, who had undergone off-season surgery for removal of a bone spur from his right heel, missed the first 65 games in 1949 because of calcium deposits in the heel. He didn't play until June 28,

Mantle (left) gets a triumphant embrace from veteran shortstop Phil Rizzuto after the Yankees' seven-game 1952 Series victory over Brooklyn.

The 1953 Yankees handled Brooklyn in six games and Game 1 heroes included (left to right) Hank Bauer, Yogi Berra, Billy Martin and Joe Collins.

Veteran catcher Berra was in the forefront of a 1956 Series celebration that also featured (left to right) Stengel, Don Larsen and Ford.

only to return with four homers in three games as the Yankees swept the Red Sox in Fenway Park.

Henrich suffered a back injury in late August and missed nearly four weeks. And Johnny Mize, purchased from the Giants for $40,000 on August 22, was soon limited to pinch-hitting duty after injuring his shoulder. Nonetheless, the Yankees beat the Red Sox in the final two games of the season to finish one game ahead of the Boston club.

Not one full-season Yankee hit .300, although DiMaggio came back to average .346 and drive in 67 runs in 76 games. The New Yorkers did get 20 home runs and 91 RBIs from catcher Yogi Berra and a .287 average, 24 homers and 85 RBIs from Henrich, whom Stengel shifted to first base. The big three of Vic Raschi (21 victories, 10 losses), Eddie Lopat (15-10) and Allie Reynolds (17-6) was capably supported by reliever Joe Page. After the struggle of the regular season, the Yankees made quick work of the Dodgers to win the Series in five games.

Winning the 1950 pennant was just about as difficult, with the Yankees' clinching not coming until September 29, two days before the end of the season. Shortstop Rizzuto had an MVP-winning year that featured a .324 batting average (he had exactly 200 hits) and a league-leading .982 fielding percentage (he made only 14 errors). DiMaggio suffered the ignominy of actually being benched for the first time as a Yankee on August 11 with his average at .270; after sitting out a week, he finished the season at .301 with 32 homers and 122 RBIs.

Raschi again won 21 games, with Lopat (18 victories), Reynolds (16) and Tommy Byrne (15) making major contributions. Help also came from Whi-

Home run hitters Bauer (above left) and Mantle (above right) flank winning pitcher Tom
Sturdivant after Game 4 of the 1956 World Series. Larsen (below left) poses at Ebbets
Field with umpire Babe Pinelli and Berra the day after his perfect game in the '56 Series.

Bobby Richardson, pictured (above) being greeted after his Game 3 grand slam, and the Yankees bombed the Pirates in three games of the 1960 Series, but still lost.

tey Ford, a brash rookie lefthander who won nine straight games after being called up on June 29 and wound up with a 9-1 record.

"He was pretty cocky," recalled Reynolds, referring to a spring-training experience with Ford. "(Pitching coach) Jim Turner came to me and said, 'I'd like to change your roommate.' I said, 'Why? I like (Cliff) Mapes.' He said, 'I've got a young pitcher I'd like to see if you can't stick a little class on.'

"I went up the first evening and walked in. He came over and said, 'I'm Whitey Ford.' I said, 'Yeah, I understand you're going to be my roommate.' We piddled around there for a little bit, didn't say anything. And I started getting dressed. He said, 'Is it time to eat?' I said, 'Yeah.'

"So I'm getting dressed and putting on a tie. He was pulling his shirt over the collar of his jacket; at

that time, that's the way kids did. And I said, 'Whitey, you can't go down there that way. You have to wear a tie.' He said, 'I don't have any ties.'

"I said, 'I've got some on the wall. Just go get one of those and wear it.' He went over and said, 'I can't wear these ties. They're all middle-aged.' "

It was Ford who beat the Philadelphia Phillies, 5-2, in Game 4 to complete a Series sweep. Despite that one-sided bottom line, the first three games were won by scores of 1-0, 2-1 (10 innings) and 3-2 (the deciding run coming in the bottom of the ninth). Nonetheless, the Yankees under Stengel had their second successive title.

"Casey to me was the perfect manager," Coleman said, "in that he understood all facets of the game. He understood the players. He understood the press. He understood the fans. He understood the

Roger Maris joined the Yankees in 1960 and began his Ruthian home run assault a year later.

front office. He really had a tremendous insight into all of these facets of the game; he really was his own PR (public relations) genius. The man was absolutely in a class by himself. I've never seen anyone who handled all phases of the game the way he did.

"But he was not an easy man to play for from the standpoint that you were a number. I'm not talking about (Mickey) Mantle or Berra or DiMaggio or people like that. But I'm talking about people like myself and the Hank Bauers and Gene Woodlings and Bobby Browns. He just used you, and there was no explanation as to why in many cases. From that standpoint, he was not a lovable guy. He was lovable to the fans but not to the players who played for him."

Bauer, who in retrospect realizes that being initially platooned with Woodling ultimately prolonged his career, refers to Stengel as "a master of, I call it, 'backwards psychology.' In regards to Gene and I, he kept us mad, and once we got in the game, we busted our asses."

The Yankees tolerated nothing less. There was a code handed down from veteran to youngster, standards that were zealously transferred. Success had instilled something in the Yankees. It wasn't just high expectations, though they certainly existed. It was the way those expectations were overtly conveyed.

"It seemed like we had a good ball club in Cleveland," said Reynolds, who was traded from the Indians to the Yankees for Gordon and third baseman Eddie Bockman after the 1946 season. "But we just beat the devil out of everybody to be fifth or sixth. New York, on the other hand, I was just amazed. When I went down to spring training, they talked about playing in the World Series.

"The manager didn't have to say anything to the players. If the players thought you were not conducting yourself in a meaningful manner, they dang sure told you about it pretty quick. And I was put in that trap one time, too.

"Spud Chandler said, 'I want to have dinner with you tonight.' So we went out to dinner, and of course that was nice for me because I was still young. And he said, 'I'm going to say something to you that you're not going to like.' I said, 'Why?' He said, 'Because it's the truth. You're not bearing down out there.'

"I was ready to punch him in the nose. I didn't feel it was true, so we debated it. After he had explained the picture he was trying to portray, I would agree I wasn't giving it what I could have. It made a big difference. And before it was all over, I was doing the same thing (with other players)."

Unlike the McCarthy clubs that bludgeoned their opponents and won by huge margins, Stengel's Yankees did comparatively more squirming. They won 100 or more games only once, and that was in 1954 when, despite 103 victories, they finished eight games behind Cleveland. The Yankees did win five of their 10 pennants under Stengel by eight or more games. And they were the focal point of baseball.

Ingrained in their play and vital to their success were a defensive soundness and the execution of baseball fundamentals, matters that were quickly emphasized to newcomers.

"Woodling and I jumped on (Bill) Skowron when Skowron first got up there," said Bauer, reflecting on the arrival in the majors of the man who would play first base for the Yankees from 1954 through 1962. "I said, 'Moose, I'm going to tell you something. Everybody makes physical errors. But the first time you make a mental error, I'm going to jump all over your ass.' And I made mental errors, too.

"I said, 'I'll tell you what, Moose. We're used to walking to the bank in October. I'll tell you something. Don't screw with our money.' "

The Yankees cashed a winning Series share in 1951 when they beat the Giants in six games. It was the conclusion of another notable season, DiMaggio's last, Mantle's first and one in which Reynolds threw two no-hitters and Berra, on the strength of a .294 average, 27 homers and 88 RBIs, won the first of his three MVP awards.

Reynolds' first masterpiece came in Cleveland on July 12 when he beat Bob Feller and the Indians, 1-0, on Woodling's homer in the seventh. Reynolds threw his second no-hitter on September 28, 8-0 against the visiting Red Sox in the first game of a doubleheader, to become the first A.L. pitcher ever to throw two no-hitters in the same season. The game ended with Williams fouling out to Berra, atonement for the catcher after he had dropped a foul popup Williams had hit on the previous pitch.

"I just thought we didn't need that much excitement," said Reynolds, 17-8 that season. "It was pretty exciting as it was."

That victory clinched a tie for the pennant. The flag was won in the second game behind Raschi, who along with Lopat wound up with 21 victories.

DiMaggio, bothered by injuries, fell to .263 with 12 homers and 71 RBIs. It was the poorest season of his 13-year major league career. And his last.

"I played three years with DiMag," Bauer said. "He was getting hurt. And I remember one incident —I think it was '51, his last year. We were having batting practice in Yankee Stadium, and he was struggling a little bit. I was just standing there watching him. He came out of the cage, and he stood next to me and said, 'Hank, what am I doing wrong?'

"I said, 'You're asking me? Well, Joe, you're getting to be about 37 years old, and your reflexes are slowing up.'

"He said, 'Oh, horseshit.' And that was his last year. He had a lot of pride. He could play. He could play with anybody, but pride was his big deal."

That insight came to Bauer late in the 1948 season upon being called up to the Yankees. He made his major league debut at Yankee Stadium in a Labor Day doubleheader, flanking center fielder DiMaggio.

"First inning," Bauer said, "I'm playing right

The Yankees' winning formula in Game 3 of the 1961 Series: (left to right) Maris, relief ace Luis Arroyo and reserve catcher John Blanchard.

field. And a fly ball went to right-center, and I called for it. He kept looking at me.

"We come in. We got the side out and ran down the runway, smoked a cigarette. He smoked Chesterfields. I smoked Camels. I said, 'Joe, did I do something wrong out there? You kept looking at me.'

"He said, 'No. But I just want to tell you something, Hank. You're the first son of a bitch that invaded my territory.'"

DiMaggio's domain soon became Mantle's, with little effect on the overall results. The Yankees won pennants in 1952 and 1953, becoming the first team to win five successive flags. The '53 team won 18 straight games from May 27 through June 14, one short of the league record established by the 1906 White Sox and matched by Harris' 1947 Yanks, both World Series championship teams. That binge by the '53 club gave New York a 10½-game lead.

Starting with the second game of a doubleheader on June 21, the Yankees then lost nine straight in a tailspin that brought fleeting excitement to the pennant race. The Yankees ultimately posted a 99-52 record and won the flag by 8½ games.

In both '52 and '53, the Yankees beat the Dodgers in the Series. Mantle hit the first of his record 18 Series homers to provide the winning margin in a 3-2 triumph in Game 6 that tied the '52 Series at three games apiece. He homered the following day in a 4-2 victory that wasn't assured until second baseman Billy Martin, with the bases loaded and the runners moving on a 3-2 pitch and two out in the bottom of the seventh, bolted for a Jackie Robinson popup near the mound. Two Dodgers had crossed home plate and another was rounding third when Martin made a knee-high catch.

Martin was the hero again in 1953, stroking a Series-deciding single and setting a record with 12 hits in a six-game fall classic. The Yankees made history by winning for a fifth straight time.

Their reign ended the following season when the Indians set an American League record by winning 111 games, eight more than the Yanks. "I remember in '54 when we didn't win it," Coleman recalled. "I said, 'That's not right.'"

It was a wrong the Yankees corrected with a vengeance. They won the next four A.L. pennants, giving Stengel nine in 10 seasons at the Yankees' helm.

Four keys to the Bronx Bombers' 1961 success: (left to right) catcher Elston Howard, first baseman Bill Skowron, Arroyo and Berra.

Seven-game Series losses to the Dodgers in 1955 and the Milwaukee Braves in 1957 took away some of the luster of that period, but not much. In 1956, Mantle won the first of two consecutive MVP honors and became the first Yankee since Gehrig in 1934 to win the Triple Crown. Besides his .353 average, Mantle slugged 52 homers, drove in 130 runs and scored 132, all figures that led the majors.

The 1956 Yankees hit 190 homers, breaking the league record of 182 set by their 1936 counterparts. And in the 1956 Series, won in seven games over the Dodgers, Don Larsen, who couldn't get out of the second inning in Game 2, reached the rarest of heights in Game 5. He pitched the only perfect game in Series history.

"This thing kept building and building," said Coleman, who was on the Yankees' bench that October 8 afternoon, "and we're all looking around. I recall vividly about the ninth inning everybody on the bench becomes a manager. 'Hey, look at the left fielder. Should we move this guy?' Everybody wanted to move people.

"Casey suddenly looked around and said, 'Goddamn it, I'm the manager. I'll tell 'em where to play.' We were all so excited that we forgot who was running the show, but he let us know in a hurry."

The Yankees decided it was going to be Ralph Houk's show soon after they lost a bizarre seven-game Series to the Pittsburgh Pirates in 1960. Two weeks after Houk was promoted to manager of the Yankees, George Weiss, a 29-year employee of the club, was replaced as general manager by Roy Hamey.

Stengel was 70 years old. Houk, the Yankees' No. 3 catcher for most of his big-league career (1947-1954), had managed New York's Triple-A farm club at Denver before returning to the Yanks in 1958 as a coach under Stengel. Since other major league clubs were making managerial overtures to Houk, it made sense for Yankee Owners Dan Topping and Del Webb to make the Houk-for-Stengel move, particularly after the galling Series.

The Yankees, who had won their last 15 games of the 1960 American League season, outscored the Pirates, 55-27, in the Series and collected 91 hits to 60 for the National League champions. Richardson drove in 12 runs and his six RBIs in Game 3 were one more than any Pirate had in the entire Series.

"Topping and Webb thought we lost the Series because Casey didn't start Whitey (Ford) the first game," said Tony Kubek, who played shortstop and some outfield for the Yankees from 1957 through 1965. "He was perfectly rested. We won the pennant early. Casey's only rationale was he wanted to save him for Yankee Stadium. Whitey only gets two starts, and he was in the midst of breaking Ruth's record for consecutive shutout innings (29) in the World Series, which he broke the next year against Cincinnati (by running his string to 32). But in '60, Whitey shut out the Pirates twice in a seven-game Series but only got two starts where he probably should have got three."

Consequently, Ford wasn't available to pitch Game 7, which the Pirates won, 10-9, on a ninth-inning homer by second baseman Bill Mazeroski. Some peculiar doings in the bottom of the eighth, which began with the Yankees ahead by a 7-4 score, were what really doomed them.

After Gino Cimoli led off with a single, Bill Virdon hit a three-hopper that bounced up and hit Kubek in the throat. Only then did Joe DeMaestri replace Kubek. In two other games in the Series, the Yankees had improved their late-inning defense by having Kubek replace Berra in left field and bringing DeMaestri in at shortstop.

"This game," Kubek recalled, "as I was going out to the field, I kind of looked at Casey. We had a lead. He said, 'Oh no, just go on out there.' It was as if we had the game wrapped up. I don't know what would have happened if I'd been in left and Joe had been at short. The same thing might have happened to Joe, but he might have been playing deeper. He might have been playing differently. Who knows what might have happened?"

A Dick Groat single cut the Yankees' lead to 7-5. Jim Coates then relieved Bobby Shantz. A sacrifice bunt moved the Pirates' runners up to second and third, where they stayed when Rocky Nelson flied out. Then came a fateful play on a grounder hit by Roberto Clemente to Skowron at first base that enabled Clemente to be safe as the Pirates cut the lead to 7-6.

"Jim Coates had come in and forgot to cover first base, which would have been the third out," Kubek emphasized. "After that, (Hal) Smith hits a three-run homer. We could have been out of the inning. It was a very unusual World Series. We were so dominant, and yet we end up getting beat."

The defeat cost Stengel his job. Houk had an entirely different approach than his predecessor. Where Stengel platooned, Houk went with a set lineup. Where Stengel virtually ignored his players, as if expecting them to perform, Houk was quick to praise them when they did deliver. For the younger players in particular, Houk was a welcome change.

"He was much easier to play for," said Richardson, who had first played for Houk in the minors. "Stengel was a man that was good with the press. He was not afraid to make a change. You might be 3 for 3 that particular day, but in his mind you didn't

have a chance that (next) time, so he'd pinch-hit for you. And Ralph would just pat you on the back and go along with you.

"For instance, in my case, from Stengel I would hear, 'He doesn't drink. He doesn't smoke. And he still can't hit .250.' From Ralph Houk I would hear, 'Well, listen, no matter what, you're my second baseman. It doesn't matter if you hit .190.' So that was the contrast; now both of them were able to mold together a team and bring the most out, but it was just the way they did it."

Houk's first Yankee team was memorable. Expansion had come to the American League after the 1960 season, stripping the Yankees of some vital bench players like Dale Long, Bob Cerv and Gil McDougald, who quickly voiced his intention to retire rather than be exposed to the expansion draft, and cutting into some of their pitching depth, namely Shantz, Eli Grba and Duke Maas. Because of those losses, Kubek believes "the '60 club was a better club, it had more depth than the '61 team." But not nearly as much drama.

Ford, backed by reliever Luis Arroyo, was 25-4 in 1961, the best season in his 16-year career. Leading the majors in victories, innings pitched (283) and winning percentage (.862) earned Ford the Cy Young Award, which was inaugurated in 1956 and until 1967 given to just one pitcher in baseball. Ford became the second Yankee to win it, following Bob Turley, who was 21-7 in 1958.

The Yankees went 109-53, winning the 1961 pennant by eight games in a dogged race with Detroit. It was the third highest victory total in league history, trailing only the 111 games won by the 1954 Indians and the 110 by the 1927 Yankees.

All summer there was a 1927 recollection more vivid than victories. That was the season Ruth hit his 60 home runs, a record that echoed throughout 1961. Mantle and Roger Maris, who in his second season as a Yankee was en route to his second successive MVP honor, chased Ruth the entire season.

Mantle finished with a career-high 54 homers and drove in 128 runs while batting .317. He was part of a wrecking crew that set a major league record with 240 homers, including six players with more than 20. Skowron hit 28, Berra had 22 and catchers Elston Howard and John Blanchard each slugged 21. Maris reigned atop the list with 61 homers.

Late in July, when it became evident that Maris with 40 homers and Mantle with 38 were seriously pursuing Ruth, Commissioner Ford Frick issued a ruling. Because expansion had ushered in a 162-game schedule, an addition of eight games, Frick decided that Ruth's 60-homer total would have to be surpassed in 154 games—154 games played to a decision, that is—to be considered a record; if it took more games, that would be duly noted by an asterisk in the record book.

On September 20, in game No. 154 (155 overall, in view of one tie game), the Yankees clinched the pennant. Maris hit his 59th homer, but failed to match Ruth. No. 60 came six days later in the Yan-

**When (left to right) Richardson, reliever Jim Coates, Hector Lopez and Clete Boyer led
the way to a Game 4 victory in 1961, the Yanks had the Reds on the Series ropes.**

kees' 159th game overall. On October 1, in the Yankees' 163rd and final game of the season, Maris hit a fourth-inning homer against Boston's Tracy Stallard. It was Maris' 142nd RBI and fittingly gave the Yankees a 1-0 victory.

The season had been an ordeal for Maris, who had grown up in North Dakota and was uncomfortable in the New York media glare. He was besieged with questions.

When Pete Rose was chasing and passing Ty Cobb's career record of 4,191 hits in 1985, he would deliver monologues before and after games. Changing his material daily, to the delight of the assembled sportswriters, Rose was clearly as comfortable behind a microphone as he was in the batter's box.

Not so with Maris, a reluctant celebrity.

In the process, a curious thing happened. Mantle, booed for years, was now viewed in tandem with Maris. It worked to Mantle's benefit.

"Mickey had gone through it with DiMaggio," Kubek said. "He became an ogre because he replaced DiMaggio. Now all of a sudden Roger comes along, Mickey becomes a hero."

And Maris something of a villain, because he had not only edged out Mantle but had dared to chase Ruth, a player whose mythical stature in the game was second to none. Maris' personality wasn't suited for an assault on one of baseball's icons.

"I think the thing that hurt Roger more than anything was his attitude," said DeMaestri, who had

Yankee righthander Ralph Terry gets a victory ride after beating San Francisco, 1-0, in Game 7 of the 1962 World Series.

played with Roger in Kansas City and along with Maris and first baseman Kent Hadley had been traded by the Athletics to New York for Bauer, Larsen, outfielder Norm Siebern and first baseman Marv Throneberry on December 11, 1959. "By attitude, I mean he always seemed to me to be on the defensive. He couldn't sit down and just say things like he probably wanted to. He couldn't express himself. And I think that was maybe why he never really got the acclaim that he should have.

"It was not unusual for somebody to say, 'Gee, what's the matter with Roger? He's always walking around with a chip on his shoulder.' It wasn't that anybody was trying to start anything. It was just that the guys would kid. Well, if you tried to kid Roger, if he didn't know who you were or wasn't that close to you, he would almost think that you were trying to be kind of a wise guy, and he'd kind of flare back at you."

Aggression was lacking from Maris and Mantle in the 1961 World Series, won in five games over the Reds. Mantle, bothered by an abscess on his right hip, played in just two games. He managed one single in six at-bats. Maris went hitless in his first 10 at-bats against Cincinnati before belting a tie-breaking homer in the ninth inning of Game 3. His only other hit in 19 Series at-bats that fall was a double.

Without the fanfare of 1961, the Yankees won pennants under Houk the next two seasons, enabling him to match Hugh Jennings as the only man to win three pennants in his first three seasons as a major league manager. Jennings managed Detroit to A.L. flags in 1907, 1908 and 1909.

Mantle had an MVP season in 1962, with a .321 average, 30 homers and 89 RBIs. It was his third such award. Richardson, who had never received more than 11 votes in the balloting (and that in 1959 when the Yankees finished third), was runner-up to Mantle. The second baseman hit a career-high .302 and led the league with 209 hits. With Kubek in the Army until early August, Tom Tresh replaced him and was selected the league's Rookie of the Year after batting .286, hitting 20 homers and driving in 93 runs.

The Yankees won the Series against the San Francisco Giants. The climactic finish came in the bottom of the ninth inning of Game 7, with the Yankees ahead by a 1-0 score, slugger Willie McCovey at the plate and runners stationed on second and third base with two out. Ralph Terry, who two years earlier had served up the Series-ending homer to Pittsburgh's Mazeroski, retired McCovey on a liner to Richardson to complete a four-hit shutout. It was to be the Yankees' last Series championship under Houk.

A year later, the Yanks scored just four runs in four games and were swept by the Los Angeles Dodgers. That Series defeat was a bitter end to a season in which New York had won the pennant by 10½ games, its largest margin since the 1947 team won by 12. A fifth straight pennant followed in

The Yankees' 1963 infield featured (left to right) Boyer at third, Tony Kubek at shortstop, Richardson at second and newcomer Joe Pepitone at first.

1964, coupled with a cessation to all the glory.

After the 1963 season, Houk took over as general manager and Berra, a player-coach, became manager. Gaining managerial respect from former teammates proved to be a difficult task for Berra.

"It really started in spring training," Richardson said, "when Yogi was going to speak to the ball club. What he was going to do was get up and say, 'Hey, listen, I'm your new manager. We're going to work hard. Nothing's going to be different. I'm going to set some rules. No swimming, tennis, golf. We're going to work hard.' Then he was going to say, 'No, I'm just kidding. I'll have fun, but we'll work hard on the field.'

"What happened is he got about three of those rules out of the way, and you heard this noise in the back. And Mantle said, 'I quit,' and started to walk out. Everybody laughed, of course. That was really kind of typical of the (1964) season."

The Yankees got an 18-13 season in '64 from Jim Bouton, a 21-game winner in 1963, and significant production from Ford (17-6 with eight shutouts), Al Downing (13-8) and rookie Mel Stottlemyre (who provided a huge lift after his August 11 recall by winning nine of 12 decisions).

First baseman Joe Pepitone hit 28 homers and drove in 100 runs, the only time he reached that RBI level in his 12-year career in the majors. Despite injuries, Mantle hit .303 with 35 homers and 111 RBIs in the last truly productive season of a career that ran through 1968. Important contributions came from Howard, .313, 15, 84, and Maris, .281, 26, 71, as well as an off-the-field assist from shortstop Phil Linz that helped propel the team to a next-to-last-day clinching of the pennant and a one-game edge over the White Sox.

On August 20, after the Yankees had lost 10 of 15 games including four straight in Chicago, Linz pulled out a harmonica as the team bus was headed for O'Hare International Airport. The third-place Yankees were 4½ games out of first, and Berra was being criticized and second-guessed by his players. On the somber ride to O'Hare, Linz started playing "Mary Had a Little Lamb."

The harmonica had been a gift from Kubek, who also had bought instruments for himself, Richardson and Tresh.

"You could have heard a pin drop," Richardson said. "Yogi, like most managers, sat in the front of the bus on the left-hand side. Phil was in the back and not paying too much attention. . . He chose that time to learn to play his harmonica.

"Of course, Yogi surely thought that was a mistake and didn't say too much. Twenty seconds later, you heard it again. Yogi jumped up and turned around and said, 'Put that thing in your pocket.' Only he didn't use those words.

"Phil was in the back of the bus. He didn't hear him and said, 'What'd you say?' Mantle over across the aisle said, 'He couldn't hear it. Play it again louder.' Then Yogi jumped up and grabbed it, and it hit Pepitone in the shin. Yogi fined Phil $200, which in that day was a lot of money."

Linz, meanwhile, parlayed the incident into a $20,000 contract with a harmonica company. And the Yankees, after losing their next two games at Boston, displayed a renewed unity and won 30 of their final 41 games to advance to the Series against the Cardinals.

After taking a 2-1 Series lead when Mantle's homer in the bottom of the ninth inning won Game 3, the Yankees lost what proved to be a pivotal Game 4. Leading 3-0 in the sixth, the Yankees faltered behind Downing. With one out and runners on first and second, Downing got Dick Groat to hit an apparent inning-ending double-play ball to Richardson. The Yankees' second baseman had trouble getting the ball out of his glove and was charged with an error when he made a bad flip to shortstop Linz.

Ken Boyer followed with a grand slam, giving the Cardinals a 4-3 lead. That proved to be the final score. The following day, Bob Gibson struck out 13 Yankees in a 5-2 Cardinals conquest that was achieved on a 10th-inning homer by Tim McCarver.

When the Series shifted to St. Louis, the Yankees evened matters as Mantle, Maris and Pepitone homered, the latter's being a grand slam, in an 8-3 triumph. The following afternoon, Mantle hit a three-run homer, his 18th and last in World Series competition. But it came with the Cardinals leading 6-0, and the resolute Gibson held on for a complete-game 7-5 victory.

The Yankees had lost two consecutive Series for the first time since 1921-1922, when they made their first appearances in the fall classic. The ultimate irony followed. The day after the Series concluded, Berra was fired and he soon was replaced by Johnny Keane, manager of the conquering Cardinals.

"Flying on the plane back from St. Louis," Richardson remembered, "Yogi was sitting by my wife (Betsy). He said, 'I'm going to meet with the Yankee brass tomorrow. Do you think I ought to ask for a two-year contract?'

"Well, my wife's a very humble person. She said, 'If it hadn't have been for Robert (that's me) making that error, you'd be the manager of the world champions.' We were driving toward South Carolina the next day when I heard the announcement that he'd been fired. . . ."

There were other changes. Topping began having health problems in 1962. He approached Webb about buying his share of the team, but Webb was too busy with his far-flung construction business. The two owners sold 80 percent of the club to CBS in November 1964. The broadcasting company, whose corporate expertise was in fields other than baseball, bought the rest of the Yankee stock in 1965. That same year, baseball instituted a free-agent amateur draft. Under that new system, teams couldn't simply sign prospects at will, but had to draft them according to the reverse order of the previous season's standings.

"I think Topping and Webb said, 'Woops, that's it. No longer can we dominate the talent pool,'" Kubek said. "I think they really started making the books look good for a sale to CBS. The stadium ran down a little bit. They let the farm system run down a bit. They'd been planning for a couple of years to sell that ball club.

"I think it showed. Ultimately, there wasn't the talent there because they probably started budgeting and pinching pennies a little bit. They scrimped in every area, and when you do that, ultimately it catches up to you. And it caught up to them pretty quick."

With lightning speed, actually. The Yankees fell to sixth place in 1965. Their 77-85 record was the club's first below-.500 season since 1925 when New York went 69-85 and finished seventh. Matters worsened for the Yankees in 1966. They tumbled to 70-89 and 10th place, last in the American League; the Yankees hadn't finished on the bottom since 1912, the final season they were known as the Highlanders.

"It was just a miserable year," said Richardson, who had wanted to retire after the 1964 season but was talked into returning in 1965. When Kubek re-

World champions 22 times: the symbolic excellence of the greatest dynastic reign in sports history.

tired because of an injury after the '65 season, Richardson agreed to play in 1966.

"And I couldn't wait for it to be over," he said. "Just wasn't used to losing. Didn't understand. It just wasn't right. For the previous years, we'd always been in contention. Knew that when the World Series rolled around, we'd be in there. Then all of a sudden, last place in the American League."

Two dynastic eras had ended with a thud. Houk replaced Keane after 20 games of the 1966 season, but the Yankees didn't rise above fifth until the second year of two-division play, 1970. In bygone days, the Yankees had visited fifth place now and then early in the season, but hastily refueled and pulled away from a league that gasped in amazement.

"We used to go to Philadelphia," Crosetti recalled, "and Connie Mack's team after a while starting finishing in the basement. We'd go there, and they'd beat us three straight. And McCarthy couldn't figure that out, why the hell they beat us three straight.

"Connie Mack said, 'Geez, I don't know how come we can beat them so. They should never lose a ball game.'"

For nearly three glittering decades, the Yankees won most of the time as they cut a championship swath through the game. Right up until 1965, when all the glory suddenly became a memory.

BOSTON CELTICS

1956·57 to 1968·69

The chief architect of the Boston Celtics' dynasty was Arnold (Red) Auerbach, a fiery, flamboyant basketball genius.

Legends aren't always a big deal while they're being made. Often, it's only with the passage of time that they become larger than life.

Perhaps the greatest example of this phenomenon is the Boston Celtics franchise. From 1957 through 1969, a span of 13 seasons, the Celtics, incredibly, captured 11 National Basketball Association championships; almost as amazing, though, is the fact that the Celts seldom sold out Boston Garden during that great run. In fact, year in and year out, the Boston club drew average crowds in the range of 8,000, leaving more than 5,500 empty seats.

"We were real fortunate from '57 on in winning championships," said Arnold (Red) Auerbach, the Celtics' coach from the 1950-51 season through the 1965-66 campaign. "People in this area (Boston and all of New England) never realized what we did in those days. They would sort of say, 'Big deal.' Whereas if we were in any other area of the country, the accolades would have been tremendous. I'm talking about New York or New Jersey or Washington, wherever, Chicago, anyplace."

If anyone ever gets around to inventing a time machine, all those unsold seats in Boston Garden from the 1950s and 1960s surely would become a hot ticket. A trip back in time to see Auerbach and Bill Russell and Bob Cousy and Sam Jones and John Havlicek surely would be a scalper's delight.

The ensuing decades have done nothing but confirm the magnitude of the accomplishments of those Celtics of yesteryear. While much was made of the Los Angeles Lakers' feat of winning back-to-back championships near the end of the 1980s—and rightly so, considering that no team had repeated as NBA kingpin since Boston achieved the feat almost two decades earlier—consider this: Auerbach's team won *eight* straight league titles in one stretch (1959 through 1966) and fashioned a .705 winning percentage in regular-season play during the 13-year dynasty.

Even when Boston didn't rule the NBA during this time frame, the Celtics remained a force. They posted a 49-23 regular-season record in 1957-58, a season in which they lost to the St. Louis Hawks in the NBA Finals; plus, the 1966-67 team reeled off 60 victories in 81 games before bowing to eventual NBA champion Philadelphia in the Eastern Division title round.

The eight consecutive crowns proved to be a stretch of success unmatched by any professional team in any major sport. Yet, in the fall following each of the first seven of those championships, the Celtics failed to sell out their home opener. Finally, in October 1966, the Celts achieved a full house for their first Boston Garden game of the season.

Today, the Celtic mystique is almost oppressive in dank, smelly Boston Garden, with the championship banners hanging high in the rafters above the chipped and aged parquet floor. But back in the mid-1950s, the Celtics were just another struggling team in a struggling league.

Dwight D. Eisenhower had won his second term

Basketball's Garden Of Eden

By Roland Lazenby

in the White House. The civil-rights movement was in its early stages, marked by a Martin Luther King-led boycott of the Montgomery, Ala., bus system by blacks. The Soviet Union was making plans to launch sputnik, man's first Earth-orbiting object. Elvis Presley was starring in his first motion picture, "Love Me Tender." Television offerings—in black and white, of course—included "The Ed Sullivan Show," "The Honeymooners" and "The Adventures of Ozzie and Harriet."

While making note of these goings-on, Arnold Jacob Auerbach, still in his 30s, was consumed with winning basketball games, so much so that he left his wife and two daughters in Washington, D.C., eight months out of each year and lived in an efficiency apartment in Boston while he coached the Celtics.

Auerbach, the son of a Russian immigrant, had grown up in Brooklyn, where his father operated a small laundry. A man steeped in the work ethic, his father frowned upon time "wasted" on athletics. But the young, red-haired Arnold played high school basketball well enough to earn a junior-college scholarship, then went on to play for Coach Bill Reinhart at George Washington University.

After a stint in the Navy, Auerbach talked his way into the head-coaching job with the Washington Capitols when the Basketball Association of America—the forerunner of the NBA—opened for business in 1946-47. Though only 29 years old, Auerbach directed the Capitols to 49 victories in 60 games and a divisional championship. The Caps lost in the playoffs, but Auerbach had made a great start in establishing his reputation. Throughout the league, opponents quickly learned that his wavy red hair was true to the stereotype.

"He was flamboyant, gutsy, on top of everything. And fiery. I mean really fiery," Celtics radio announcer Johnny Most said of the young Auerbach. "But the important thing about him was that he knew the rules better than the officials. And he pulled the rule book on the officials all the time. . . . And he had the bite of intimidation. Like when his team was not playing well or playing lethargically, he'd go out there and start to scream at the fans or the referee and get them on him."

After a falling-out with the management in Washington, Auerbach left the Capitols after three seasons and took over as coach of the league's Tri-

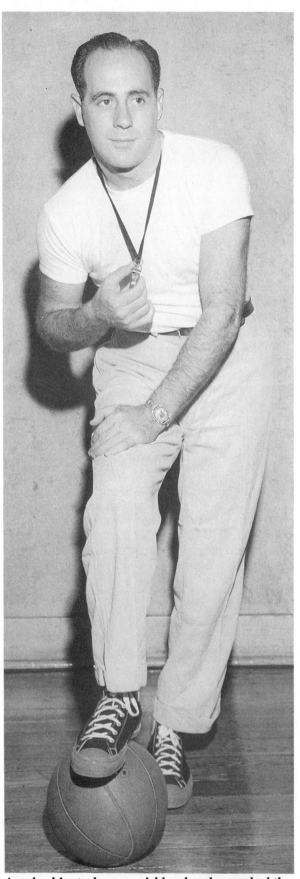

Auerbach's stock rose quickly when he coached the Washington Capitols of the Basketball Association of America to a 49-11 record in 1946-47.

Cities Blackhawks (whose home court was in Moline, Ill.) early in the 1949-50 campaign, then moved to Boston for 1950-51. The Celtics had been losers in their first four seasons of operation, and Owner Walter Brown figured Auerbach was gritty enough to change that. The young coach jumped at the chance to effect a turnaround.

It was a perfect marriage. Auerbach had found an owner who wanted to win as badly as he did.

"Walter Brown was one of the pioneers of professional basketball," Auerbach said. "He was a true sportsman. His word was his bond. He gave his whole material being and everything else to basketball. He was a guy who never knew basketball. He grew up in hockey. He came to the point where he loved basketball. That was his baby. He was one of the truly great men that affected my life."

Most important, Brown had staying power when things were difficult financially in those lean early years. He didn't break and run under the pressure.

"Holy Moses," Auerbach said. "He mortgaged his house and everything else. He believed in it (basketball). See, I never had a written contract with him. When I came here, I signed a contract—I didn't know him. After the first year, we tore up the contract. We had a handshake, year by year. I'd say, 'What's the deal next year?' 'What do you want?' Boom. Boom. We'd take five minutes and it was over. Nothing ever written down."

On occasion, Brown's good-heartedness would extend beyond Auerbach's business sense. Red watched his nickels closely and guarded Brown's money as if it were his own.

"Walter Brown would fall in love with players," Auerbach recalled. "Some of the players would wait until I was out of town and play golf with him and sign with him and make more money. He was a great man. I always compare people to Walter Brown by saying, 'Yeah, he's got some of Walter Brown's traits, but he's no Walter Brown.' Which means he's no sportsman. Walter Brown dedicated his life to sports. He used to subsidize it out of his own pocket, and he was never a real wealthy man."

When Auerbach assumed Boston coaching duties in the fall of 1950, pro basketball was in its second season under the banner of the National Basketball Association. A year earlier, the Basketball Association of America and the older National Basketball League had merged into the NBA. After an unwieldy 17-team alignment at the start, the NBA evolved into a league of eight to 10 teams in the '50s but hardly was national in scope. With franchises in such cities as Rochester, N.Y., Syracuse, N.Y., and Fort Wayne, Ind., as well as Boston, New York, Philadelphia and Minneapolis, the focus was the Northeast and, to some extent, the Midwest.

It was a life of long train rides, cold gymnasiums, dim lighting, lopsided balls, fickle fans and fight-marred games. It was so rough around the league that players automatically disliked anyone who had a propensity toward flashiness or exhibited leaping ability. Slater Martin, a standout guard with the

The Celtics gained respectability in the early 1950s as Auerbach made good use of frontcourt star Ed Macauley (left) and flashy guard Bob Cousy (right).

Minneapolis Lakers and St. Louis Hawks, once said: "In those days, you couldn't leave your feet. They'd just knock you into a wall."

Auerbach pushed Boston to a 39-30 finish that first year—the team had staggered to a 22-46 record the year before—but the job of building the Celtics had just begun. New Englanders cared little about basketball in the early '50s, choosing instead to spend their time and money on hockey. Asked his most important accomplishment in developing the Celtics, Auerbach has a ready answer: "Educating New England about basketball. The Bruins were here much before we were, and being the cold climate and all, the colleges played hockey. It was the accepted thing.

"Take schools like Boston College. The Number 1 sport was football, and then hockey for years and years. But through a process, we educated the people who became fans. That took quite a while. We made talks to the high schools, junior high schools. We did clinics all over. We would take a portable court and go to supermarket parking lots to conduct clinics and things like that, in order to teach our future fans."

Guard Bob Cousy, the so-called "Houdini of the Hardwood," became another major factor in the popularization of basketball in New England, although he had to overcome Auerbach's skepticism to do it. For the Celtics' draft in the spring of 1950, Brown suggested that Boston pick Cousy, an All-America guard at nearby Holy Cross, a selection that would please the fans. The coach, however, was opposed to the idea and he told reporters that he had been hired to win championships, not to please "the local yokels."

Boston selected 6-foot-11 Charlie Share of Bowling Green in the first round and then picked Chuck Cooper of Duquesne, the first black player ever drafted by an NBA team, in the second. Cousy, meanwhile, was taken in the first round by Tri-Cities, then quickly traded to the Chicago Stags. But the Chicago franchise folded and, as fate would have it, Boston drew Cousy's name out of a hat in a dispersal draft.

Auerbach believed deeply in the running game, the style of play he had learned while playing under Reinhart at George Washington. And Cousy wasted little time proving he was just the player to take the running game to a new level. In his rookie season, he averaged 15.6 points (the ninth-best mark in the league) and 4.9 assists (fourth in the NBA).

"He was the greatest innovator in the game," Most said of Cousy. "He had such a fabulous imagination. I think the greatest passer who ever lived. He could throw any kind of pass.

"The minute he touched the ball his head was up and he was looking down court for the open man. It was his philosophy to do it with the pass rather than the dribble. But if he had to dribble, if they forced the dribble, he could make you look like a fool. He really could. He had all the moves of a Globetrotter. And he never was lacking in confi-

Auerbach on the Celtics' bench in the 1956-57 season with newcomer Bill Russell, the biggest piece to the championship puzzle.

dence."

Just before hiring Auerbach, Brown had obtained Easy Ed Macauley, a 6-8, 190-pound center, in yet another dispersal-draft maneuver. Macauley had spent the 1949-50 season, his first in the pros, with the headed-for-extinction St. Louis Bombers. Macauley was no intimidator, but he had a graceful offensive style and could run the floor. The next year, 1951-52, Auerbach added Bill Sharman, the sharpshooting guard and defensive hawk out of Southern California, a versatile athlete who also was playing baseball in the Brooklyn Dodgers' organization.

With the Cousy-Macauley-Sharman triumvirate as the core of the franchise, the Celtics compiled such records as 39-27, 46-25 and 42-30 but couldn't advance beyond the divisional championship round.

Then came a milestone decision. The NBA, beginning with the 1954-55 season, adopted a 24-second shot clock. Much to Auerbach's liking, the game became significantly faster. Not at all to the coach's liking, the clock exposed his team's weaknesses. Boston had the greyhound guards in Cousy and Sharman to run other teams off the floor, but it didn't have a powerful rebounding center who could pull the ball off the defensive boards and throw the outlet pass to start the fast break. Macauley was a fine shooter, but he simply didn't have the muscle and inside knack to fill the role of a power player.

Auerbach had begun looking for that special inside man when his old college coach, Reinhart, raved about Bill Russell, a standout collegiate cen-

Dynasty Data

Yearly Record
1956-57 to 1968-69

Season	W	L	Pct.	Avg. Score Bos.-Opp.	—Finish in Division— Place	GA(+)/GB	Coach
1956-57—(Eastern Division)	44	28	.611	106-100	1	+ 6	Red Auerbach
1957-58—(Eastern Division)	49	23	.681	110-104	1	+ 8	Red Auerbach
1958-59—(Eastern Division)	52	20	.722	116-110	1	+12	Red Auerbach
1959-60—(Eastern Division)	59	16	.787	125-116	1	+10	Red Auerbach
1960-61—(Eastern Division)	57	22	.722	120-114	1	+11	Red Auerbach
1961-62—(Eastern Division)	60	20	.750	121-112	1	+11	Red Auerbach
1962-63—(Eastern Division)	58	22	.725	119-112	1	+10	Red Auerbach
1963-64—(Eastern Division)	59	21	.738	113-105	1	+ 4	Red Auerbach
1964-65—(Eastern Division)	62	18	.775	113-105	1	+14	Red Auerbach
1965-66—(Eastern Division)	54	26	.675	113-108	2	1	Red Auerbach
1966-67—(Eastern Division)	60	21	.741	119-111	2	8	Bill Russell
1967-68—(Eastern Division)	54	28	.659	116-112	2	8	Bill Russell
1968-69—(Eastern Division)	48	34	.585	111-105	4	9	Bill Russell

Playoffs

Season	—Eastern Division— Semifinals	Finals	Championship Series	Total Playoff Record
1956-57	Earned bye	3-0 vs. Syracuse	4-3 vs. St. Louis	7-3
1957-58	Earned bye	4-1 vs. Philadelphia	2-4 vs. St. Louis	6-5
1958-59	Earned bye	4-3 vs. Syracuse	4-0 vs. Minneapolis	8-3
1959-60	Earned bye	4-2 vs. Philadelphia	4-3 vs. St. Louis	8-5
1960-61	Earned bye	4-1 vs. Syracuse	4-1 vs. St. Louis	8-2
1961-62	Earned bye	4-3 vs. Philadelphia	4-3 vs. Los Angeles	8-6
1962-63	Earned bye	4-3 vs. Cincinnati	4-2 vs. Los Angeles	8-5
1963-64	Earned bye	4-1 vs. Cincinnati	4-1 vs. San Francisco	8-2
1964-65	Earned bye	4-3 vs. Philadelphia	4-1 vs. Los Angeles	8-4
1965-66	3-2 vs. Cincinnati	4-1 vs. Philadelphia	4-3 vs. Los Angeles	11-6
1966-67	3-1 vs. New York	1-4 vs. Philadelphia		4-5
1967-68	4-2 vs. Detroit	4-3 vs. Philadelphia	4-2 vs. Los Angeles	12-7
1968-69	4-1 vs. Philadelphia	4-2 vs. New York	4-3 vs. Los Angeles	12-6

ter for the San Francisco Dons. College basketball received modest publicity in those days. There was no national television, no basketball poop sheets, no cable connection, no Dick Vitale touting the stars. Because he competed on the West Coast, Russell was largely unknown to the Eastern basketball establishment. Plus, he was an unusual package. He stood 6-9½, was exceptionally athletic and possessed excellent speed for a big man.

Russell's sense of timing made him an excellent rebounder and shot-blocker. Yet his offensive skills were unrefined to the point that much of his scoring came from guiding his teammates' missed shots into the basket. His knack for this ability was a factor in the development of offensive goaltending rules in college basketball.

Russell's reputation gained a terrific boost in the '54-'55 season as he and guard K.C. Jones led the Dons to the first of two straight NCAA championships. Still, his lack of an offensive game left most pro teams skeptical about the potential of the USF pivotman. Auerbach, however, knew Russell was just the player he was looking for.

"I had to have somebody who could get me the ball," Auerbach recalled. "...Bill (Reinhart) said Russell was the greatest defensive player and greatest rebounder he'd ever seen."

Rochester had the first selection in the regular phase of the 1956 NBA draft—Boston actually led off the proceedings by making Holy Cross sensation Tom Heinsohn a territorial pick—and the Royals opted for Sihugo Green of Duquesne. The Celtics, because of a deal they had swung the day before, then had claim to the next choice, which belonged

to St. Louis. The Hawks had yielded the draft position to Boston in exchange for Macauley and the rights to Cliff Hagan, a 1953 Celtics draftee who had yet to play a game of pro ball because of military service.

Who did the Celtics wind up with as a result of their wheeling and dealing with St. Louis? None other than one William Felton Russell. And, later in the draft, Boston nabbed Russell's USF teammate, playmaker Jones.

The only hitch involving Russell was that the big man had made clear his intentions to play for the 1956 U.S. Olympic team, meaning that he wouldn't be able to join the Celtics until well into December. The Celtics weren't exactly shorthanded, though, when the 1956-57 NBA season got under way. They had a muscular front-line player in Jim Loscutoff, a second-year man out of Oregon; a gifted swingman in Frank Ramsey, who was returning to the team after a year of military duty; a solid rookie in Heinsohn, and proven stars in Sharman and Cousy. Because of a service hitch, Jones, also a '56 Olympian, wouldn't join the Boston club until the fall of 1958.

After helping the United States roll to the Olympic gold medal, Russell, who had rejected a contract offer from the Harlem Globetrotters, joined the Celtics in mid-December and made his pro debut in a nationally televised game against St. Louis. In that December 22 contest, Russell scored only six points but grabbed 16 rebounds in 21 minutes of action. Maybe it wasn't obvious in that first game, but the NBA would never be the same.

The impact on the Celtics was almost immediate. Russell struggled a bit in his first few games, but his

The 1957-58 Boston Celtics: (front row, left to right) Frank Ramsey, Andy Phillip, Owner Walter Brown, Auerbach, treasurer Lou Pieri, Cousy and Bill Sharman; (back row) Lou Tsioropoulos, Jim Loscutoff, Jack Nichols, Russell, Arnie Risen, Tom Heinsohn, Sam Jones and trainer Harvey Cohn.

presence unshackled the rest of the team. The rookie center was such an awesome defensive rebounder that Heinsohn's and Loscutoff's roles shifted from battling on the boards. The forwards merely boxed out their men, then released quickly for the fast break while Russell was snaring the rebound and whipping the outlet pass to Cousy.

Sharman and Cousy, meanwhile, were ecstatic with this development, after having spent the previous seasons frustrated by the team's lack of inside strength. Plus, Russell's intimidating presence allowed them to gamble on defense. If they made a mistake, Russell more often than not covered for them.

But most pleased was Auerbach, who considered Russell's shot-blocking to be one of the major developments in the evolution of pro basketball. The first-year man exuded a confidence that bordered on arrogance. But as he later revealed in his book, "Second Wind," Russell was far more insecure about his offensive skills than he let on. He was aware of his detractors—that most coaches, players and writers believed that the ideal big man had to be an offensive force.

When Russell arrived, though, Auerbach called him in and told him not to worry about offense, that his primary responsibilities were rebounding and defense. The coach also promised that statistics

such as scoring averages would never be a part of contract discussions. Auerbach's understanding of Russell's unique skills was the single-most important element in the genesis of this dynasty.

Like Auerbach, Russell really cared only about winning. Player and coach didn't have to spend much time together to sense this in each other. "He was the ultimate team player," Cousy said of Russell. "Without him there would have been no dynasty, no Celtic mystique."

Beginning in his college days (he received little playing time until his senior year in high school), Russell had turned shot-blocking into a science. By the time he reached the pros, he possessed a very special skill. He seldom swatted the ball so that it went out of bounds. Instead, he brushed it, or caught it, or knocked it away, so that most times it remained in play and became a turnover, sparking the Celtics' fast break the other way. Such a defensive weapon sent shock waves across the league.

"Nobody had ever blocked shots on the pros before Russell came along," Auerbach said. "He upset everybody."

The oft-cited example is that of Neil Johnston, the Philadelphia Warriors' star who dominated NBA scoring with his rather flat hook shot. Russell was so effective in blocking Johnston's shot that the three-time NBA scoring champion became tentative

Bob Cousy, a basketball Houdini who took the NBA running game to a new level, threads his way through the Cincinnati defense during a 1958-59 game.

Bill Sharman (left) teamed with Cousy to give the Celtics a dynamic backcourt in the team's formative years. Tom Heinsohn (right) and Russell arrived in 1956 to provide much-needed inside punch.

and ineffective on offense against the Celtics. Because he was basically a one-dimensional player, Johnston was unable to adjust.

Two weeks after Russell began play in the NBA, Philadelphia Owner Eddie Gottlieb protested that the newcomer was playing a one-man zone (a zone defense was illegal in the NBA) and goaltending as well. Other coaches and owners around the league joined the chorus. But Auerbach fended them off.

"When we made the deal for Russell, nobody thought he was going to be good (at the pro level)," the Boston coach told reporters. "He has far exceeded everybody's expectations. None of his blocks of shots has been on the downward flight. He has marvelous timing. He catches the ball on the upward flight."

When the league supervisor of officials said Russell's play was clearly within the rules, Gottlieb dropped his beef. The age of a new athleticism had dawned, and coaches everywhere looked for a way to counter it. Mostly, other teams tried to muscle and bang Russell. But as tough and proud as he was, Boston's man in the middle wasn't about to back down.

Russell clearly was not your average NBA rookie. A Celtic tradition called for first-year players to haul the bag of practice balls from game to game. Heinsohn had been handling this chore and he hoped he could pass the job over to Russell when the center joined the team. But Russell's fierce frown made his teammates think better of asking. So Heinsohn carried on.

The 1956-57 Celtics finished the regular season 44-28, six games ahead of Syracuse in the Eastern Division, as Russell averaged 14.7 points and 19.6 rebounds over 48 games. Cousy led the league in assists for the fifth consecutive season and was voted the NBA's Most Valuable Player. As the playoffs began, Heinsohn was selected the Rookie of the Year. In the locker room before the first playoff game, he opened the envelope containing the $250 prize. Always a needler, Russell eyed the money and suggested that half of it should be his. At least half, some observers thought.

Boston swept Syracuse in the Eastern Division title round, but Western playoff kingpin St. Louis, which managed only a 34-38 regular-season record, made the 1957 NBA Finals a series to remember. Featuring Bob Pettit at forward, Macauley at center and Jack McMahon and Slater Martin at the guards, the Hawks were talented and ready to play.

Sharman scored 36 points for the Celtics in the first game at Boston Garden, but Pettit scored 37 and the Hawks won the opener in double overtime on a late shot by Jack Coleman. After the clubs split the next two games, Boston won twice to seize the series lead, three games to two. The Hawks, though, deadlocked the playoff with another narrow victory. All three of St. Louis' triumphs had come by two points.

Game 7 was a classic, except for the performance of Boston's backcourt. Cousy made only two of 20

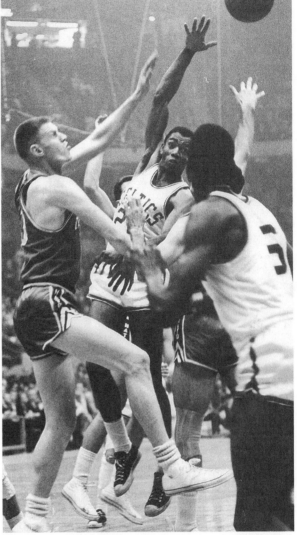

Sam Jones is surrounded by Syracuse players as he battles for a rebound during play in the 1959 Eastern Division title round.

field-goal attempts, and Sharman sank just three of 20 tries. The load fell upon the rookies, Heinsohn and Russell, and they delivered. Heinsohn netted 37 points and pulled down 23 rebounds; Russell scored 19 points and collected 32 boards.

With the Celtics ahead, 103-101, in the closing seconds, Pettit sank two free throws to send the game into overtime. Then, as the first extra period was about to end, Boston again was up by two points, 113-111, when first-game hero Coleman drilled another clutch basket. In the late going of the second overtime, Ramsey hit a foul shot and a field goal to send Boston into a 124-121 lead and Loscutoff sank a key free throw. As time was about to expire with Boston guarding a 125-123 lead, the Hawks mapped strategy for a floor-length pass to Pettit. Alex Hannum, St. Louis' player-coach, planned to bank the ball off the backboard, with the hope that Pettit could tip it in. Incredibly, Hannum was able to ram

It was shower time for Auerbach in 1960 after the Celtics' seven-game victory over the St. Louis Hawks. The chief revelers are Ramsey (left), Sharman (holding the banner) and Cousy.

the ball off the board, to Pettit, but the final shot rolled off the rim.

The Celtics celebrated by shaving Russell's beard in the locker room, downing a few cold ones and going out to dinner. It was the first of the good times for Boston. With Russell's special talents deflating opponents while inflating league attendance, the Celtics were struggling no more and the NBA was making major public-relations inroads as pro basketball edged into the second half of the 1950s.

About the only thing undermining the glorious beginning of Boston's dynasty was the undercurrent of racial problems. The NBA and the Celtics were integrating ahead of society; there were few, if any, problems on the team. But Boston was a racially troubled city, a not uncommon condition in the United States at that time. A couple of sportswriters in Boston made little effort to mask their contempt for Russell. And road games were sometimes rough, particularly in St. Louis, where the fans weren't averse to shouting racial epithets. As with the rough play on the court, Russell wasn't about to back down.

"Russ has always been extremely militant," Cousy said. "He came into Boston with the proverbial chip on his shoulder. His militancy had been honed before he arrived. Of course, there were good reasons for the way he reacted, and I've said many

times I would have been far more radical than he was. He couldn't play golf at the local courses. At one point, vandals broke into his house and defecated in his bed."

Russell's anger was justified, Johnny Most agreed. "I knew where he was coming from deep down," Most said. "And for a lot of it, I didn't blame him. He faced a lot of irritating, irritating prejudice."

In Auerbach's system, winning stood above all else. Neither the coach nor his players would let racial differences interfere with the main objective. Russell has said many times that, above all, he could trust his coach not to be petty.

A master psychologist, Auerbach created an atmosphere of give and take, a unique mix of toughness and fun in which pranksters thrived amid grueling practices. Exploding cigars and other silly gags were allowed, serving to bring a soft edge to Auerbach's hard drive for winning. Within this system, the Celtics liked each other and got along.

When Russell arrived, veteran frontcourt player Arnie Risen took him aside and talked about the ins and outs of the competition around the league. Another veteran on another team might not have imparted such knowledge to a rookie about to move into his territory, Russell later noted, but Auerbach surrounded himself with people who cared only about being No. 1.

The Jones boys, K.C. (left) driving for a layup against the Philadelphia Warriors, and Sam (right) were solid performers through Boston's glory years.

The Celtics' sixth straight title in 1964: (standing, left to right) Willie Naulls and K.C. Jones; (seated) Russell, Auerbach, Ramsey, Larry Siegfried and Jack McCarthy; (in the foreground) John Havlicek and trainer Buddy LeRoux.

That's not to say there weren't problems. Overall, the press exhibited little sophisticated knowledge of pro basketball in those years, and the reporters fawned over Cousy, the local hero, while virtually ignoring Russell's brilliance. Auerbach, however, sensed these injustices and constantly praised Russell and other unrecognized players while talking to reporters.

It was in this spirit that Frank Ramsey, the first of the Celtics' ballyhooed sixth men, grew in the public mind. Auerbach didn't invent the idea of the sixth man, but he tirelessly touted and promoted it to the writers covering Boston's games. In so doing, the coach wrapped his athletes in the ever-pervasive "team" concept.

The next season, 1957-58, Boston added Sam Jones, a surprise first-round pick in the draft, out of little North Carolina Central. Bones McKinney, who had played under Auerbach in the pros before gravitating to the coaching ranks at Wake Forest, had tipped off the redhead that this 6-4 guard was something special. In time, Jones would prove it. But for his rookie season, he fit in nicely coming off the bench.

With Russell leading the league in rebounding (22.7 average) and Cousy doing the same in assists (7.1 mark), Boston ran past Syracuse to win the Eastern Division title by eight games. St. Louis prevailed in the West, also by eight games, so a rematch was in the works in the NBA Finals.

In perhaps a telling commentary, Russell was voted to the All-NBA second team—but won the league's MVP award. The all-league team was determined by a vote of writers and broadcasters, who obviously still hadn't tumbled to the impact that the Boston center was having on his team, opposing clubs and the game itself; the MVP was decided by a balloting of NBA players, with Russell's peers knowing full well what he meant to the Celtics' success.

Boston seemed a good bet to win its second straight NBA title—until, that is, Russell suffered an ankle injury in Game 3. He appeared only briefly in the remainder of the Finals, and St. Louis won the championship in six games. In the decisive contest, Pettit broke loose for 50 points as the Hawks scored a one-point triumph (and thereby ran the cumulative margin in their four victories to eight points).

The Celtics renewed their efforts in 1958-59 with the addition of Gene Conley, the veteran backup bruiser who had played with the club six seasons earlier before achieving a modicum of distinction as a big-league pitcher, and service returnee K.C. Jones, a rookie who teamed well with Sam Jones off

The already-dominant Celtics added Tom (Satch) Sanders (right) in the 1960 draft and sixth-man supreme Havlicek (left) two years later.

the bench when Auerbach wanted to step up the defensive pressure. Again, Russell and Cousy led the league in rebounds and assists, respectively. And, once more, Boston powered to the Eastern Division title, this time by 12 games with a 52-20 record. St. Louis ran away with the regular-season crown in the West, building a 16-game margin, but the Hawks lost in the playoffs to the Minneapolis Lakers, who featured rookie sensation Elgin Baylor.

Boston had a scare in postseason play but, unlike St. Louis, survived. The Celtics were extended to seven games in the Eastern title round by a Syracuse team that had played sub-.500 ball in the regular season. At one point in Game 7 of the Eastern championship playoff, Most got so excited he nearly lost his dentures over the rail of the upper press deck.

"We were down at the half (by eight points)," Most recalled, "and it looked as if the Celtics' dynasty would be over before it ever got started. In the second half, it was the most perfectly played basketball game I've ever seen. Heinsohn often said it was

the best game he ever played in."

The Celtics charged back for a 130-125 triumph over the Nationals and rode the momentum of that victory to a sweep of the Lakers in the NBA Finals.

The dynasty was off and running, and once it got started, nothing seemed capable of stopping it—not even the arrival upon the scene of 7-2 Wilt Chamberlain, who joined the Philadelphia Warriors for 1959-60 after a stint with the Harlem Globetrotters. Chamberlain, an All-America at Kansas, proceeded to lead the league in scoring in his first seven seasons and he topped the NBA in rebounding in five of those years. But it was Russell who took home the championship rings.

The Celtics won an NBA-record 59 games in '59-'60, a season in which Chamberlain scored at a record-breaking 37.6 clip and helped boost league-wide attendance by 23 percent. But Wilt and company finished 10 lengths behind a Boston club that went on to outlast St. Louis in a seven-game Finals. A year later, Auerbach's athletes notched 57 victories and dispatched the Hawks in five games for the

Celebratory beer baths were becoming an annual rite by 1965, when the Celtics captured their seventh consecutive title with a five-game triumph over the Los Angeles Lakers.

NBA championship.

Then, in 1961-62, the Celtics broke their own record by winning 60 regular-season games before battling Chamberlain and Philadelphia in a seven-game Eastern title series. The two teams didn't like each other and fought to prove it. With 10 seconds left in Game 7 and Boston clinging to a three-point lead, Chamberlain, who had averaged an unbelievable 50.4 points per game during the regular season and scored 100 in one outing, dunked over Russell and was fouled. He made the free throw, tying the game at 107, but Sam Jones pumped in a game-winning jump shot with two seconds left.

"I thought they'd be looking for me to go right, so I went left," said Jones, who had lofted the game-winner over Chamberlain after Russell set a pick on Philadelphia's center. "I figured that if I could get the ball over Chamberlain's head, Russell could probably tip it in even if I missed."

The Finals pitted Boston against the Lakers, who by now had moved from Minneapolis to Los Angeles and boasted the likes of Baylor and Jerry West. The Celtics won big to open the series, but the Lakers stormed back for a 3-2 lead in games. Los Angeles' victory in Game 5 was spiced by Baylor's

61-point performance at Boston Garden. The redoubtable Celtics battled back, however, and prevailed in Game 6 in Los Angeles before going to overtime in Game 7 at Boston when the Lakers' Frank Selvy missed a bank shot at the end of regulation.

"I would trade all my points for that last basket," said Selvy, who once had tallied 100 points in a college game. "It was a fairly tough shot. I was almost on the baseline." The ball came off the rim, and Russell, who would finish with 30 points and 40 rebounds, wrapped it into his arms.

The Celtics made off with their fourth straight title in the extra period, taking a 110-107 decision. Sam Jones scored five of his 27 points in the overtime. Ramsey finished with 23 points.

While the championship banners had begun to proliferate, the Celtics weren't standing pat. They added reserve strength in the frontcourt for the 1962-63 season by obtaining veteran Clyde Lovellette, who had averaged more than 20 points per game for St. Louis in each of the three previous years. Additionally, Boston selected John Havlicek of Ohio State in the 1962 draft, and two years earlier the Celts had plucked Tom (Satch) Sanders of

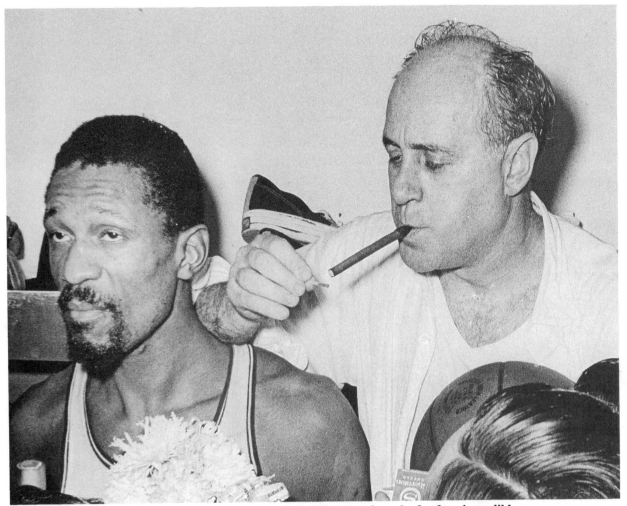

Auerbach's traditional victory cigars have punctuated Boston triumphs for four incredibly successful decades.

New York University out of the collegiate pool. Havlicek would become the quintessential sixth man in pro basketball, while Sanders' defense and rebounding already had figured prominently in Red's winning formula.

The '62-'63 season would be Cousy's last, meaning the Jones duo of Sam and K.C. would take on an ever-expanding role (although Sam already had demonstrated his talents with an 18.4 scoring average in '61-'62). Built around the incredible Russell, the team retooled with ease.

Boston's flamboyant coach and its "franchise" center clearly had come to dominate the NBA, and Auerbach toasted each victory with a cigar. There would be considerably more lighting up in the years ahead.

"At first I didn't like Red Auerbach," a rival NBA coach once said. "But in time I grew to hate him."

If anything, Auerbach's Celtics were so efficient, their fans almost acted as if they were boring. Average Boston Garden crowds in the 1961-62 season fell to 6,852, the lowest figure in nine years. "Once we started to win, we almost did it too easily," Cousy said.

Boston claimed the Eastern Division crown again in Cousy's farewell season, ringing up a 58-22 record before finishing off the Lakers in six games in the NBA Finals. Seven Celtics averaged more than 10 points per game in that '62-'63 campaign, with Sam Jones pacing the club in scoring for the first time with a 19.7 figure.

Cousy's retirement necessitated a change or two in Boston's philosophy. After all, the Celtics were losing a man who had averaged 18.5 points per game in his pro career, once made the All-NBA team in 10 consecutive seasons and led the league in assists eight straight times in another stretch.

"Red always added up what the starters would score," K.C. Jones said. "I was not a shooter, and Red figured with Cousy gone on offense we would lose seven or eight points. We made that up by increasing our defensive intensity."

There indeed were some adjustments, Heinsohn said. "Cousy was the greatest ever running the fast break," Heinsohn contended. "We still ran with the ball, but we didn't run the same way because K.C. was now the middle man in the break. He wasn't the same type of passer as Cousy. But with Sanders and Russell and the Joneses, we had four excellent defensive players."

The 1963-64 and 1964-65 Celtics kept the title streak intact. The sixth consecutive Finals conquest came against the Warriors, who now were based in San Francisco, and No. 7 was at the expense of the Lakers.

It was during the march to No. 7 that the makeup of the Eastern Division changed markedly. On January 15, 1965, the Western Division's Warriors traded Chamberlain to the East's Philadelphia 76ers (the onetime Syracuse Nationals franchise), and the 76ers—already possessing such talents as Hal Greer, Chet Walker and Lucious Jackson—suddenly were turned into a potential powerhouse.

Boston wound up well atop the standings with a 62-18 record but had to go seven games to escape the 76ers in the Eastern Division title round. In fact, Chamberlain's team wasn't vanquished until Havlicek stole an inbounds pass under Philadelphia's basket with five seconds remaining in Game 7, which Boston won, 110-109. Most's delirious "Havlicek stole the ball!" call is a broadcasting classic.

After Boston went on to defeat Los Angeles in the Finals for the third time in four years, Auerbach announced he would coach one more season and then retire to the front office. He explained privately that coaching had become a burden, a drudgery.

Perhaps more than any coach in NBA history, Red Auerbach loved winning, but success had taken its toll. Red was nearing 50 and feeling 70. Celtics Owner Walter Brown had died in September 1964, and the administrative load was heavier. Auerbach also was serving as Boston's general manager.

Chamberlain and company came back the following season, 1965-66, to take some of the steam out of the dynasty. Heinsohn had retired at the end of the previous season, and while the Celts found a nice replacement in Don Nelson, the Boston club—for the the first time in a decade—failed to win the Eastern Division title. The 76ers won 55 games and Boston 54. But Auerbach's charges regrouped in the playoffs. Philly had received a first-round bye and was caught flat in the Eastern title series as Boston won, four games to one.

The 1966 NBA Finals, again matching Boston against Los Angeles, quickly turned into another scrap. The Celtics had a good lead in Game 1 at Boston Garden, but the Lakers fought back to win, 133-129, in overtime. Afterward, Auerbach announced that Russell would be his replacement as coach the next fall. Working as a player-coach, Boston's center would be the first black head coach in a major American sport in modern times. (Auerbach had talked briefly with Heinsohn about taking the job, but both men agreed no one could better motivate Russell than Russell himself.)

With the future leadership of the team settled, the Celtics got down to business and won the next three games. But the Lakers fought back to tie the series at three victories apiece, setting the stage for another classic contest. Boston led Game 7 by six points with 20 seconds remaining, so it appeared time for Red

Auerbach plots strategy during a 1966 game as future coaching notable Don Nelson (left) and Naulls (right) listen intently.

to light another victory cigar. The Lakers took exception to that, cutting the margin to two points with four seconds left. But Havlicek took the inbounds pass and dribbled out the clock. Celtics 95, Lakers 93. *Eight* consecutive NBA championships for the Boston Celtics.

At Auerbach's retirement dinner, Russell addressed the gathering—and directed some special remarks at his longtime coach. "When I took this job," Russell started out, "somebody said, 'What did you take it for? You have nothing to gain. You've got to follow Red Auerbach.'

"I don't think I'm going to be another Red Auerbach. Personally, I think you're the greatest basketball coach that ever lived. You know, over the years . . . I heard a lot of coaches and writers say the only thing that made you a great coach was Bill Russell. It helped. But that's not what did it.

"Now this is kind of embarrassing, but I'll go so far, Red, as to say this: I like you. And I'll admit there aren't very many men that I like. But you, I do. For a number of reasons. First of all, I've always been able to respect you. I don't think you're a genius, just an extraordinarily intelligent man. We'll be friends until one of us dies. And I don't want too many friends, Red."

With Russell handling the coaching reins and contributing 21 rebounds per game as well, Boston won 60 regular-season games in 1966-67. Only problem was, Philadelphia was now a full-fledged juggernaut. The 76ers cruised to a record-breaking 68 victories (against only 13 losses) and routed Boston in five games in the Eastern championship round. Chamberlain and company then beat San Francisco in the Finals.

The amazing string of league titles had come to an end. But this reign of terror wasn't quite over. Not with Russell still around. And Sam Jones. And

By 1968, the veteran Russell was seeing double duty as a still-dominant center and Auerbach's successor as coach.

Auerbach, now general manager of the Celtics, gives Russell and Havlicek a victory hug after Boston's six-game title victory over the Lakers in 1968.

Havlicek. And Nelson. And Sanders. And Bailey Howell, a high-scoring forward who had been acquired from the Baltimore Bullets in September 1966. Something else was still around too: Celtic mystique.

With the pluses outweighing their one big minus, advancing years, the Celtics rebounded for NBA championships in 1968 and 1969. In the 1967-68 season, Boston again finished eight games behind Philadelphia, but the Celts outlasted the 76ers in the playoffs, four games to three, and then whipped the Lakers in six games in the NBA Finals. In the clincher against Los Angeles, Havlicek tossed in 40 points.

The 1968-69 season found Russell struggling with leg injuries that forced a brief hospital stay. With Sam Jones also hurting, Boston came to rely on Havlicek and Howell, who for the third straight season combined for more than 40 points per game.

Philadelphia had traded Chamberlain out of the Eastern Division—to the Lakers—over the summer, but the Celtics still struggled in the East. However, after finishing fourth with a 48-34 record, the Boston club drew upon Celtic pride in the playoffs and chased off the pretenders to the throne one more time. First, Philadelphia fell; then it was the New

York Knicks. The final chapter brought one more dramatic series with the Lakers, who were bolstered this time by Chamberlain.

Each team won three games on its home floor, bringing about Game 7 in Los Angeles. The Lakers found themselves down by 17 points with a little less than 10 minutes remaining in the game, but mounted a scorching comeback. The aging Celtics were fading fast with about five minutes to go when Chamberlain injured his knee and left the game. Later, when his knee felt better, Chamberlain asked Coach Butch van Breda Kolff to return. But the Lakers' coach decided to stay with Mel Counts.

The Celtics hung on for a 108-106 victory, thereby scoring their sixth Finals triumph of the 1960s over the thoroughly frustrated Lakers. And although they had been friendly through their careers, Russell later criticized Chamberlain for leaving the game. Nothing short of a broken leg should have taken Chamberlain out of the fray, Russell contended.

The game marked the last NBA playing appearances for the 35-year-old Russell and Sam Jones, nearing 36, and was Russell's swan song as the Celtics' coach as well. After three years on the job, he was ready to turn over the coaching rigors to some-

Boston Garden, with its parquet floor and the championship banners hanging majestically from the rafters, still exists as a museum of basketball excellence.

one else (and that someone else turned out to be Heinsohn). It also marked the end of an unparalleled period of team success in pro sports.

Oh, the Celtics would resurface as a power in the mid-1970s, with Dave Cowens leading the way, and they would scale the heights once more in the first half of the 1980s, thanks largely to the brilliance of Larry Bird. But the achievements of those teams paled in comparison with what the Celtics accomplished beginning with the 1956-57 season and ending with the 1968-69 campaign: 11 NBA titles in 13 seasons, one runner-up finish and 60 regular-season victories in the one season in which they didn't reach the Finals.

In 1985, the Celtics honored Auerbach for his work in building the team and for his 35-year contribution overall. Dozens of old Celtics returned, stars and role players alike, long-termers and short-timers, all to honor Red. The occasion prompted Bill Russell to reflect on exactly what set Auerbach apart.

"He never made any pretensions about treating players the same," Russell recalled. "In fact, he treated everybody very differently. Basically, Red treats people as they perceive themselves. What he did best was to create a forum, but one where indi-

viduals wouldn't be confined by the system. And he understood the chemistry of a team. People tend to think teamwork is some mysterious force. It can really be manufactured, and he knew how to do that, to serve each player's needs."

Explaining Boston's success as the 1990s drew near, Auerbach said: "Everything is basics. We care what happens to our players when they're through playing. The Celtic pride is not involved only in winning; it's the pride of being a Celtic. The pride of your performance, the pride of so many, many aspects. The pride that you take in your loyalty and the loyalty that's extended to you.

"When you retire we care what happens," he reiterated. "Obviously, we can't go after everybody who played here. But if a guy played all or most of his career here, I can tell you where every one of those players are, how they're fixed, what they're doing and that stuff. You look here at our games during the year, you'll find Havlicek, Cousy, Cowens, Heinsohn, Sanders . . . I can go on and on. Guys who are out of town are always welcome. They come up to the office. They never have to buy a ticket. They are always welcome."

In other words, the welcome mat is always out at Boston Garden. Just like a championship banner.

GREEN BAY PACKERS 1961 to 1967

The driving force behind the Green Bay Packers' success was Vincent Thomas Lombardi, pictured during his team's 1967 NFL title showdown—a.k.a. the Ice Bowl—against Dallas.

Even now, the achievement seems improbable. At the time, it seemed nothing but impossible.

The Green Bay Packers in 1958 finished 1-10-1, the absolute low point in the history of a once proud little franchise. And somehow, the outlook was even worse than their record.

Green Bay was still a village by National Football League standards, a mill town of about 65,000 inhabitants located at the mouth of the Fox River in northeastern Wisconsin. On the football map of the day (or any map, for that matter) it was a cold, remote spot seemingly more suited to ice fishing than professional football—kind of a Siberia of the NFL. If your play was flawed or your conduct faulty, this was the standard threat in the league: "If you don't shape up, we will trade you to Green Bay." The place was perceived as the end of the road—or somewhere north of it.

The Packers were, literally, run by committee. The team was a public trust, dating from the days when the citizens of the area bought shares in the franchise to prevent it from folding. That community effort represented a unique and noble chapter in American sports. But what the Packers were left with for leadership was their Executive Committee, a group of interested and influential local businessmen who were not particularly knowledgeable in football matters. The group guided the franchise as best it could. And the best, in the 1950s, wasn't very good.

The Packers for many years had been a powerhouse under founder Earl (Curly) Lambeau, who had coached the club to six league championships, including an unprecedented three straight titles from 1929-31. But Lambeau's post-World War II teams had gradually slipped, and the Packers had last posted a winning record in 1947. Gene Ronzani, Lisle Blackbourn and, finally in 1958, Ray (Scooter) McLean had subsequently failed as coaches.

If there was a silver lining around this cloud, it was the fact that the Packers actually had some talented players on hand. For all of their failures, they had been in a position to draft well, which they did. The rookie class in 1958 included fullback Jim Taylor, guard Jerry Kramer and linebacker Ray Nitschke, three future All-Pros who, nevertheless, couldn't prevent the Packers from sinking to terrible depths that year. Green Bay scored the fewest points in the league, surrendered the most points and suffered what still ranks as its worst beating ever, a 56-0 loss to the Baltimore Colts. "Scooter was a great guy," wide receiver Max McGee said in defense of McLean, "but nobody really cared."

The Green Bay coaching job was no plum. It was a coffin. When the Packers searched for a new coach for 1959, the Executive Committee considered such marquee names as Forest Evashevski of Iowa and Otto Graham, the former Cleveland Browns quarterback. In the end, the committee chose a relatively unknown offensive coach from the New York Giants: Vincent Thomas Lombardi.

A Proud Little Franchise

By Mike Bauman

Lombardi was 45 years old, perhaps best remembered as a former guard at Fordham and one of the "Seven Blocks of Granite." He had been an assistant coach at Fordham, Army and then New York, carrying with him a belief that he had been passed over for head coaching jobs because of his Italian heritage. But with Green Bay, Lombardi was made not only coach, but also general manager. In one bold stroke, the committee had acknowledged that this organization sorely needed direction.

Lombardi would spare no effort, or no person, to make certain this opportunity, often dreamed of and so often postponed, would lead only to greatness. The Green Bay players had no idea what they were getting in the person of Lombardi. He wasted no time in letting them know.

The Packers had for too long been characterized by complacency, a shrugging attitude toward training, toward practice, toward the whole business. McGee and Howie Ferguson, a veteran running back on those 1950s Packer teams, checked into a local hotel for a few final nights of enjoyment before their first camp under Lombardi was to begin. The rookies were already training, quartered at nearby St. Norbert College. McGee and Ferguson dropped by the college cafeteria for what they figured would be a free dinner with the team. They dined and then hit the streets.

The next morning, the two veterans returned for a free breakfast. Lombardi spotted them and pulled them into his office. He told them, in no uncertain terms and with trademark bursts of temper, that since they had eaten with the team, they now were officially members of the team. They would immediately start working out and keeping curfew. Ferguson protested, saying they were not due to report for two days. Lombardi gave the players a choice: follow his orders or get out for good. It was, McGee said, quite an introduction.

"Here we were, meeting him for the first time, and he really chewed our asses out," McGee said. "It sure gave me a sign of what was to come. I guess the object was to show that he was dead serious. It was probably normal for him. What the hell, I checked into the dorm. Ferguson, he didn't last through training camp."

A few nights later, Lombardi gathered all of the troops together for his first formal address. He challenged them, threatened them and, finally, promised them that greatness was within their reach if only they fully accepted his leadership, his system. The players saw in this man a presence, a personality, a determination that had been absent in the Packer organization. In that moment, Lombardi won over the players and took total command.

"He said, 'Anybody who doesn't want to play winning football, get the hell out of here right now,'" McGee recalled. "I said to myself, 'Hey, this guy's got something.' It was like Sinatra singing on stage. There was a presence there.

"We were better immediately. The difference between '58 and '59 . . . so help me God, it was night and day. From the top to the bottom, everything was totally different. We went first-class, we played first-class, the whole thing was professionally run.

"A couple of weeks later, after that speech, he called me in. He said: 'Maxie, when I made that speech, I was scared to death. I thought the whole damn group would just get up and walk out.' I said: 'Coach, you didn't have to worry. You had them by the ass.'"

From that moment, what was to be recorded was more than the development of a team, more than the resurgence of a lovably eccentric franchise. What would occur was the growth of a legend, or a pair of legends, intertwined. There were the Packers and there was Lombardi. Or perhaps it would be, there was Lombardi and there were the Packers.

At first, it was sudden enough to seem miraculous. After finishing 7-5 in 1959, their first winning season in 12 years, the Packers played for the NFL championship in Lombardi's second season. Green Bay would lose that 1960 title game to the Philadelphia Eagles, a defeat that left Lombardi bitterly disappointed. Most everyone else in the organization was astonished to be anywhere near a championship.

It would be the last time Lombardi lost a championship game. Over the next seven years, he would win five NFL titles and the first two Super Bowls.

By the third season, the Packers moved from being figures of ridicule to domination. They did not merely win the championship, but took apart the New York Giants in the title game, 37-0. The Packers had finished 11-3 during the regular season, a year in which three starters—halfback Paul Hornung, receiver Boyd Dowler and Nitschke—were summoned to Army reserve duty due to the Berlin crisis. It was a disruption, no doubt, but the players managed to get weekend passes and play in nearly every game. Hornung, perhaps the most versatile player of the era, won his third straight league scoring title, then victimized the Giants for a championship-game record 19 points on a touchdown run, four extra-point conversions and three field goals.

After the game, Lombardi, not generally given to overly generous praise, told the team: "Today, you were the greatest team in the history of the National Football League." President John F. Kennedy added his blessings, sending a telegram to Lombardi that read: "Congratulations on a great game today. It

was a fine victory for a great coach, a great team and a great town."

That set the tone for what was to follow. The Packers were, somehow, even better in 1962, finishing 13-1. The one blemish was a 26-14 Thanksgiving Day loss to the Detroit Lions. Berated by Lombardi for this one failure, the Packers were back on top in a week, routing the Los Angeles Rams, 41-10. Playing the Giants again for the championship, the Packers prevailed, 16-7.

"One thing about Lombardi, he was a student of the game, and he had this burning desire to win three world championships in a row," said linebacker Dave Robinson, the Packers' No. 1 draft pick in 1963. "He knew that the only team that had done that was the Packers, from 1929 to 1931. He was a fanatic about it. He was determined to go and win the third in a row."

Ordinarily, the Packers' performance in 1963 would have been good enough to earn a shot at the championship. But this was the year of a great Chicago Bears defense, led by Bill George, Doug Atkins, Joe Fortunato and Richie Petitbon. Chicago throttled the Packers twice, limiting Green Bay to a total of 10 points in both losses, and finished 11-1-2 to the Packers' 11-2-1 to claim the Western Conference title. The Packers had lost Hornung for the season to a suspension for gambling, and Lombardi had lost in his quest for three straight championships. But this dream turned out to be not really lost, only

Dynasty Data

Yearly Record
1961-1967

Season	W	L	T	Pct.	Avg. Score Pitt.-Opp.	Place	Coach
1961	11	3	0	.786	28-16	1	V. Lombardi
1962	13	1	0	.929	30-11	1	V. Lombardi
1963	11	2	1	.821	26-15	2	V. Lombardi
1964	8	5	1	.607	24-18	2†	V. Lombardi
1965	10	3	1	.750	23-16	1†	V. Lombardi
1966	12	2	0	.857	24-12	1	V. Lombardi
1967	9	4	1	.679	24-15	1	V. Lombardi
Total	74	20	4	.776	26-14		

Playoffs

Season	NFL Championship	Super Bowl (NFL vs. AFL)	Total Playoff Record
1961	37-0 New York		1-0
1962	16-7 New York		1-0
1963			
1964			
1965	23-12 Cleveland		1-0
1966	34-27 Dallas*	35-10 Kansas City*	2-0
1967	21-17 Dallas*	33-14 Oakland*	2-0
Total			7-0

*Game played in January of following year.

Additional Data

Best Year—1962 (13-1-0).
Worst Year—1964 (8-5-1).
Most Lopsided Victory—56-3 over Atlanta, 1966.
Most Lopsided Defeat—45-21 to Baltimore, 1961.
Most Consecutive Regular-Season Victories—11 games from Dec. 17, 1961 through Nov. 22, 1962.
Most Consecutive Regular-Season Defeats—2 games from Oct. 18 through Oct. 25, 1964; from Oct. 31 through Nov. 7, 1965.
Shutouts—The Packers held opponents scoreless in 7 games.
Times Shut Out—The Packers were never shut out during their dynasty years. Only once were they held to only 3 points.

The many faces of Lombardi: contemplative, warm and endearing, intimidating. Lombardi (below) makes his point during a 1967 game.

Two key figures in Green Bay's rise to football prominence in the 1960s: quarterback Bart Starr (left) and linebacker Ray Nitschke.

delayed.

There was, however, no hope in 1964 when the Packers slipped to 8-5-1. Second place—for the second straight year—was just not enough. "Vince always said, 'Once you've accepted second place, it's easy to accept third,' " Robinson recalled.

The Pack came back in 1965. Tied for first at the end of the regular schedule, the 10-3-1 Packers won a thrilling conference playoff game from the Baltimore Colts, 13-10. Then, on a snowy day at Lambeau Field, in the mud and the slush, Green Bay overcame the Cleveland Browns, 23-12, to regain the NFL championship. "This team has more character than any other team I've had," Lombardi said after the game.

Lombardi's final two seasons at the Packer helm were perhaps the most glorious. The rise of the Packers coincided with the emergence of the NFL as a television event. The league was receiving more exposure and the team from Green Bay became a national phenomenon. The rivalry with the American Football League was leading to the merger that would take the professional game to an even higher level.

All of this came together on January 15, 1967, in the Los Angeles Coliseum, for Super Bowl I. To get

there, the Packers had compiled a 12-2 record in 1966, then defeated the Dallas Cowboys for the NFL championship, 34-27, with Bart Starr throwing four touchdown passes. Playing the Kansas City Chiefs for the "world championship," the Packers seemed to be in a no-win situation. They carried the prestige of the NFL into a game against the champions of an upstart league. A loss would be unthinkable. Even a narrow victory would be inadequate. But the Packers defeated the pressure and the Chiefs, pulling away in the second half for a decisive 35-10 victory that left no doubt about the superiority of the team and the league.

After the game, reporters tried to coax Lombardi into a comparison of the NFL and AFL. He resisted initially, but finally stated the fact. "That's a good football team," he said of Kansas City. "But it is not as good as the top teams in our league. That's what you want me to say and now I've said it. It took me a long time."

Poised on the brink of history, the three straight championships in the modern era, Lombardi pushed his players perhaps harder than ever in 1967. The Packers were beginning to age, they were bothered by a string of injuries and every team in the league saw a game against Green Bay as a life-

The devastating Packer sweep: guards Jerry Kramer (64) and Fuzzy Thurston roll out to clear a path for powerful fullback Jim Taylor.

time opportunity. Gone were such stars as Hornung and Taylor.

Through all this, the Packers displayed an indomitable quality. Perhaps they did not blow out opponents with regularity, but they still won when they had to, taking the Central Division title with a 9-4-1 record in the first year of the NFL's four-division format. In the Western Conference playoff, they met the Rams, who had posted an 11-1-2 record and beaten the Packers just weeks before. Touted as the team of the future, the Rams were humbled by the Pack, 28-7.

The NFL championship game, December 31, 1967, became more than an athletic contest, but a test of will. The "Ice Bowl," as it became known, between the Packers and the Cowboys, was played in conditions suitable to a performance by Admiral Byrd, not the NFL. The temperature at Lambeau Field was minus-13 degrees and the wind chill 40 below.

But the vision remains, of the clock running down, the Dallas defenders digging in, trying to find a foothold in the frozen tundra that passed for turf, and Starr, keeping the ball from a yard away, behind the blocks of, most famously, Kramer, and, less famously but just as important, center Ken

Bowman, and finding the end zone.

The Packers won, 21-17. They had defeated the best of the NFL and endured the worst of the elements in claiming their third straight NFL title and fifth in seven years. An ensuing 33-14 victory over the Oakland Raiders in Super Bowl II made it official: This was a coach and team that had come from the bottom to the top of their sport, through ability, through cohesion, through sheer will. They would transcend their own era and become American legends. Little Green Bay, regarded by the metropolitan types as nothing more than a dot in a distant province, proudly became "Titletown U.S.A."

There was, and still is, a religious quality about Green Bay Packer football. Lambeau noted this early, calling the team "a community project and a regional religion." The people of Green Bay cared not just about every game, but about every play. They cared not just about every player's position, but about every nick and scratch he might suffer. "The only crime here," the police chief remarked, "is when the Packers lose."

There was no place like Green Bay, and for many players who might have initially thought otherwise, it was the only place they wanted to play.

"I didn't really know at first how this little town could be a football town," Nitschke said. "But it didn't take long to figure out how important the Packers were, and are, to the people of this city and of this state. Then I started to understand the loyalty and the knowledge and the support."

Packer football is the focal point of life outside the home in Green Bay. Perhaps, between July and January, it becomes the focal point of life inside the home, as well. There is not a wealth of cultural diversity in this setting. But there are not many distractions, either. This would be the ideal place for Lombardi, the New Yorker, to work his coaching magic. He would be completely focused on football. His directives, and these circumstances, would ensure that his players had the same focus.

Lombardi would bring with him a religious nature, both in the traditional sense and in the way he approached this game. Lombardi was a devout Catholic, a daily communicant. This was noted with a mixture of respect and skepticism by the players, who heard the coach regularly indulge in a sweeping variety of profanities.

"We used to say that if you talked to him once, you knew why he had to go to church every day," Starr said. "He always said that there were three central things in life, in this order of priority: Number 1, religion. Number 2, family. Number 3, the Green Bay Packers. We used to accuse him of getting those turned around."

Religion represented, at least in part for Lombardi, a striving toward personal perfection, and the players saw that philosophy applied to them daily on the football field. They would be driven and then driven some more to reach Lombardi's vision of what they could be as individual players and as a team. But perfection would always be elusive. Lombardi could be toughest on his players not in defeat, but after a victory in which he thought their performance had been shabby.

"There would be this fanny-chewing after we'd won," Starr said. "You'd think, 'My God, he has the wrong team in here.' But then when we saw the film, we knew what he was talking about."

The Packers never became perfect, but they became champions. Whatever they achieved, they achieved by living up to Lombardi's view of football and of life. His views were embodied in a cluster of phrases that have come down to us as cliches. But they were not cliches with Lombardi. They were reality, they were necessity. Mental toughness, paying the physical price, playing hurt, the willingness to excel—these were the qualities that he had to instill in the Packers. "He sold it," Starr said. "Everybody bought it."

There are two quotes, one by Lombardi, the other about him, that symbolize the man for posterity. One is his statement: "Winning isn't everything. It's the only thing." The media have seized upon that and made it his credo. But Michael O'Brien, in a definitive work on Lombardi, "Vince: A Personal Biography of Vince Lombardi," points

out that Lombardi said, at least as often, "Winning isn't everything; trying to win is." That's a lot more human and realistic. Total effort was probably the only thing.

The other quote was by defensive tackle Henry Jordan, a Packer for 11 seasons. "Coach Lombardi is very fair. He treats us all the same—like dogs." That was a great one-liner. But it wasn't, in a literal sense, true. It was Lombardi's genius, in the midst of the religious fervor about winning, to identify the precise way to motivate each individual.

Lombardi could rise to great heights of verbal abuse, humiliating players who responded to that kind of criticism. A favorite target was Nitschke. Before Lombardi's arrival, Nitschke was regarded as a linebacker with great potential, but a player with little discipline, on or off the field. Nitschke took the abuse regularly, learning not only to understand it but, in a way, to appreciate it.

"Lombardi never let up, man," he said. "The guy never let up. But he was consistent. You had to admire that guy. He was just never satisfied. He didn't give up many compliments, but when you got those (championship) rings, then you knew that it was all worthwhile.

"And I knew that he was for me. He wanted me not only to be a good player, but to be a good guy. I needed that. Before I got married, I was kind of runnin' them streets."

Marv Fleming, a Packer tight end from 1963 through 1969, was another frequent recipient of Lombardi's wrath. "Every time he would say something complimentary about Marv Fleming in the paper, Marv would have a bad game," Robinson remembered. "So after awhile, he very rarely gave Marv any accolades, even though he said later that Marv Fleming was one of the best tight ends he ever saw. I told Marv, 'You should have played lousy after he yelled at you. That's the only way he's going to quit.' "

One of the best examples of the one-on-one relationship between player and coach involved defensive end Willie Davis, a cornerstone of the Packers from 1960 through 1969. Davis, like many players of the era, had dreaded his arrival in Green Bay. After spending his first two years with the Cleveland Browns, he heard on his car radio one day after the 1959 season that he had been traded to Green Bay.

"For the first time in my life," he said, "I thought of pulling across the highway into the oncoming traffic lane. That's how bad the thought of going to Green Bay was."

Lombardi's reputation as the strictest of taskmasters was not something that gave him cause for cheer, either. But the Lombardi he found was nothing like what he expected. "He was so friendly, so warm, that there was a kind of chemistry immediately created with the man," Davis said.

Lombardi told Davis that with his quickness and ability to react to unfolding plays, he could be a great football player in Green Bay. He asked what kind of contract Davis had with the Browns. "I was naive enough at the time to believe that he didn't know," Davis said. "I told him and he gave me a $1,000 raise on the spot. He had me pretty well locked up even before I left the office."

Davis became, over the years, extremely close to Lombardi. Lombardi respected his performance, his competitive nature and the fact that Davis was, like himself, a perfectionist. Davis watched and saw how every player got what he needed from Lombardi in terms of motivation. "He knew that I was my own worst critic. He once said to me, 'Willie, I know why you have to play the way you play.' He understood me."

Davis may have been an ideal Lombardi player because of his pride and self-motivation, but he wasn't exempt from criticism. "Some people will tell you that Willie Davis was one of Lombardi's favorites," Davis said. "But I can remember after one game, Lombardi came in there and looked dead at me and said, 'You ought to apologize because we didn't have a defensive line out there today.' He

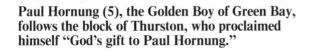

Paul Hornung (5), the Golden Boy of Green Bay, follows the block of Thurston, who proclaimed himself "God's gift to Paul Hornung."

Nitschke, one of nine Hall of Fame players from the Packer dynasty, was an intense middle linebacker who thrived on contact.

looked at me dead in the face and said, 'Willie Davis, you ought to be ashamed of yourself.' "

Nobody else was totally immune, either. "There was no one above the system," Davis said. "Even a Bart Starr . . . was treated the same as the 45th guy on the squad."

Of all the relationships on a football team, the one between coach and quarterback is the most delicate and the most demanding. Starr became, over time, an extension of Lombardi's philosophy on the field—fiercely competitive, resourceful, precise, the epitome of football leadership and intelligence.

But the relationship did not begin with much promise. Starr is a man who prizes civility, in himself and in others. He also possesses grim determination, though not in a flamboyant way. Consequently, to those who don't know him, Starr the quarterback might appear too gentle for the task at hand.

When Lombardi took over the Packers, Starr was a struggling young quarterback, a 17th-round 1956 draft choice from Alabama. To Lombardi, at first, Starr was too self-effacing, lacking in the outward signs of leadership. Veteran Lamar McHan was brought in to compete at quarterback until Starr's performance in 1960 finally lifted him into Lombardi's favor and the starting job, for keeps. The Packers also launched an era of excellence few sports franchises have matched.

"It was a vacillating period," Starr said of the first year and a half under Lombardi. "The quarterbacks were playing the game of merry-go-round; one of us on the horse, the other one next to it."

Starr said his confidence never failed him, but added: "He misread me. He mistook meekness for weakness."

Time, and Starr's success, took care of that. "Over time, we developed trust and respect," he said. "My father had always told me that those are qualities that are earned. They are not given away. I had to earn his trust, his respect, his confidence."

Some perceived McGee and Hornung to be Lombardi's favorites, but both players also learned that where discipline was concerned, there was no preferential treatment.

"I thought, 'He loves those guys.' " Robinson recalled. "But every time I turned around, he was fining Max. I thought, 'Hell, he loves Max. He probably hates me. I better keep my nose clean.' That kept me on the straight and narrow."

McGee and Hornung, the Golden Boy, were the two Packers with the playboy images. McGee maintains that at least part of his reputation is myth, built by succeeding generations of writers. He has played along with the script, in an amused sort of way. "I liked to go to parties, sure," he said. "But Number 1, I wasn't much of a drinker. I really was something other than the local drunk who went out every night. But it's my reputation and I've gone along with it. I haven't killed it.

"I broke some rules, but I didn't mind paying the fines if I got caught. But I was in the best shape of my life every time I played under Vince Lombardi. If I was half as bad as all those stories, Vince Lombardi wouldn't have had me around."

One memorable episode occurred as the fines against McGee for breaking curfew escalated from $50 to $100 to $500. In a team meeting, Lombardi angrily told McGee that the next fine would be $1,000. Then, lowering his voice, he suggested: "Max, if you can find anything worth sneaking out for, for a thousand bucks, hell, call me and I'll go out with you."

There was, indeed, more to Lombardi than the raging tyrant that some have portrayed. "I knew Vince Lombardi well enough to know the type of life he led," McGee said. "He wasn't always deadly serious. I think he envied, in a way, the kind of life led by Paul Hornung and Max McGee."

Starr believes that Lombardi "relished" a player who challenged his rules at times, because he saw in that behavior the sign of a strong-willed person, a competitor. The classic example was again McGee.

In 1966, McGee's career was winding down. Thirty-four years old, he played little during the regular season, catching only four passes over the 12-game schedule. But in Super Bowl I, when starting wide receiver Boyd Dowler was injured early in the game, McGee was summoned off the bench. He caught seven passes for 138 yards and two touchdowns, sparking Green Bay to a 35-10 victory over Kansas City. And, as legend has it, on Super Bowl Eve, McGee was everywhere but his hotel room.

In that historic moment, when Lombardi had other receivers ready to play, younger and doubtlessly better-rested receivers, he turned to McGee. The fact that McGee was still around indicates Lombardi could be pragmatic about iron discipline when it involved a competitor.

"You could never count on something like that," McGee said of his Super Bowl opportunity. "But I had watched Kansas City's defensive backs on film and I knew they weren't great. I said to Ray Scott, our broadcaster then, 'If they let me in there, I'm going to bust this thing wide open.' I'll be damned, I got the opportunity. I had hardly played all year. But I knew that if it ever got to a big game, I'd be the first substitute wide receiver. I was a gamer and Lombardi liked that."

Just as Lombardi looked upon his players as individuals with specific needs, whether saints or sinners, needing little direction or constant direction, each player saw the coach in a slightly different way.

There is no single picture of Lombardi that will suffice. There was too much of a man for that, too many shifts of mood, too many volcanic eruptions of temper followed by moments of gentleness. But it also was part of the genius of Lombardi that he could become what the players needed him to be. For some, he was a father figure. For others, he was a great coach but a difficult, at best, human being. But even those who did not particularly like him could not avoid respecting him.

Talented cornerback Herb Adderley was a ballhawk who returned seven of his 48 career interceptions for touchdowns.

Tackle Forrest Gregg (left) and center Jim Ringo (right) were intelligent, scrappy players who fit the Lombardi mold.

Kramer, in his book "Instant Replay," characterized Lombardi as a "cruel, kind, tough, gentle, miserable, wonderful man whom I often hate and often love and always respect." Had that been written about almost any other public figure, the author could be accused of overwriting to create an effect. In Lombardi's case, the man was all that Kramer described and more.

"Lombardi was a very emotional man," Davis said. "Lombardi would have to fight back tears at the drop of a hat, and yet he could show anger that was so intense that it could almost instill fear in you.

"I never met anyone else who could kick the living hell out of you one moment and in the next moment restore every good feeling you ever had."

Robinson was a high-spirited player, a man with a quick and ready wit. Yet he saw the need for direction. Lombardi entered his life at what was for him a perfect time.

"Vinnie and I got along very well," Robinson said. "I questioned everything, I wanted to know everything, I wanted to know the why, the theory. But he understood that.

"I always had the feeling that he was rough and gruff and exacting. But my father died when I was

in high school and he became a father figure for me. At that time, I had a fear of Vince Lombardi. But it was like the fear you have for your father. You know he loves you, but you also know that if you screw up, he'll punish you."

Robinson remembers, humorously and pointedly, breaking (sort of) a standing Lombardi rule. The team ran on what the players called "Lombardi time," which meant they were to show up 20 minutes ahead of the scheduled time. Lombardi was obsessed with punctuality, which to him was an indication of commitment. "He always used to say, 'Every morning before you leave, plan to have a flat tire and run out of gas,'" Robinson related, chuckling.

One particular morning, Robinson planned to stop at a diaper service before 10 a.m. practice. "I played in the days before they had Huggies," he said. Once under way, however, he had a flat tire. Losing time to the diapers and the flat, he finally made it to the Lambeau Field locker room, obsessed with time by this point. He frantically dressed, declining to have his ankles taped by the trainer, and was on the field by 9:40, feeling relieved. Robinson knew the Packers levied a $250 fine against a player who suffered an ankle injury when his ankles

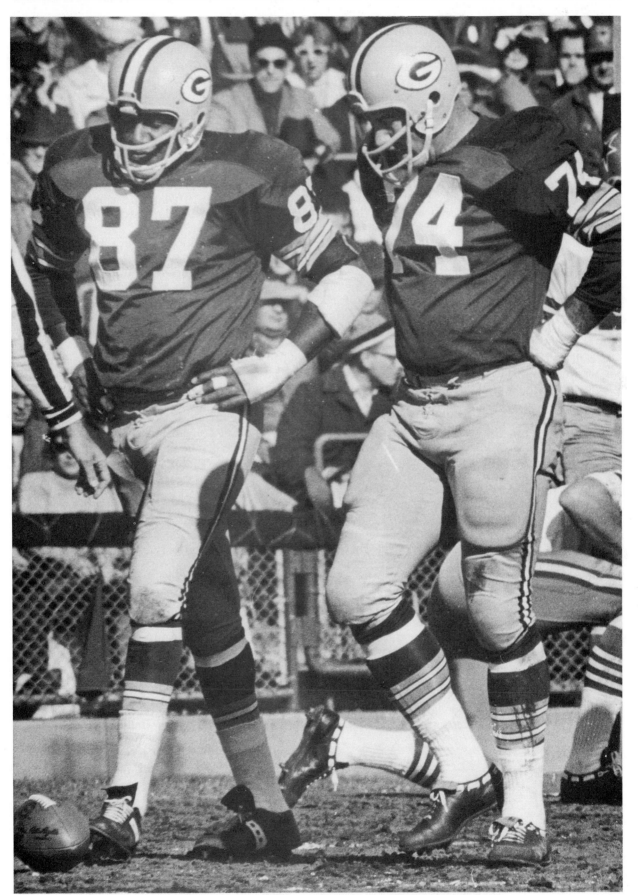

Defensive end Willie Davis (87) and tackle Henry Jordan, the Pack's ferocious pass rushers, return to the huddle after dropping Dallas quarterback Craig Morton.

weren't taped. Obviously, he had not yet violated this rule.

Lombardi, in something other than a happy mood, approached Robinson. "He comes over to me and says, 'Your ankles aren't taped, what happened?'" Robinson said. "I couldn't tell him that I had a flat tire, because he always said to plan for that. So I said, 'I have no excuse.' So he fined me $50."

Lombardi had made Robinson feel very guilty for not quite being late. He had fined him for not yet violating a rule. "Ron Kramer came over to me and said, 'That fine isn't fair; you should appeal it to the Packer Executive Committee.' I said, 'Right, I'm going to the Packer Executive Committee over $50.' But then Lombardi came over, hit me on the back of the head, laughed and that was it. There were no more words between us about it."

This was another part of Lombardi that some of the mythmakers have overlooked. He could push and push and push. But he knew when to stop pushing.

And when he had pushed too far. Ken Bowman was Hall of Famer Jim Ringo's successor at center for the Packers of the mid-1960s, into the '70s. He was an independent-minded, intelligent man who did not accept Lombardi's approach as readily as others did.

"I didn't get onto the Jerry Kramer bandwagon or the 'father figure' thing," Bowman said. "I had a father and I loved him very much and I knew that my father wouldn't have treated me the way Lombardi treated me."

Bowman regarded Lombardi with more ambivalence than many other players. While he says: "I will always admire and respect the man and the greatness of what he achieved as a football coach," he also will say: "I've often said that if he was not so successful, he would have been a miserable human being."

But again, Bowman saw how Lombardi found the limits for dealing with each individual. "He knew exactly how far he could push and he knew exactly when he had pushed too far," Bowman said. "He really knew how to handle people and that was the key to his strength."

Bowman recalled one practice session when he found himself being pushed too far. The offense was in a two-minute drill, trying to move the ball 80 yards. "You put your mind in neutral and just pass-block," he said. There was an incomplete pass, so the offense huddled. The snap count was changed and then Starr changed the play. Bowman snapped the ball and backed up, intending to protect the passer. The new play, however, called for a run by Taylor, and Bowman backpedaled into the charging fullback. Lombardi exploded.

"Lombardi called me stupid, he called me ignorant, he called me an ass, he called me everything he could think of," Bowman said.

Practice ended and Bowman fumed as he trudged off the field. He was tired. He was smarting from the insults. He was a rational man in an irrational situation.

"I was thinking, 'I have had it,'" he remembered. "I was walking back across the parking lot thinking, 'I don't have to do this. I don't have to put up with this. I've got to be a masochist to put up with this. I could play anywhere in this league. What am I doing up here, playing for this idiot?'"

And at that moment, of course, Lombardi came up to Bowman, gave him a hearty pat on the back, told him "Way to go," and congratulated him for the way he was helping the team get ready for Sunday's game.

Bowman still thinks of that, how Lombardi made him feel like an outcast one moment, and in the next, not only brought him back into the fold, but made him feel like the most essential member of the Green Bay Packers. Bowman still asks: "How can you stay mad at a guy like that?"

Starr was one player who didn't find Lombardi that far out of his personal experience. But then, Starr had grown up as the son of a master sergeant. "Actually, my father was tougher," he said.

Starr heard statements that Lombardi made and remembered statements his father made. The striving for excellence was at the heart of what both men taught Starr. And so were the lofty expectations and the rigid discipline. "From his first day there, Lombardi always talked about striving to be the best you can be," Starr said. "So today, every time I see one of those U.S. Army commercials, I'm reminded of Lombardi's teachings."

Somewhere in the process of the endless conditioning drills and grueling practices, Lombardi penetrated the minds of these players with the inescapable thought that such drudgery would lead directly to their being a championship football team. At first, it had to be hard to accept. The Packers were used to neither winning nor this kind of labor. Yet, they were worked as if they already were champions.

"If you had told me back then, out there doing those grass drills, that we would have ended up with all of these championships, with all of these people in the Hall of Fame, I would have said, 'You gotta be crazy,'" Nitschke said.

"But we had a lot of people who wanted to win, and that was combined with having a special leader. You learned that people many times have a lot

Green Bay vs. Most Frequent Opponents

1961-1967
(5 or More Regular-Season Games)

Opponent	W	L	T	Pct.	Avg. Score G.B.-Opp.
Chicago	11	3	0	.786	20-11
Minnesota	11	3	0	.786	30-16
Los Angeles	9	3	1	.731	25-17
San Francisco	9	3	1	.731	23-15
Detroit	9	3	2	.714	20-13
Baltimore	9	4	0	.692	24-17

Jordan closes in for the kill against New York Giants fullback Alex Webster during the 1961 NFL Championship Game won by the Packers, 37-0.

more than they're willing to put out, both physically and mentally. Physically, the human body can go through a lot of abuse. Mentally, it's the same thing. It's amazing what people can do when they're emotionally strong. And you can build on that. It was something where you pushed yourself as hard as you could. And then you had Lombardi pushing you that much more."

The players recall most vividly the grass drills, especially Lombardi's favorite, the "up-downs." In this drill, they ran in place, lifting their knees as high as they could, pumping as hard as they could, and then, on command, hit the ground, bellies first. On command, they popped up again, driving the legs once more until they performed probably 70 repetitions, maybe 75, who knew after awhile?

The players remember reaching a point where they knew they could go no further, yet they were made to go further. And when they did, they felt a sense of exhilaration, of stretching beyond physical limitations. Lombardi was planting the seeds of an idea, that this training—painful, exhaustive, repetitious though it was—represented the one path that would lead directly to victory. This was where the

Packers would have an edge.

"I've sat back and I've tried to analyze it," Bowman said. "Maybe the secret was in the grass drills, getting the guys exhausted, then controlling them mentally. He had you so dog-tired that your mind was not working. And then, you just went on. Up-downs. It's early in training camp and you're on maybe your 70th one. And then he starts in on how you're going to thank him in December.

"When the mind was too weak to fight it off, he would then try to persuade you that you were going to be a superior-conditioned athlete, that nobody else could be in this kind of shape, that this was part of being a champion. He would implant that in the mind when the mind didn't have any resistance. That's probably how he did it, as I look back."

There was no questioning the old axiom that you play the way you practice. And if you didn't practice the Lombardi way, you didn't play. "We were not allowed to jump offside on third-and-one," McGee said. "If you jumped offside in practice, you didn't play on Sunday."

The players accepted the system, because as hard as Lombardi drove them, he drove himself at least

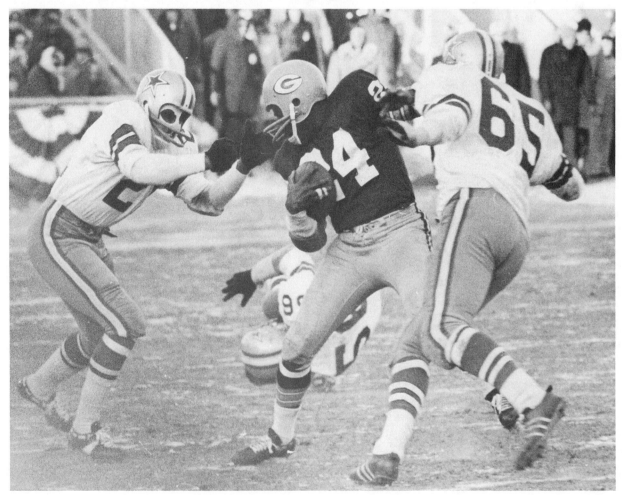

One of the classic games in NFL history occurred on December 31, 1967, when Green Bay met the Cowboys for the league championship in arctic-like conditions at Lambeau Field. Adderley (26) prepares to dive on a Dallas fumble (above). Willie Wood (below) encounters an unfriendly masked man while returning a punt.

Lombardi, backup quarterback Zeke Bratkowski and Starr plot Ice Bowl strategy moments before Starr's game-winning plunge into the end zone.

as hard. Bowman and others remember driving past the Packer offices at midnight, routinely seeing Lombardi's car parked outside, seeing light flickering in his office, knowing that he was going over films one more time, looking for that one edge that might spell the difference between victory and defeat.

The Packer assistant coaches were treated no differently. Players recall visiting the offices in the off-season and observing assistants diagramming plays as if it were midseason.

Lombardi was able to foster a kind of togetherness that is extinct today, in an era of inflated salaries, avaricious agents and rampant jealousies. Lombardi preached that no one could win with selfish players. Oh, maybe a selfish player could find selfish reasons to get up for a game or two and win a couple that way, but over the long haul, no.

"From Day One he stressed teamwork, the team concept," Starr said. "He told us unequivocally that the people who were members of this organization must be willing to submit their own desires to the good of the team."

There were good football players traded or released by Lombardi, but they were not what he regarded as good team players. Before his first camp,

he traded wide receiver Billy Howton, twice an All-Pro pick and the Packers' leading receiver from 1952 through 1957. After one game that season, he released rookie Timmy Brown, who would become one of the league's most versatile and exciting running backs with Philadelphia.

"There was a cohesion among the members of the team and I think Lombardi instilled that," Bowman said. "He got rid of a lot of players who were good football players, but who didn't fit in."

The players were urged to stay together and socialize together. In Green Bay, there were not always many other alternatives, anyway. "There are a lot of great things that people don't realize about playing in a small town," Nitschke said. "You get to know your teammates a lot better. Socially, you kind of depended on your teammates. Playing there, after awhile, I really appreciated it."

After home games, the Packers met for a ritual party, which Robinson described as a "debriefing" session. Players aired any complaints they had with each other, and the game was replayed, for better or worse. The discussions remained strictly private business.

"Guys would get things off their chests before they went out into public, downtown for dinner, whatever," Robinson said. "When I went to the Washington Redskins later, everyone went their own way. But in Green Bay, the result was that you never had teammates second-guessing each other in the press. There was none of those comments getting back to reporters."

Some of the factors that exacerbate envy among players today did not exist then. Salaries were a pittance compared with current money, and there was less economic disparity. And unlike today, when bonus money for postseason play is just a fraction of a player's total salary package, the playoffs for players of the 1960s were, on a percentage basis, a real windfall. What was good for the team was, financially and literally, good for the individual player.

Some of that could have changed in 1966 with the arrival of running backs Donny Anderson and Jim Grabowski, the "Gold Dust Twins," who were to be the heirs to Hornung and Taylor. In the midst of a bidding war with the American Football League, Lombardi signed the two draft picks to multiyear contracts totaling close to $1 million. That, of course, was more money than many of the veterans would see over their entire careers. The thinking around Green Bay was that this would tear the team apart. "The line won't block for these guys," the reasoning went.

That was just not a consideration. Bowman laughed at it then and laughs at it now. "You heard that sort of thing," he said. "But there would be 50,000 people in the stadium and all of those people watching on TV. Not blocking for those guys with the big price tags? I may as well have taken out a knife and fallen on it, samurai-style, to show everyone how to commit suicide. It was the pride factor.

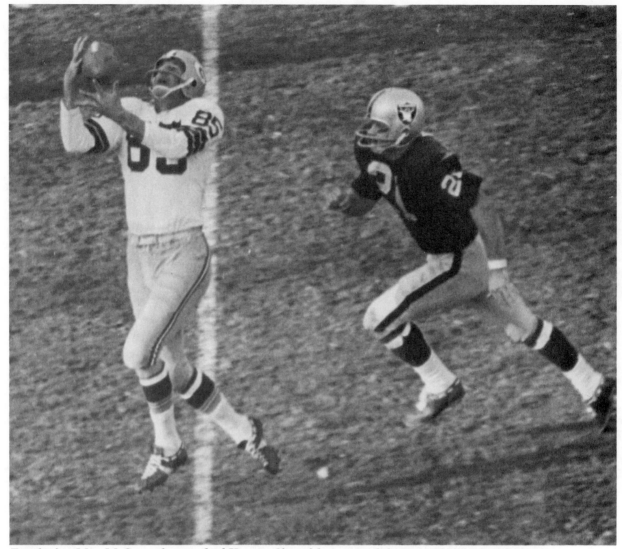

Fun-loving Max McGee, who wrecked Kansas City with two touchdown catches in Super Bowl I, pulls in a 35-yard pass from Starr to set up a Super Bowl II touchdown against Oakland.

The pride was bigger than the money."

Said Nitschke: "We didn't have all that envy, that jealousy. We really had that attitude of all-for-one. Nobody cared about who was making the most or who was getting the most interviews. The attitude was, you've got to be family, you can't be selfish. You can't worry about what the other guy gets. We accepted that. Lombardi focused on it, but you have to have people who respond and accept it.

"When Anderson and Grabowski came in, I really don't think anybody was jealous. They were happy that they got the big money. You didn't care about the money so much. You just wanted to make the team better. The great teams, or the great companies, have the same quality—everybody working toward one goal, winning. We had people who felt just that way."

Lombardi took extra steps to make sure that the family feeling was extended. After one championship, he bought mink stoles for the players' wives. After another title, the Packer families received stereos as gifts. Other clubs were less than thrilled

with this expensive precedent. But Lombardi had the wives behind him in this drive for excellence. He had just drafted some of the most influential people in America.

And so the Packers—offense, defense, husbands, wives—pulled together. Some of this was Lombardi being astute, whether in dealing with individuals or gathering about him the type of people who would view life through the eyes of a team player. Some of it was good men rising above the pitfalls of jealousy and envy. Lombardi frequently spoke of the feeling on the team as "love." Whatever the terminology, the bond was formed and it held, year after year.

"The crucial thing with those teams was togetherness," Robinson said. "Lombardi would tell us, 'Individually, you guys are nothing. There are lots of guys in the league who are bigger, faster, stronger. But together, you are the Green Bay Packers, the greatest team in the world.'"

Said Bowman: "The way that whole team fit together was the crucial element. Nobody was a misfit. Nobody was out of place. That is, I think, what

Jerry Kramer (right) and Gregg (left) hoist a happy Lombardi after Green Bay's "Super" victory over the Raiders.

created the championship fever that we had in Green Bay. There were other teams with great players. The Los Angeles Rams of that era, for instance, had some great players. But they never played consistently the way Green Bay did."

But there is no overlooking the individual talent that thrived within the Packer system. Nine members of the dynasty, in addition to Lombardi, are in the Hall of Fame: Starr, Hornung, Taylor, Gregg, Ringo, Davis, Nitschke, Herb Adderley and Willie Wood. "I really believe that when all the dust has settled, upwards of half the squad will have been enshrined," Davis said.

Starr was, to Lombardi, "a perfectionist, a great student of the game" who made up for what he lacked in flair with a methodical, analytical approach that made him arguably the greatest quarterback of the 1960s.

"Unitas may be able to burn you faster because

of his arm," Detroit Lions safety Bruce Maher said in 1966, "but Starr will frustrate you to death. He will find the weakness in your defense and keep after it until you adjust. Then he will find the new weakness. And when you do something about that, he'll be back after the old weakness."

Sometimes criticized for being conservative ("All Starr has to do up at Green Bay is hand off to Taylor and Hornung," Bobby Layne once said), Starr nevertheless led the league in passing in 1962, 1964 and 1966. He was a master of unerring execution, throwing 294 consecutive passes without an interception at one point to set a standing NFL record. In 1966, he was intercepted only three times, tying a single-season league record.

"The Packers never let loose of the darn ball with their 'three, four, six, move-the-sticks' offense," said Norm Van Brocklin, the former championship quarterback who coached the Minnesota Vikings from 1961 through 1966. "Bart Starr is the master of all situations. He is the smartest quarterback in pro football."

When he retired in 1971, a Packer for 16 seasons, Starr had compiled a .574 completion percentage, the best in NFL history at the time. Yet always, he deflected praise to his blockers, his receivers and the powerful backfield of Hornung and Taylor that chewed up yard after yard.

Hornung never found the spotlight too bright, not as the 1956 Heisman Trophy winner as a senior quarterback at Notre Dame, not when he was suspended for betting on NFL games, or when he stepped out on the town with a fetching young lady.

His image aside, Hornung was the single most dangerous weapon in the Packer offense. "Hornung did it all," Adderley said. "He ran the ball. He threw the halfback option pass better than anybody. He was a good receiver. He kicked extra points and field goals. He was a triple threat, plus.

"Paul didn't have blazing speed but he was smart, he set up his blockers real well. He ran the power sweep to perfection. Vince called him our money player. Get the ball inside the 10 and Paul would find a way to score."

A Packer through 1966, Hornung came into his own under Lombardi, winning the NFL scoring title three consecutive seasons (1959-61) after playing only sparingly (at quarterback, fullback and halfback) his first two years. In 1961, he set a standing league record by rolling up 176 points (an average of 15 points per game), though he never believed he was a special target for enemy defenders.

"They can't set their sights on me with the likes of Jim Taylor there with me," he said. "When they stop me, he gets away. And if the defense is set to stop him, it helps my plays go."

Taylor was the Packer powder keg, a straight-ahead runner who often sought out opponents to blast head-on. "You've got to make tacklers respect you," he explained. "You've got to punish them before they punish you."

Taylor earned respect as a ballcarrier, though he liked to antagonize opponents for a more spirited battle. "You tackle him and he'll say, 'I thought you could hit harder than *that*,'" linebacker Carl Brettschneider once said. "So you try to do it."

Playing in the shadow of Hornung and Cleveland's Jim Brown, Taylor was the first player in NFL history to rush for 1,000 yards in five consecutive seasons, a feat he managed from 1960 through 1964. In 1962, Brown was denied the only rushing title of his career by Taylor, who ran for a league-high 1,474 yards and 19 touchdowns, an NFL record for scoring runs at the time.

"Taylor is every bit as good as Brown," Lombardi said flatly. "I've never had a better fullback. I've never seen a quicker-starting fullback. He blocks superbly. It's common knowledge that Brown rarely blocks."

"The impact of meeting Taylor after five yards is greater than meeting Brown at the same point," testified Sam Huff, the Hall of Fame linebacker with the New York Giants and Washington Redskins. "Brown is strong, but he doesn't shock you like Taylor does. Brown would rather slide off to one side and keep going."

Taylor blasted away for Lombardi through the 1966 season, capping his final Packer season by scoring a touchdown and leading all rushers in Super Bowl I. After a final campaign with the New Orleans Saints in 1967, Taylor retired with 8,597 rushing yards in 10 seasons, second to Brown on the all-time scrolls at the time.

Throwing the blocks and leading those Packer sweeps was a line that may have had no peer. With a lineup of Jerry Kramer and Fuzzy Thurston at guard, Gregg and Bob Skoronski at tackle and either Ringo or Bowman at center, the Green Bay front wall fulfilled half of Lombardi's twofold philosophy that reduced football to its basics:

"Football is two things," he said. "It's blocking and tackling. You block and tackle better than the team you're playing, you win."

Gregg, an All-Pro eight consecutive years, was once acclaimed "the practically perfect football player" by Lombardi, but Thurston was dubbed "God's gift to Paul Hornung" . . . by himself.

"You are so right, baby," Hornung agreed, "You are so right."

One of the first players Lombardi acquired in 1959 (from Baltimore), Thurston was short and squat for a lineman (6-foot-1, 245 pounds) but an excellent pass protector who was seldom turned away by a rushing defender. Gregg was a versatile player who switched to guard when necessary (he was an All-Pro pick at *both* tackle and guard in 1965) and incredibly durable, playing in 187 consecutive games to set a club record.

In Ringo, Lombardi had a center whose outstanding blocking ability belied his size (6-1, 235). "Starr, Taylor and Hornung would be only a trio, not a triumvirate," a writer once mused, "were it not for Ringo up front calling blocking assignments for the interior linemen, keying the start of each play and then leading the blocking downfield or setting up to protect the passer."

After Ringo was traded to Philadelphia following the 1963 season, Bowman stepped in at center, playing alongside Jerry Kramer, an All-Pro selection five times. "Nothing upsets him," Lombardi said of Kramer, "so you can bawl him out anytime."

Ron Kramer, described as a "misplaced tackle" by Van Brocklin, was a 245-pound tight end who revolutionized his position. "In the past, the end often used to double-team with the tackle on blocks," a Packer assistant explained, "but we were able to give Ron blocking assignments where he was wiping out one man by himself."

Traded to Detroit in 1965, Kramer was succeeded by Fleming, who endured Lombardi's criticism and played some excellent football through 1969.

To do the tackling, Lombardi had a defense led by Davis and Jordan up front, Nitschke at line-

Lombardi could be gruff and intimidating on the football field, but warm and accommodating when dealing with the devout Green Bay fans.

backer, and Adderley and Wood in the backfield.

"Coach Lombardi tells us, 'Pursuit is the name of this game,' " said Jordan, acquired from Cleveland in the Howton trade. "But that doesn't mean foolish pursuit. When a player first comes up to the pros, he tries to make all the tackles himself. That's not only dangerous, it doesn't work.

"The first thing with our defense is make sure of your responsibility. This is a team thing. After you've taken care of your responsibility, then you pursue."

Jordan and Davis were ferocious pass rushers, regarded as more dangerous than bigger linemen, who didn't have the Packer twosome's agility and quick moves to the inside or outside. In the Packer defense, the linebackers blitzed infrequently, leaving the front line to put pressure on the passer.

"After I play Green Bay," said Baltimore guard Jim Parker, "my ankles hurt all week. I have to stay up on the balls of my feet against Jordan because I never know what he's going to do next. Other tackles I don't have to stay up like that. They don't have Henry's moves."

Davis never missed a game in his 12-year career but played every one as if it would be his last. He was always running wild in backfields, "always towering over you, coming, coming all the time," said Y.A. Tittle.

Nitschke was equally dynamic in a primitive way, the epitome of unbridled energy. Whether burying a ballcarrier with a hellish tackle or covering a receiver one-on-one (he intercepted 25 passes in his career), the Packer middle linebacker was most happy wherever there was likely to be body contact.

"It's not so much his speed or even his quickness," one opponent said of Nitschke's ability. "In his case, it's a desire to make the play, an ability to get to the right spot ahead of everybody else."

Set to either side of Nitschke were such standouts as Bill Forester, an All-Pro from 1960 through 1963, Lee Roy Caffey and Dave Robinson. Though Nitschke received much of the attention during the glory years, the others were no less a factor in the defensive scheme, much like unsung linemen Dave Hanner, Lionel Aldridge and Ron Kostelnik.

The big names in the Packer secondary were, of course, Adderley and Wood. But again, the Packer backfield played as a unit, and this club had a stellar supporting cast in Hank Gremminger and Jess Whittenton on the early championship teams, then Bobby Jeter and Tom Brown.

Wood, a 12-year veteran, was rock-steady at safety and an exciting punt returner, as well. Adderley, the Packers' No. 1 draft pick in 1961, was a ball-hawk at left cornerback in nine seasons with the team. A running back in college, he became an offensive weapon whenever he picked off a pass, returning seven of his 48 career interceptions for touchdowns. He liked to play all receivers tight, regardless of their reputation.

"You have to recognize that you are going to get beaten once in a while," he said. "You just can't dwell on it. You just have to concentrate on not letting the same man beat you again."

The Packer receivers themselves believed that a play-it-safe defensive back was making a big gamble.

"Over in Philadelphia, when I'd run at (Irv) Cross, he'd back up fast when I'd get a few yards from him," McGee said in 1962. "I just told Bart on the sidelines that instead of running the pattern 12 or 15 yards deep, I'd make my cut at seven yards, when Cross was the farthest from me. It paid off in a long play when he missed the tackle on me after I'd got the pass and turned upfield.

"I always figure that if I can beat my man by enough to catch the ball and then turn upfield, I ought to have a pretty good chance to get by him."

The Packer receivers reflected efficiency, not flamboyancy. They made their mark silently but steadily, rarely ranking among the league leaders in catches. McGee, Dowler and flanker Carroll Dale were classic receivers with rangy power and sure hands.

"We've had a lot of championships, and a lot of times you find that the guys who are out in front in pass catching are on teams that aren't championship-caliber," Dowler said at one point. "We've always thrown to the open man, and that's fine. Any other way and you're reflecting an imbalance in your attack, or maybe your receivers, and that isn't good."

From the devout, such as Starr and Gregg, to the fun-loving, McGee and Hornung, the Packers had the full range of personal styles, as well.

"I told Mike Ditka the year that the Bears went to the Super Bowl," Starr said, "that the only thing you guys have this year that we didn't have was a video. We had our characters."

There were times when someone had to break the tension, reset the mood. You don't think of the Lombardi Packers in terms of laughter, but their grim determination was not unbroken. McGee was a valuable character in that regard.

Before one typically big game against the Browns, the Packers were practicing in Cleveland's Municipal Stadium. Lombardi was all business and then some, stressing the importance of the game, noting that the cavernous stadium would be filled on Sunday with 90,000 fanatics, none of whom would be fond of the Green Bay Packers. "You look afraid," Lombardi said. "What are you afraid of?"

McGee could not resist. "Hell," he said. "we're afraid that they're not going to show up."

These were the Packers and they defied the easy categorizations that were reserved for them. Their offense depended on execution and precision, rather than deception. The Packer sweep was the embodiment of that. Opponents knew it was coming, but it would be flawlessly executed and impossible to stop. But then Starr would seize the moment to do the least conservative thing. On third-and-short, he'd run a play fake and throw long—and com-

When the Packers shocked the football world by winning the 1961 NFL championship, the 39,029 fans at City Stadium (now Lambeau Field) celebrated into the night. Green Bay was on its way to becoming "Titletown U.S.A."

plete. This was not the mark of a team that played conservatively. This was the mark of a team that played with intelligence.

The years only add meaning to the Packer story. There are teams today that dominate one year and then fall back into the pack. There are teams that rise to the top periodically. There are teams that are almost always competitive and represent models for the way a modern football franchise should be operated. But there are no teams winning three straight NFL championships and five in seven years.

"Lombardi was never satisfied with us, so it was hard for us to be satisfied with ourselves," Nitschke said. "Now, a team wins one year and then they fall by the wayside. Then, we had people who were willing to go on as far as they could. Once you know how to win, you want to keep it, you want to keep that feeling. We liked winning. We wanted to pay that price. But you have to push yourself, dedicate yourself, re-dedicate yourself. These were people of character, combined with a special leader."

Vince Lombardi was not a saint. Lombardi was not perfect. In his nine seasons at the Packer helm, Lombardi posted an overall coaching record of 98-30-4. Yet the Packer story isn't about perfection. It is about trying very hard to be perfect and coming closer than anybody else on a football field.

Lombardi also imparted lessons to live by, the kinds of things that transcended football. "I don't have everything today," Robinson said, "but whatever I have, I owe it all to Vince Lombardi."

The men who played for Lombardi were more than just a concentration of great talent. They had a great will, too. Lombardi led, all right, but these were not simply workaday followers. They embodied values that sometimes seem to have been misplaced along society's way—teamwork, hard work, ingenuity, sacrifice for the common good, fair play, a fair shot for anybody. You want "America's Team," there it was. In the heartland, in small-town America, in first place.

Vince Lombardi and the Green Bay Packers were just a football coach and a football team, but what they accomplished told us something very good about human possibilities. They represented a kind of nobility of spirit that is difficult to find these days; not only in sports, but in politics, economics and sometimes even in religion. We look back and we admire them and respect them. And sometimes, when we think of how much they meant then, and the way things have become now, we miss them, too.

U C L A
BRUINS
1963·64 to 1974·75

Though UCLA won national championships before his arrival and after his departure, tall and talented Lew Alcindor was the centerpiece in the Bruins' dynastic showcase.

Nobody on the West Coast knew much about John Wooden when he vacated the Indiana State basketball coaching position after the 1947-48 season to take over the top job at UCLA, so the Bruins' publicist allowed his imagination to run wild.

"For those of you who go to the record books for a criterion of success," began the introductory paragraph in UCLA's 1948-49 press brochure, "there is a new face among the coaching staff of UCLA who could well become the phenomenon of basketball coaching circles in the West.

"...We must warn the worthy gentlemen of the Pacific Coast coaching ranks that they are in for a rough time," continued the personality sketch. It was pure hyperbole at the time, yet the years ahead made that publicist a prophet and the glowing praise an understatement.

It took 15 more seasons before Wooden would become a household name, but in 1963-64 his pressing Bruins unleashed a streak of success—10 NCAA championships in 12 years—that made them the envy of the college basketball world.

UCLA basketball became the symbol of excellence, a standard by which all others would be measured for years to come. Those Bruins were to the college game what the Boston Celtics were to the professional ranks, with the big difference being that the cast of characters kept changing at UCLA. The results did not.

The common thread, of course, was Wooden. A stern taskmaster who starred as a three-time All-America guard at Purdue, Wooden won with a variety of players because the individual—even one of superstar caliber—was sacrificed for the good of the team.

"The beauty of it was that he was able to win with every different style, size and shape," said Louisville Coach Denny Crum, an assistant under Wooden when UCLA won national titles in 1969, 1970 and 1971 and a Bruin player in the late 1950s.

"We probably weren't aware of the significance at the time. Everyone knew UCLA was dominant, and everyone expected them to keep winning. It was almost automatic. Wooden was a great coach who adjusted to great players.

"He won with Bill Walton and Lew Alcindor, but he also won without them. He had the ability to organize, teach and be competitive with all different styles of teams. It's really an awesome achievement."

Gary Cunningham, athletic director at Fresno State, also played under Wooden and was on the Bruins' coaching staff for eight NCAA titles. He said the impact of UCLA's accomplishment wasn't evident until he left the school.

"We didn't realize how great it was at the time," recalled Cunningham, who himself took a crack at coaching the Bruins in the late 1970s. "Coach Wooden kept things in balance. There was pressure, but we never thought about it. We became a very intimidating program.

The Wooden Legacy: 10 Out of 12

By Nick Peters

"Everyone was playing us hoping not to get blown out. We developed a mystique. It became a standard to go to the Final Four, and it became an expectation to win it. The whole thing was unbelievable."

Walt Hazzard, the key player at the start of the dynasty and an All-America in 1964, traces the Bruins' success to Wooden's practice sessions. That was the coach's classroom, and he was a master teacher.

"He was a great practice coach," Hazzard said. "He didn't do much as a bench coach, but we were so well prepared, it really didn't matter. Everything we did was reflective and instinctive. We were very precise.

"Coach Wooden deserves all the credit. He had the ability to withstand the pressures, the expectations and the jealousies. He wouldn't allow the players to become complacent. He kept driving the team to excellence."

Silky-smooth forward Keith Wilkes, an All-America toward the end of the dynasty in 1973 and 1974, said the success of his predecessors created added pressure to maintain the Bruins' dominance.

"When it was happening, it sometimes felt unreal," Wilkes remembered. "As part of the Walton Gang, we felt the coach had us so primed to play, we couldn't possibly lose. There was a pressure not to be the first team to lose.

"The expectations were so high, you were always aware of the tradition. All you had to do was walk into practice at Pauley Pavilion and look up at all those championship banners hanging from the ceiling. There were constant reminders."

Wooden, reflecting at age 78 on the Bruins' glory years, said in 1989 that he was oblivious to the pressure of maintaining a high level of excellence. Unlike most observers, he thinks the Bruins' records may be broken.

"I never gave much thought to pressure," Wooden said. "I hope I'm not showing excessive ego, but I always had faith in my ability to do things. If I didn't get a coaching job, I'd have been content being a good teacher.

"But if anyone had told me we'd win 10 championships in 12 years, I'd have said it was impossible. I never thought a team could dominate as we did. But the fact it happened means it could happen again.

When guard Walt Hazzard (42) arrived at UCLA, he teamed with John Green (45) and helped the Bruins garner national attention in the 1961-62 season.

"They talk of parity today and the talent being distributed," he added, "but in some ways, it might be easier to do it today. There are more good players, so if a coach got it going, there's no reason not to have good talent for a number of years."

Wooden's contention notwithstanding, UCLA's achievements during the dynasty are staggering. It was a 12-year reign of terror that likely never will be challenged. A sampling of the remarkable accomplishments:

● Seven consecutive NCAA crowns and 10 in 12 years. Previously, no other Division I school had won more than two national championships in a row.

● Eighty-eight consecutive victories, shattering the previous Division I record of 60 straight by San Francisco. The Bruins also had winning streaks of 47 and 41 games during the dynasty.

● Thirty-eight straight NCAA Tournament triumphs, more than three times as many as any other school has recorded.

● Four 30-0 seasons, three 29-1 campaigns and two 28-2 records in those dozen dazzling years. The 10 champions fashioned a 291-10 record. By comparison, the 1979-80 Bruins finished as national runners-up with a 22-10 mark.

● A 41-1 conference record, an 88-2 ledger overall and three NCAA titles in the Alcindor Era, which ran from 1966-67 through 1968-69.

● Two national championships, 40 triumphs in 42 league games and 86 victories in 90 outings overall during the rampage of the Walton Gang, 1971-72 through 1973-74.

● Wooden's emergence as the first Division I coach to post back-to-back unbeaten seasons. (His 1971-72 squad set an NCAA record by outscoring opponents by an average of 30.3 points per game, 94.6 to 64.3.)

● A 163-11 record against conference opponents over the 12 seasons (158-11 in league games). Among league rivals, Oregon enjoyed the most "success" against the Bruins by winning three of 22 games.

Two important members of UCLA's first championship team: forwards Keith Erickson (left) and Kenny Washington.

Oregon State was 2-20, Stanford 2-23 and Southern California 2-28. Washington and Washington State each managed one victory in 25 games. California was 0-25.

"I never felt it was difficult to prepare for UCLA," said longtime coach Ralph Miller, who went head-to-head against Wooden in the first five of the 19 seasons he spent at Oregon State, a Pacific-8 Conference rival of the UCLA juggernaut. "You knew what they were going to do, but they did it so darn well. It was a matter of execution on your part. If you played a great game, you could beat them."

With a little luck, UCLA could have been even more dominant, if that can be imagined. The Bruins might have won 12 NCAA championships in a row—running from 1964 through 1975—and captured 13 national crowns in 14 years were it not for some tough tourney losses and the absence of the freshman-eligibility rule (implemented in the 1972-73 season, seven years after the arrival on the UCLA campus of one Ferdinand Lewis Alcindor Jr.).

Beginning with the 1961-62 campaign, UCLA failed to make the Final Four in only three of 14 seasons. The 1961-62 Bruins lost to Cincinnati, 72-70, on a last-ditch shot by Tom Thacker in an NCAA Tournament semifinal. The 1962-63 UCLA squad, the one aggregation in this stretch that doesn't quite fall into the "almost" category, ran into a torrid-shooting Arizona State team in the West Regional and was blitzed by the Sun Devils to the tune of 93-79. In 1965-66, Alcindor played on an unbeaten freshman team while the varsity went 18-8 and was supplanted by Oregon State as the league's representative in the NCAA Tournament.

UCLA's lone tournament loss during the dynasty was North Carolina State's double-overtime triumph in 1974.

"I think we would have won at least one more if Lew were eligible as a freshman, don't you?" Wooden asked rhetorically. The answer is a resounding yes.

The NCAA tourney field clearly got a break with

the no-freshmen rule. Not only did Alcindor have to confine himself to freshman-team duty as a UCLA newcomer, but Walton, the kid from the San Diego area, also met the same fate five years later. Nevertheless, Alcindor and Walton helped the Bruins to five of the seven consecutive NCAA crowns they won starting in Lew's sophomore season. (And while UCLA didn't reach the heights when Alcindor played on the freshman team, the Bruins did cop the national title even as Walton was forced to bide his time on the yearling squad.)

It wasn't all smooth sailing, of course. There were problems with the media over the sheltering of Alcindor and with the free-spirited Walton, and most of all there was resentment over what was perceived as UCLA arrogance. "Anyone could win with Wooden's talent" was a common remark.

"Anyone would have had success with his talent," allowed Marv Harshman, former Washington and Washington State coach. "But not everyone would have won more than one or two championships, let alone 10.

"My measure of Wooden's genius is that he took great players and made great teams. A lot of coaches can't control great talent, but John had the ability to get players to play his way."

Fellow Basketball Hall of Famer Pete Newell had the distinction of beating Wooden and UCLA eight straight times prior to his retirement from the coaching business after the 1959-60 season, but that doesn't reduce his admiration for the Wizard of Westwood.

"John was a different coach when I went against him," Newell noted. "He grew, like any great coach would. John had the ability to sustain that winning attitude regardless of the obvious pressures.

"It was a tremendous coaching feat, one which never has been duplicated. Others didn't win the NCAA championship with great centers, including Wilt Chamberlain's two years at Kansas. No school can dominate like that again.

"Jealousies naturally develop when you have so much success," Newell said. "John also wasn't a West Coast guy and a lot of coaches didn't warm up to him, and vice versa. He also wasn't very outgoing, so their success bothered people more."

If the criticism bothered Wooden, he seldom showed it. Seven-foot centers notwithstanding, he was the program's tower of strength, providing a consistency and a stability amid constant intensity.

"Our winning brought about an air of envy and suspicion," Wooden said. "Too much of anything can be as big a problem as too little, but I'd rather have problems while winning instead of losing.

"I also heard many times how anybody could have won with our talent, but that never bothered me. I know nobody wins without talent, but there are some who don't win with it.

"There were times when I would have traded my talent with other coaches at the beginning of a season. I remember one coach asking me at the end of a season whether I thought I could win with his

Fast-shooting lefty Gail Goodrich was the top scorer on the Bruins' first two title teams.

Dynasty Data

Yearly Record
1963-64 to 1974-75

	W	L	Pct.	Avg. Score UCLA-Opp.	Coach
1963-64	30	0	1.000	89-70	John Wooden
1964-65	28	2	.933	86-71	John Wooden
1965-66	18	8	.692	84-73	John Wooden
1966-67	30	0	1.000	90-64	John Wooden
1967-68	29	1	.967	93-67	John Wooden
1968-69	29	1	.967	85-64	John Wooden
1969-70	28	2	.933	92-73	John Wooden
1970-71	29	1	.967	83-69	John Wooden
1971-72	30	0	1.000	94-64	John Wooden
1972-73	30	0	1.000	81-60	John Wooden
1973-74	26	4	.867	82-63	John Wooden
1974-75	28	3	.903	85-72	John Wooden
Total	335	22	.938	87-67	

John Wooden, UCLA coach and master builder, with his first championship team in 1964.

talent.

"I told him yes, but that I didn't think he could win with mine. All the dynasties like the Yankees and the Packers had great talent. We had it, too, but we also had great team play. If they wanted to play, they had to play together as a team."

Wooden's system was based on old-fashioned values. Everyone around the Bruins was well aware of his Pyramid of Success, a collection of virtues he regards as the most original work he has ever penned.

Alongside the blocks in the pyramid were these words: "Success is peace of mind, which is a direct result of self-satisfaction in knowing you did your best to become the best you are capable of becoming."

Wooden also listed three things instrumental to success: (1) an emphasis on conditioning, (2) skillful execution and (3) teamwork. Lectures on the above would greet each UCLA team when practice began in October.

"All of our work in two hours of practice would have been wasted if the players didn't stay in shape," he explained. "I always told them we won because we were in better shape than our opponents.

"I demanded execution, but the main thing was that the execution be done quickly. We tried to do everything with quickness, and we had several drills in practice to keep us sharp.

"They also knew I would not tolerate individual play," Wooden said. "That was the best way for someone to land on the bench despite individual talent. I wanted them to work together and to acknowledge a pass or a screen with a wink or a smile."

The formula worked to near-perfection. Those talented Bruins utilized a methodical effectiveness that wore opponents down. Even at the tournament level, UCLA seldom was tested.

The Bruins went 10-0 in NCAA Tournament championship games under Wooden, beating title opponents by an average of 13.4 points. In the 44 NCAA tourney games that UCLA won in those dozen years, foes were clobbered by an average of 15.4 points.

"It bothered us that nobody else in the conference could go to the tournament in those days," Harshman said of the one-representative-only situation that wasn't changed until the 1975 tourney. "The Bruins dominated the tournament better than they did the conference. We saw them more often and were better prepared.

"I remember one year (1970-71) when both of USC's losses (in a 24-2 season) were to UCLA, and the Trojans had to stay home. I remember (USC Coach) Bob Boyd giving them trouble with a slow-down game and (Oregon's) Dick Harter playing them very physical."

Wooden didn't see anything wrong with the UCLA monopoly. "I'm a compassionate man," he said, "but it didn't bother me that only one team could represent the conference. I don't think teams that finish second, third or fourth should go anywhere. That diminishes the importance of winning.

"We didn't expect to go anywhere if we finished second. My 10 NCAA championship teams lost a total of 10 games! Now, they might as well let everyone in the tournament."

Wooden, however, never placed as much emphasis on winning as he did on his teams playing their best. In fact, his players can't recall him ever using the word win.

"Coach Wooden never asked us to win," Wilkes said. "He just asked that we play well and hard. He was a very remarkable person. With him in charge, it took a lot of the edge off. He made us supremely confident."

Cunningham concurred.

"The 10 championships and the 88 straight victories were tremendous achievements," he said, "but I don't think they meant that much to the coach in perspective.

"He didn't mention the accomplishments, so they weren't uppermost on our minds. Coach Wooden made winning the conference championship our first goal, and then getting to the Final Four."

Actually, Wooden was a successful coach long before the champion Bruins vaulted him to more prominence. Serving his apprenticeship in the Indiana prep ranks, he posted a 218-42 record prior to going 44-15 in two seasons at Indiana State. At the end of the 1947-48 season, his Sycamores were runners-up to Louisville in the National Association of Intercollegiate Basketball Tournament (the NAIB being the forerunner to today's National Association of Intercollegiate Athletics, the umbrella under which many small colleges compete).

He was an immediate hit at UCLA, guiding the Bruins to a 22-7 record in his rookie season of 1948-49. The next year, his team finished 24-7. Wooden never coached a losing team at UCLA.

In the 15 seasons prior to his first NCAA champion at UCLA, Wooden won at least 18 games on 11 occasions and reached the national tournament five times. Willie Naulls, a front-court player who averaged 23.6 points per game in the 1955-56 season, was his first great Bruin.

But Wooden's early accomplishments didn't create much of a stir on the West Coast. The great Phil Woolpert-coached San Francisco teams, featuring Bill Russell and K.C. Jones, commanded the most attention with NCAA crowns in 1955 and 1956 and the 60-game winning streak that stretched from December 1954 to December 1956.

Newell also made a splash by coaching USF's Dons to the 1949 National Invitation Tournament championship and taking Cinderella California to an NCAA title in 1959. Newell retired as coach after directing the Golden Bears to a second-place national finish in 1960.

With Cal on the decline, the Wooden dynasty took root. In his early years, the Wizard recruited almost entirely in California. The Bruins weren't

Four talented sophomores in the 1966-67 season: (left to right) Alcindor, Lucius Allen, Kenny Heitz and Lynn Shackelford.

UCLA's Results in NCAA's Tournament
1963-64 to 1974-75

| Season | Opening Round | West Regional | | Championship | |
		1st Game	Championship	Semifinal	Final
1963-64		95-90 Seattle	76-72 San Francisco	90-84 Kansas State	98-83 Duke
1964-65		100-76 Brigham Young	101-93 San Francisco	108-89 Wichita State	91-80 Michigan
1965-66		Not in NCAA Tournament			
1966-67		109-60 Wyoming	80-64 Pacific	73-58 Houston	79-64 Dayton
1967-68		58-49 New Mexico State	87-66 Santa Clara	101-69 Houston	78-55 North Carolina
1968-69		53-38 New Mexico State	90-52 Santa Clara	85-82 Drake	92-72 Purdue
1969-70		88-65 Long Beach State	101-79 Utah State	93-77 New Mexico State	80-69 Jacksonville
1970-71		91-73 Brigham Young	57-55 Long Beach State	68-60 Kansas	68-62 Villanova
1971-72		90-58 Weber State	73-57 Long Beach State	96-77 Louisville	81-76 Florida State
1972-73		98-81 Arizona State	54-39 San Francisco	70-59 Indiana	87-66 Memphis State
1973-74		111-100 Dayton (3 OT)	83-60 San Francisco	77-80 N.C. State (2 OT)	78-61 Kansas (C)
1974-75	103-91 Michigan (OT)	67-64 Montana	89-75 Arizona State	75-74 Louisville (OT)	92-85 Kentucky
(C) Denotes consolation game.					

exactly big league, either, practicing in an old gym and playing home games all over the Los Angeles area.

Two things altered the pattern. First, a flashy ballhawk from Philadelphia, Hazzard, went westward to play his college ball and, along with Cunningham and John Green, he shot UCLA into prominence during the 1961-62 season. Second, Pauley Pavilion was built to showcase UCLA's basketball team. The glittering facility opened for basketball in the fall of 1965; along with the school's NCAA-title banners from '64 and '65, it proved quite a lure for top-rated prospects. Indeed, one freshman on campus when the arena doors swung open for Bruin basketball was a New York import named Lew Alcindor.

"We were winning more conference championships than anyone in those early days," Wooden recalled, "but we didn't have an adequate place to practice or play. There really was no home court.

"There were poor practice conditions for 17 years, including the first two championship teams. There were all sorts of things going on during our practices. We had wrestling mats on one side of the gym and a trampoline on the other.

"When I was a schoolboy back in Indiana," the Martinsville native continued, "nothing interfered with basketball practice. I just couldn't understand it, and I still don't know how we won two championships under those conditions.

"When I think of all the accomplishments, I'm not as impressed by the 88 victories in a row or the seven straight NCAA championships as I am with those first two championships without our own gym and with only two baskets with which to practice. I'd like to see how many coaches would stand for that today."

Wooden, an old-school coach who didn't relish recruiting, concedes that a lot of good luck prefaced the start of the dynasty. Hazzard, for instance, arrived in Westwood almost by accident.

"The Southern schools, including Maryland and Georgetown, were segregated," Hazzard said. "I didn't know anything about John Wooden. I probably would have gone to Temple or St. Joseph's, but UCLA appealed to me because Jackie Robinson had been my hero all my life.

"I wanted to go to UCLA because of what it stood for. It had a legacy of giving an opportunity to everyone, from Jackie to Kenny Washington to Woody Strode...."

Hazzard spent one year in junior college and made his UCLA debut in 1961-62 with a team that started the season 4-7. The Bruins went 14-4 the rest of the way and just missed making the NCAA final because of that two-point loss to Cincinnati.

"Had we won that game, I think we would have had the momentum to win a couple more championships," the stellar guard said. "We had Cincy beat, but I gave up the ball on a turnover (a charging foul, actually). And Thacker, who was my man, hit his only basket of the game to beat us.

"Jerry Lucas got hurt in the other semifinal (and was not up to par for the championship game), and Cincinnati beat Ohio State for the title. I think we would have beaten the Buckeyes, too. It was a different world then. We played our home games all over L.A."

Yet the Bruins still had appeal. In a region known for its great defense, as practiced by USF and Cal, Wooden attracted players to his wide-open style. By 1962-63, the high-powered offense blended with a devastating press.

Those Bruins went 20-7 in the regular season and headed for the West Regional supremely confident. But Arizona State had other plans, bolting to a 33-13 lead and coasting to victory. The Bruins had to wait one more year.

"The way we were playing the end of my junior year, I knew we'd be a great team by 1964," Hazzard said. "We just ran into a buzz saw against ASU

Alcindor prepares for the jump ball in a much-publicized rematch against Houston and Elvin Hayes in the 1968 NCAA Tournament.

(which rolled to a 62-31 halftime cushion on the way to its 14-point triumph).

"We had a truly unique group of individuals on that 1964 club. Fred Slaughter was the No. 1 200-meter man in Kansas, a 230-pounder who could fly. Gail Goodrich was the Player of the Year in L.A. (as a high school basketball star). . .Keith Erickson simply was a great athlete who could do anything." Plus, Jack Hirsch had been selected Co-Player of the Year in Los Angeles during his prep days.

Slaughter was the Bruins' under-sized center, while Erickson and Hirsch held down the forward slots and Goodrich played alongside Hazzard in the backcourt.

With the 6-foot-5 Slaughter anchoring the middle in a high-post offense and volleyball star Erickson being the key to UCLA's vaunted full-court press, the 1963-64 Bruins went 30-0 without a starter taller than 6-5.

Alcindor after the Bruins' 1967 title victory (above) and with his father after UCLA's 1969 championship win.

Mike Warren, who later would gain fame as an actor on the hit television series "Hill Street Blues," was a starting guard on UCLA's 1968 title team.

The relentless press paralyzed opponents and created numerous turnovers to fuel fast-break opportunities. A 113-71 romp over Brigham Young in the opener set the tone for an amazing season. Baylor was pummeled, 112-61. Washington State was throttled 121-77.

By January 6, the Bruins had attained the No. 1 ranking for the first time in their history. By season's end, Goodrich had compiled a 21.5 scoring average, Hazzard had been named College Player of the Year and Wooden had earned Coach of the Year distinction.

NCAA Tournament games had been relatively close until Duke was demolished, 98-83, in the '64 national final for the first of 10 UCLA championships. Goodrich sparked that victory with 27 points and swingman Kenny Washington came off the bench to add 26 points and 12 rebounds.

"Wooden didn't press in the early years, but then he and (assistant) Jerry Norman applied it with those mid-'60s teams," Newell noted. "They did it as well as I've ever seen. The trademark of those 1964 and 1965 teams was defense, but he also believed in simplicity and execution."

The Bruins' style of play captured the imagination of the nation's fans. Because of their lack of height, UCLA players were branded as overachievers and viewed as an underdog riding the essence of team play to success.

"We had a degree of toughness, but we also had poise—and that's an unusual combination," Slaughter said. "Our success was based on acquiring an understanding of roles."

It was Wooden's first major test in proving you could mold diverse characters into a tightly knit team. Erickson and Hirsch were basically undisciplined, and Goodrich probably wanted to shoot whenever he had the slightest opportunity.

"I was just having a good time," Erickson recalled. "It was perfect. We were naive on one hand and kind of arrogant on the other. Wooden was a wise man, a great man. Of course, I didn't know it at the time. I didn't listen to anything he said."

Someone listened, because those Bruins were the epitome of teamwork, a cohesive unit that averaged 88.9 points and yielded but 70.1 per game.

Wooden over the years steadfastly has declined to compare his teams, but he admits having a soft spot for the 1964 group that triggered so much success and began the Bruins' dominance of the college sport.

"Winning in 1964, of course, was a big breakthrough," Wooden allowed. "We attracted a lot of attention and a lot of TV exposure. That concerned me, too, because I didn't permit fancy play. I didn't want my teams playing for the cameras.

"Yes, there was something special about that 1964 championship. It's like your first-born, always special. But I truly have no favorite. Some of the teams that didn't win were joys to work with."

But Wooden's admiration for the 1964 champions is obvious, especially in light of the fact they

The high-flying Allen was the steadying force in the Bruin backcourt in the first two of the "Alcindor years."

Steve Patterson (left) had the unenviable task of filling Alcindor's center position in 1969-70, while John Vallely (right) started at guard.

didn't have a real home and were forced to practice in the third floor of a rickety old gymnasium without air conditioning. That's where the luck factor surfaces.

"Everything sort of fell into place for us when we started our string of championships," Wooden said. "We won the first two years with Slaughter and (Doug) McIntosh as our centers. Alcindor was a junior in high school (Power Memorial Academy in New York) when we won the first one.

"His coach (Jack Donohue) called me after the season because our success attracted Lew's attention. He narrowed his choices down to five schools, and we were among them. Without that championship, it wouldn't have happened.

"When we repeated in 1965," the coach continued, "it solidified his attention. When Lew came out for his visit, I took him to show him Pauley Pavilion as it was being built. I told him he'd dedicate it as a freshman and that he'd have a great facility in which to play his college games.

"Suppose we had to climb three flights of stairs to our old gym with wrestling mats and trampolines in the way. Or if we had to play our games at Venice High, Santa Monica and Long Beach. The timing was right."

Hazzard was not around, of course, in 1964-65, so Goodrich picked up the pace and averaged 24.8 points en route to All-America honors. Furthermore, the press was even more effective as the Bruins put together a 28-2 season.

UCLA averaged 86.3 points and surrendered 71.3 per game. During the NCAA Tournament, Wooden's athletes averaged 100 points. Goodrich set a championship-game record with 42 points in a 91-80 victory over Michigan.

The following season produced an oddity: The freshmen stirred more of a commotion than the varsity following Alcindor's heralded arrival, 23 years before he was to announce his retirement as

Wooden with bookend forwards Sidney Wicks (center) and Curtis Rowe after UCLA's 1969-70 title run.

Kareem Abdul-Jabbar of the Los Angeles Lakers. Cunningham returned to the school and was named freshman coach. His debut was in the inaugural basketball game played at Pauley, a contest in which the freshman squad—led by Alcindor's 31 points—roughed up the varsity by 15 points.

The Brubabes, who also had standout players in guards Lucius Allen and Kenny Heitz and forward Lynn Shackelford, went on to a 21-0 season. Cunningham's phenoms, who averaged 113.2 points and yielded 56.6 points a game, won one game by more than 100 points (Citrus Junior College was obliterated, 152-49) and prevailed by 50 or more points 13 times. Meanwhile, the varsity finished second behind Oregon State in the conference race and won 18 of 26 games overall.

"Winning those first two years couldn't have

been predicted," Wooden said, "but when Lew came, I said at the time that only three things could keep us from winning the NCAA championship.

"I was concerned about him being injured or getting sick, and I doubted my ability to coach a true big man. I remember calling people like Wilt Chamberlain and George Mikan. I also facetiously mentioned the men in striped shirts."

Wooden had nothing to fear. With Alcindor averaging 29 points and making two-thirds of his field-goal attempts, the Bruins went 30-0 in 1966-67 and outscored opponents by an average score of 89.6 to 63.7. They scored at least 100 points one dozen times.

UCLA's winning streak reached 47 games in Alcindor's junior year before a gloating Elvin Hayes erupted for 39 points to muscle No. 2-ranked Houston to a 71-69 upset over the top-rated Bruins before a record 52,693 fans at the Astrodome on January 20, 1968. The Cougars had entered the game with a 16-0 season record.

It was billed as the greatest game in college basketball history at the time, but it actually was a mismatch because Alcindor had an eye scratched in a game against Cal the previous week and suffered blurriness and double vision. He struggled with 4-for-18 shooting from the floor and managed only 15 points. Hayes won the battle on the backboards, too, pulling down 15 rebounds compared with Alcindor's 12.

The Bruins had to endure Hayes' long-distance taunts for the remainder of the regular season, but justice was served. In what seemed as improbable as many a Hollywood script, second-ranked UCLA, 27-1, was matched against No. 1 Houston, 31-0, in a 1968 NCAA Tournament semifinal game at the Los Angeles Sports Arena. The Bruins exploded for a 101-69 victory, with Alcindor collecting 19 points and 18 rebounds and Hayes geting only 10 points and five rebounds.

"That was the most satisfying victory we had," Alcindor said. "We wanted to teach them some manners." The Bruins did it with balance, getting 17 or more points from four players.

"That's the greatest exhibition of basketball I have ever seen," Houston Coach Guy Lewis marveled. In the tourney final, Alcindor's 34 points helped the Bruins bury North Carolina, 78-55.

"This is the best team of all time, and Alcindor is the greatest player who ever played college basketball," summed up Tar Heels Coach Dean Smith, who didn't hear many arguments.

Alcindor, of course, was the force, but those Bruins also had a dandy backcourt of Allen and Mike Warren, who later starred as a policeman on the hit television show "Hill Street Blues."

One year later, those guards were gone (Warren had graduated and Allen was an academic casualty), but sophomore forwards Sidney Wicks and Curtis Rowe hooked up with Alcindor and fueled a 25-0 start. After a 46-44 loss to Southern Cal in the regular-season finale—the defeat was the Bruins' first ever at Pauley Pavilion in an official game—Wooden's troops regrouped for the NCAA Tournament.

UCLA swept aside New Mexico State and Santa Clara in the tourney before scrambling to beat Drake by three points in a national semifinal. Alcindor then completed a brilliant three years with 37 points and 20 rebounds in a 92-72 whipping of Purdue in the NCAA championship game. In three years, he had scored 2,325 points and averaged 26.4 points, both still school records.

Wooden was only halfway to his 10 championship banners, yet resentment grew because of the Bruins' dominance. West Coast schools, obscured by UCLA's accomplishments, were particularly unhappy.

"I think it helped West Coast prestige," Wooden said. "Lincoln, my favorite American, once said

Steady guard Henry Bibby was a senior when the Walton Gang arrived for the 1971-72 season.

The red-haired Walton was tall, talented and always controversial.

Wooden and Walton did not always see eye to eye, but they did share some tender moments during their three-year association.

The fierce and dominating Walton was complemented nicely by silky-smooth forward Keith Wilkes (52).

that you don't build up the weak by tearing down the strong. I believed that. It was good for baseball when the Yankees were dominant. Having a real strong team can only make the others better."

Cunningham concurred: "We knew there would be a lot of jealousies. Our winning so much placed people in a position of saying it wasn't good for basketball. I personally felt it was very good, contributing to an awareness of the sport."

Newell, a more objective observer, agreed. "The UCLA era helped to bring college basketball to the forefront," he said. "It took it out of the back rooms and into the big leagues.

"Athletic Director J.D. Morgan deserves a lot of credit, too. He put together a TV package which gave them more exposure. The Bruins made the game glamorous for TV, elevating the Final Four into one of the greatest events around."

Wooden went back to his high-post offense after Alcindor advanced to NBA stardom. The 1969-70 squad adjusted quite well without the big man, compensating with a diversified attack that had each starter averaging at least 12.5 points per game.

Wicks led the way at 18.6, followed by guards John Vallely (16.3) and Henry Bibby (15.6), Rowe (15.3) and center Steve Patterson (12.5). Those bal-

anced Bruins scored more than 100 points 10 times and averaged 92 points per game.

That team had ample incentive to sustain UCLA's excellence. The players wanted to prove they could win without Alcindor, and that goal was accomplished with an 80-69 championship victory over Jacksonville for a 28-2 finish.

"Every time somebody mentioned the three championships in a row, they said Lew did it," Rowe observed following UCLA's fourth straight NCAA title. "We just proved four other men from that (1968-69) team can play basketball."

The Bruins also proved it was no fluke by doing even better in 1970-71. Wicks (21.3 average) and Rowe (17.5) were a formidable one-two scoring punch and Patterson enjoyed the game of his life with 29 points in a 68-62 NCAA title victory over Villanova.

Those two UCLA squads perhaps were the least remembered of Wooden's 10 champions. After all, they lacked the wizardry of a Hazzard or a Goodrich, or the imposing presence of an Alcindor or a Walton. Still, some observers regarded Wicks, Rowe and Patterson as the best front line in college history.

Following an 89-82 defeat at Notre Dame on Jan-

With the departure of Walton, Richard Washington became UCLA's center of attention in the 1974-75 season.

uary 23, 1971, the Bruins won their last 15 games to finish 29-1 and lay the foundation for the greatest winning streak ever in college basketball, one completed by the Walton Gang.

With Bibby providing a steadying hand as a senior and Walton and Wilkes exhibiting incredible poise as sophomores, the 1971-72 squad presented a case as the mightiest college team of all time, one that started the season scoring more than 100 points in seven straight games.

Walton averaged 21.1 points and 15.5 rebounds to lead the way in what turned out to be a perfect season. UCLA won 28 of its 30 games by 13 or more points, with its closest call coming against Florida State in the NCAA final. The Seminoles bowed, 81-76. The Bruins' 30-0 mark extended their winning streak to 45 games.

The pressure and the victories mounted when Walton and Wilkes powered another 30-0 steamroller in 1972-73, presenting Wooden with his ninth NCAA crown in 10 years and his seventh consecutive championship. In the process, the Bruins stretched their winning string to 75 games.

Walton capped a fantastic tourney with a record 21-for-22 shooting performance in an 87-66 championship rout of Memphis State. Walton finished with 44 points and 13 rebounds, erasing Goodrich's title-game scoring mark.

But the big news that season was the consecutive-victory record. The Bruins played what they regarded as their best game of the season when the streak reached 58 with a 92-64 trouncing of, curiously, USF, which was still clinging to the standard of 60 straight triumphs.

Providence was a 101-77 victim for No. 59, and then the Bruins headed for the Midwest to play Loyola of Chicago and Notre Dame. UCLA tied the record with an 87-73 victory over Loyola behind Walton's 32 points and 27 rebounds.

Notre Dame was beaten, 82-63, in the record-breaker, and Wooden attempted to relieve the pressure by telling the players the streak no longer was significant.

"The streak was not a problem until we got into the high 50s," Wooden recalled. "The game I remember most was the one against USF, because they were the school that held the record.

"I also remembered what a tough trip we anticipated to Chicago and South Bend. We were very conscious of the streak then. Once we won that 61st game, though, the thought of the streak left our minds. I told them we hold the record and not to worry about it. Our opponents thought about it more than we did."

Cunningham agreed.

"We really didn't think much about the 88-game streak," he noted. "The media mentioned it a lot. We just went about our work in a blue-collar way. Coach Wooden never looked too far ahead."

But Wooden made a concession at the end of that second straight 30-0 season and suggested the Walton Gang might have been his most impressive

Larry Farmer, a future UCLA coach, begins the net-cutting ceremony with a lift from Swen Nater after the Bruins' NCAA title victory in 1973.

champion. After all, those two teams seldom were tested seriously.

"I've never had a greater team when you consider both offense and defense," Wooden declared. "We won almost every game by the middle of the second half. I'd rate Bill with Lew as the best I've ever coached. They're both completely team-oriented, totally unselfish ballplayers."

Walton's senior year produced a 13-0 start and an extension of the winning streak to 88 games, but the string was snapped at Notre Dame, against the last school to beat the Bruins. As was the case when UCLA tied and broke USF's mark, the Bruins were on a Midwest trip.

Only Maryland, a one-point loser to Wooden's team in the Bruins' second game of the season, had come close to UCLA in the 1973-74 campaign. Iowa, the first opponent on the two-game swing, absorbed a 68-44 pounding at Chicago as the streak reached 88. "So much had to fall in place for all this to happen," Wooden noted. "We've weathered a lot, including injuries, slowdown games and bad games by certain players."

It seemed the streak would continue at South Bend, Ind., where UCLA enjoyed a 70-59 lead with 3 minutes, 32 seconds remaining. The Bruins somehow didn't score again, and Dwight Clay's jump shot produced a 71-70 upset for the Fighting Irish.

The outcome was stunning because the Bruins heretofore had never lost their poise. The inability to nail down a "sure" victory set a precedent that ultimately would deny UCLA an eighth consecutive championship.

A measure of revenge was gained when the Bruins returned to Pauley and downed the Irish, 94-75, one week later, but UCLA soon was to lose a pair of games on the road to Oregon State and Oregon. The shield of invincibility was no more.

There also was a three-overtime scare against Dayton (111-100) in the NCAA West Regional before North Carolina State, down by 11 points with 10:56 left in regulation, roared back for an 80-77 double-overtime victory against the Bruins in a national semifinal. The Bruins also were ahead in that one by seven points with 3½ minutes to play in the second overtime. And, earlier in the season, they had pounded the Wolfpack by 18 points in a game played in St. Louis.

North Carolina State, featuring jumping-jack sensation David Thompson and 7-4 Tom Burleson, wound up with a 30-1 record. The Wolfpack clearly benefited from the fact that all its NCAA Tournament games—regional competition through the Final Four—were played in North Carolina. Nevertheless, no one would argue that Coach Norm Sloan's team was anything but a full-fledged powerhouse.

"During our senior year, we became more aware of the resentment toward UCLA and we became a lot more sensitive about it," said Wilkes, who in his pro career became known as Jamaal Wilkes. "We kept more to ourselves, and it felt like we were in a vacuum at times.

"Looking back to the N.C. State game, I just always give them the credit. They had gone undefeated (27-0) the previous year, but they were on probation and couldn't go to the tourney. They were a great team. We just had a lapse and they capitalized."

There weren't many major lapses during the dynasty, yet two of the biggest—against Notre Dame and North Carolina State—came in the senior year of two great players. Walton nonetheless finished with 1,370 rebounds, a 15.7 rebound average and a .651 field-goal percentage, all school career records. Only Alcindor scored more points than Walton's 1,767. Wilkes, meanwhile, concluded his UCLA career with scoring and rebounding averages of 15.0 and 7.4, respectively.

So, Wooden had to rebuild again, producing another miracle with a relatively new team after losing four starters from 1974. But the tradition lived on and UCLA rolled into the NCAA Tournament with a 23-3 record.

En route to the Final Four, the Bruins were forced into overtime by Michigan and beat an upstart Montana team by only three points. Then, following a stem-winding 75-74 victory over Louisville in an NCAA Tournament semifinal at San Diego, Wooden announced his retirement. He was rewarded with a 92-85 going-away present over Kentucky in the championship game.

Center Richard Washington had 28 points and 12 rebounds against Kentucky and forward Dave Meyers added 24 points and 12 boards. Reserve center Ralph Drollinger came off the bench and netted 10 points and 13 rebounds.

"That last team gave me great pleasure," Wooden said. "We'd lost Walton and Wilkes, plus. . . starters at guard, so I felt we had very little chance to win again.

"I didn't have to retire that early, but I had a heart problem for which I've taken medication every four hours for 17 years. I could have coached three more years, but it was a family decision and I have no regrets.

"When I retired, I wanted to make sure I left my successor with a great team, and I did (the 1975-76 Bruins advanced to the Final Four)," added Wooden, who inadvertently created tremendous pressure for his successors, all of whom futilely have been chasing a legend.

It's significant to note that Gene Bartow (52-9, .852), the immediate successor to the Wizard of Westwood, and Cunningham (50-8, .862) finished their brief UCLA stints with better winning percentages than Wooden's final .808, based on a 620-147 record.

What they couldn't do was win the big one. The name of the game is to win championships consistently, and that's what sports dynasties are all about.

Nobody did it better than UCLA and John Wooden.

The dynasty's last stand: Wooden's final NCAA title team in 1975.

MONTREAL
CANADIENS
1955·56 to 1978·79

Eight Stanley Cup championships and 500 regular-season victories were part of the legacy of Montreal Canadiens Coach Hector (Toe) Blake.

Three Generations Of Success

By Tim Burke

Like Yankee pin stripes, the bleu-blanc-rouge sweaters adorned with the "CH" crest have become a symbol of supremacy. The legend of the dynasty is etched upon the Canadian imagination, passed on to succeeding generations who hold the "Flying Frenchmen" and the rest of Les Habitants in reverential awe: Rocket and Pocket, Doug and Dickie, Beliveau and Boom Boom, Lemaire and Lafleur.

Since the founding of the National Hockey League in 1917, the Montreal Canadiens have won 22 Stanley Cup championships in 31 final series appearances. They rose to dominate hockey at a time when the game reached its zenith, winning an unprecedented—and unequaled—five consecutive Stanley Cups from 1956 through 1960 after winning only six in the league's first 38 years. Playing with a panache and fury unsurpassed before or since, they had a power play so overwhelming that the NHL was forced to tame it with legislation, and a defense so disciplined that goalie Jacques Plante won the Vezina Trophy all five championship seasons.

Save for losses in the seventh game of the finals in both 1954 (in overtime) and 1955, the Canadiens would have strung together eight consecutive Stanley Cup titles, beginning with a five-game victory over the Boston Bruins in 1953.

When it was over, nine Canadiens who formed the backbone of the 1950s dynasty, as well as General Manager Frank Selke and Coach Toe Blake, would be elected to the hockey Hall of Fame. *Two entire lines* would be enshrined—Jean Beliveau centering left wing Bert Olmstead and right wing Bernie Geoffrion, and Henri Richard centering brother Maurice on right wing and Dickie Moore on the left—as well as the pillars of the Montreal defense: Plante in goal, and defensemen Doug Harvey and Tom Johnson. Defenseman Emile (Butch) Bouchard, who played his last of 15 seasons with the Canadiens in 1955-56, also would be called into the Hall.

Even the supporting cast chiseled out its niche of immortality, honest blockers such as Marcel Bonin, Donnie Marshall, Claude Provost, Bob Turner, Andre Pronovost, Dollard St. Laurent, Floyd Curry, Jean-Guy Talbot and Phil Goyette.

They forever established the standard by which all Canadiens teams would be measured. Understandably, it hasn't been easy for those that followed, even the Canadiens who won four of five Cups from 1965 through 1969, or the team that streaked to four straight titles from 1976 through 1979. When flaws were still being found with the dynasty of the 1970s, star left wing Steve Shutt said ruefully: "We are doomed to be compared to the ghosts of the past."

Which is, of course, better than being haunted by the ghosts.

No other dynasty was ever as closely identified with the city it represented. On each of those 1950s championship teams, no fewer than 15 players came from Montreal or the Quebec hinterland—and these were days of 20- to 25-man rosters. The Canadiens were truly an extension of their people, who elevated hockey to a form of religion, of provincial pride. In the province of Quebec, the Club de Hockey Canadien became the flagship of a national destiny.

Indeed, fans had rioted at a March 17, 1955, game at the Montreal Forum, enraged by NHL President Clarence Campbell's suspension of native son Maurice (Rocket) Richard for the balance of the season and the playoffs. Though Richard had punched a linesman in the face in a game against Boston, the penalty (rendered March 16) was viewed as excessively unfair, and it was fresh on the embittered crowd's mind as Campbell took his seat near the Forum ice. Before the end of the first period, debris rained down from the rafters and Campbell was physically threatened. A tear gas canister was thrown as hooligans pressed around the league's highest executive. The game was forfeited to archrival Detroit, and the angry crowd spilled outside, joining a mob gathered there on a looting spree down St. Catherine Street.

It is the opinion of some Canadian sociologists that it was actually the Richard Riot that ignited Quebec's "quiet revolution," a movement begun to make the province increasingly French in character —and an ongoing fermentation that threatens to divide Canada to this day. It is ironic that the players themselves were the most apolitical individuals imaginable, driven to greatness not by any sense of provincial duty, but by a pride in their abilities as a hockey team.

In the wake of the riot, the Canadiens lost the Stanley Cup finals for the second straight year to Detroit. A defeatist attitude had begun to fester in Montreal over the Red Wings. Led by goaltender Terry Sawchuk, defenseman Red Kelly and the "Production Line" of Ted Lindsay, Sid Abel and Gordie Howe, the Red Wings owned a lock on first place in the six-team NHL from 1949 through 1955, winning four Stanley Cup championships during their reign. They failed to reach the finals only in 1951 and 1953, when the Bruins' upset victory in the semifinals ultimately helped the Canadiens claim the Cup.

Harvey, for one, dismisses Montreal's '53 championship as an aberration. "We weren't the best team," he said, "we were just lucky Boston beat De-

Blake despised losing and drove the Canadiens incessantly in his quest for perfection.

troit."

In view of the unhappy events in the spring of 1955, Selke decided it was time for change. He replaced Coach Dick Irvin, a veteran of 15 seasons behind the Habs' bench, with Hector (Toe) Blake, the popular former Canadiens star who had played left wing on the famous "Punch Line" with Elmer Lach and Maurice Richard. Nicknamed the "Old Lamplighter" for his scoring touch (235 career goals and 292 assists), Blake understood the importance of team harmony and motivation. He knew the difference between elan and complacency, after watching the latter reduce one great Canadiens team from Stanley Cup contender to pretender. "During my playing days, we lost a few games and the players weren't particularly worried," he said. "They kept telling themselves they'd win the next one. But the next one never came around. By the time we started to play up to our potential, we were out of the playoffs."

Blake became a master handler of players, driving them incessantly and always getting total effort in return. Perhaps, he was helped by a nugget of advice from the shrewd Selke when he took over the coaching chores.

"What can I teach players like Beliveau, Richard and Harvey?" Blake wondered. "They're all great."

"It isn't the coach's job in major league hockey to teach," Selke counseled, "it is to manage and remind."

It is unlikely that this greatest of all hockey dynasties could have happened without Blake. Where

the rigid Irvin was characterized as a "management coach," a product of an earlier era, Blake opened up a line of communication with his players, many of whom had once been his teammates—the Rocket, Harvey, Bouchard, Curry and Ken Mosdell.

Even with the Canadiens' staggering array of individual talent, his coaching philosophy—beyond an emphasis on team spirit and commitment—was decidedly basic, stressing conditioning and fundamentals. The players, lean and hard from a regimen of grueling scrimmages, often looked forward to a game as a respite.

Most of the Canadiens genuinely liked Blake, even if his Vesuvian temper shook the walls of the Montreal dressing room in defeat. He would roar in not-so-general terms so that the trembling malefactors never missed his message. Many were afraid of him, a few even disliked him, but everyone respected Blake, who never got to his team through the press.

"The team came first with Toe," Moore said. "When we won, he was at the back of the line. When we lost, he was the first one up front."

And Blake probably detested losing more than any coach in hockey. For the sake of those around him, he won more often than not—exactly 500 games during the regular season and eight Stanley Cups over his 13-year coaching career.

Blake's arrival in 1955 was an auspicious one. Beliveau, Moore and Geoffrion, all 24 years old, were coming into their own. Coming up from the junior and minor league ranks were Henri Richard, Talbot and Provost. No one gave the 19-year-old "Pocket Rocket," as Henri soon became known, a chance at cracking the lineup, but by the end of camp an astonished Blake reasoned: "How can I cut him? He's always got the puck."

Only 5-foot-7 and 155 pounds, Henri was a fearless, stylish skater who would be a wheel horse for the Canadiens for the next 20 seasons. He would tally more than 1,000 points in his career (358 goals and 688 assists) and play on an NHL-record 11 Stanley Cup champions. But Henri's legend is best put into context when one considers that his addition in 1955 gave the Canadiens an advantage no team had enjoyed before: two formidable offensive lines, Olmstead-Beliveau-Geoffrion and Moore-Henri-Maurice Richard.

And that, pointed out Harvey, explained the Canadiens' mastery over the NHL. "We always had at least six guys breaking in on the net," he said. "The other guys had only three."

Irvin had been content to use only one big line for production, sending out the other skaters to contain and punish the opposition. Moore, who would win league scoring titles in the 1957-58 and 1958-59 seasons, felt he was initially "one of the cannon fodder. Irvin measured your performance in hits, and hits only counted when you knocked the guy to the ice. He figured you were doing your job if you had 21 hits in a game."

Irvin's obsession with contact, Harvey believed,

was based on an unfounded fear "that we'd get run out of the rink in Toronto."

Moore had been an exciting and daring junior player, hockey's version of a kamikaze pilot. After joining the Canadiens, he earned a reputation as a cocky player, one who carried his stick and elbows high. Wherever he played, he challenged not only the opposing players, but their fans, too, often requiring a police escort out of hostile arenas.

"I've always played to win, and sometimes you've got to play against certain teams in a certain way," he said at the time. "If I've carried my stick high against some club, it's because you have to play against that team that way."

But until Blake came along, Moore recalled in retirement, he was insecure and frustrated, "always either on the trading block or on the verge of being sent down to the minors." A rash of crippling in-

juries in his second and third seasons had left him with fragile, aching knees. But under Blake's guidance, he left behind his insecurity for immortality. "Toe wanted *every* line to produce," he said.

In their first year under Blake, the Canadiens placed three players among the league's top four scorers. Consequently, the rest of the league was buried in the standings, crushed under the weight of Montreal's NHL-record 45 victories.

Olmstead, who finished fourth in the scoring race with 70 points (one point behind third-place Rocket Richard), set a single-season record by assisting on 56 goals. Beliveau's 47 goals were the most ever scored by a center, helping him claim league scoring honors with 88 points and the Hart Trophy as its most valuable player.

The Habs' scoring talent simply ran too deep to be contained. Of the top five goal scorers active

Dynasty Data

Yearly Record
1955-56 to 1978-79

Season	W	L	T	Points	GF	GA	—Finish— Div.	Overall	Coach
1955-56	45	15	10	100	222	131		1	Toe Blake
1956-57	35	23	12	82	210	155		2	Toe Blake
1957-58	43	17	10	96	250	158		1	Toe Blake
1958-59	39	18	13	91	258	158		1	Toe Blake
1959-60	40	18	12	92	255	178		1	Toe Blake
1960-61	41	19	10	92	254	188		1	Toe Blake
1961-62	42	14	14	98	259	166		1	Toe Blake
1962-63	28	19	23	79	225	183		3	Toe Blake
1963-64	36	21	13	85	209	167		1	Toe Blake
1964-65	36	23	11	83	211	185		2	Toe Blake
1965-66	41	21	8	90	239	173		1	Toe Blake
1966-67	32	25	13	77	202	188		2	Toe Blake
1967-68	42	22	10	94	236	167	1	1	Toe Blake
1968-69	46	19	11	103	271	202	1	1	Claude Ruel
1969-70	38	22	16	92	244	201	4†	4†	Claude Ruel
1970-71	42	23	13	97	291	216	3	4	Claude Ruel, Al MacNeil
1971-72	46	16	16	108	307	205	3	3	Scotty Bowman
1972-73	52	10	16	120	329	184	1	1	Scotty Bowman
1973-74	45	24	9	99	293	240	2	4	Scotty Bowman
1974-75	47	14	19	113	374	225	1	1†	Scotty Bowman
1975-76	58	11	11	127	337	174	1	1	Scotty Bowman
1976-77	60	8	12	132	387	171	1	1	Scotty Bowman
1977-78	59	10	11	129	359	183	1	1	Scotty Bowman
1978-79	52	17	11	115	337	204	1	2	Scotty Bowman

Playoffs

Season	Preliminary Round	Quarterfinals	Semifinals	Stanley Cup Finals	Total Playoff Record
1955-56			4-1 vs. N.Y. Rangers	4-1 vs. Detroit	8-2
1956-57			4-1 vs. N.Y. Rangers	4-1 vs. Boston	8-2
1957-58			4-0 vs. Detroit	4-2 vs. Boston	8-2
1958-59			4-2 vs. Chicago	4-1 vs. Toronto	8-3
1959-60			4-0 vs. Chicago	4-0 vs. Toronto	8-0
1960-61			2-4 vs. Chicago		2-4
1961-62			2-4 vs. Chicago		2-4
1962-63			1-4 vs. Toronto		1-4
1963-64			3-4 vs. Toronto		3-4
1964-65			4-2 vs. Toronto	4-3 vs. Chicago	8-5
1965-66			4-0 vs. Toronto	4-2 vs. Detroit	8-2
1966-67			4-0 vs. N.Y. Rangers	2-4 vs. Toronto	6-4
1967-68		4-0 vs. Boston	4-1 vs. Chicago	4-0 vs. St. Louis	12-1
1968-69		4-0 vs. N.Y. Rangers	4-2 vs. Boston	4-0 vs. St. Louis	12-2
1969-70			Did not make playoffs		
1970-71		4-3 vs. Boston	4-2 vs. Minnesota	4-3 vs. Chicago	12-8
1971-72		2-4 vs. N.Y. Rangers			2-4
1972-73		4-2 vs. Buffalo	4-1 vs. Philadelphia	4-2 vs. Chicago	12-5
1973-74		2-4 vs. N.Y. Rangers			2-4
1974-75	Earned bye	4-1 vs. Vancouver	2-4 vs. Buffalo		6-5
1975-76	Earned bye	4-0 vs. Chicago	4-1 vs. N.Y. Islanders	4-0 vs. Philadelphia	12-1
1976-77	Earned bye	4-0 vs. St. Louis	4-2 vs. N.Y. Islanders	4-0 vs. Boston	12-2
1977-78	Earned bye	4-1 vs. Detroit	4-0 vs. Toronto	4-2 vs. Boston	12-3
1978-79	Earned bye	4-0 vs. Toronto	4-3 vs. Boston	4-1 vs. N.Y. Rangers	12-4
Total					176-75

when the franchise annexed its fifth straight Cup in 1960, three wore the bleu-blanc-rouge of Montreal: Rocket Richard, Beliveau and Geoffrion. The Canadiens placed at least three players among the league's top 10 scorers each championship season and consistently dominated the playoff scoring lists.

Despite their arsenal of scorers, the Canadiens eschewed the easy blowout. "Doug (Harvey) wouldn't let us run up the score," Moore said. "He said: 'Never embarrass them. We only have to win by one goal.'"

Moore traces part of the team's dominance to the intense but positive internal rivalries. The Canadiens were a team of supercharged temperaments. "The Rocket wanted to show that he was still better than Beliveau and the others wanted to show they were as good as the Rocket," Moore said. "I wanted to show that I belonged with the rest of them."

In his first camp, Moore tried to justify his reputation as a terror in juniors by running the Rocket into the boards. When defenseman Tom Johnson warned him about it after practice, Moore snarled, "Don't worry, your turn's coming tomorrow."

When Henri Richard came up in 1955, he wanted to prove he belonged on his own, not as the kid brother of the Rocket, 15 years his senior. Yet at the outset, the combative Maurice jumped to his brother's defense whenever the action turned chippy. That changed one night in Boston when Henri took on three of the toughest Bruins, one right after the other. "It was all we could do to keep ourselves from giving Henri a standing ovation," recalled one Bruin who had witnessed the feat from the Boston bench.

In a 1971 interview in The Sporting News, Henri maintained that playing center on a line with his brother "was all a dream for me."

"I realize possibly now I would have been better off with another team," he said. "I know I pass the puck too often . . . because when I was with Maurice, I was always looking for him.

"People say my career has been overshadowed by my brother. . . . But I would never change anything, not even my name. I did what I wanted and always dreamed of doing."

But throughout his 20 seasons in Montreal, he fought a battle to be recognized for who he was—Henri Richard, not just the Rocket's brother. And that wasn't so bad, Henri would admit, for Rocket was regarded in Canada as not just a sports idol, but the national idol. "Maurice Richard was not only the best of the French but of the English, as well," explained one fan. "He came to epitomize the desire of the French-Canadian nationalists. He was one of their best expressions. But he has no personal interest in it. Maurice Richard never did a thing to accentuate it. He was a person to fix their eyes. . . ."

Indeed, the Rocket paid little attention to the symbolism of his feats on an entire nation. "It was to win for the team," he often said. "It was a matter of pride."

Inside the enemy blue line, the Rocket was the most fearsome attacker ever, his intensity rising with the urgency of the situation. Picking up the puck from Harvey or Moore or Henri, he would stride powerfully up the ice, then veer suddenly on goal, carrying one defender on his back and fending off another with his powerful left arm. His eyes—"straight from the nut house," one opponent said—lit up like two blazing coals as he hurtled toward the net. He could beat a goaltender from any angle but was deadly from his backhand. Sometimes, he would be flat on his back under a melee in front of the net, wristing the puck into the upper corner.

Not a particularly graceful skater, Richard combined speed and power to dominate hockey in the 1940s and '50s. His strength, especially in the legs and wrists, was legendary. "It was those legs of his," recalled Bep Guidolin, a forward with Boston, Detroit and Chicago during the era. "Once in a while I could budge Gordie, but never the Rocket."

No one was ever more tormented by opponents, who pushed, slashed, elbowed, held and battered the Rocket mercilessly. "It's a shame what we do to Maurice," said Jack Adams, the longtime coach and general manager of the Red Wings. "But if we didn't stop him by fair means or foul, he'd beat every team in the league single-handed."

Many of those fouls were either missed or overlooked by referees, and the Rocket was forced to mete out justice with his own two hands. The penalty box soon became his second home, and his frequent brawls came to be as sensational as his patented rushes on goal. Some teams hired designated hit men in an effort to tame hockey's ultimate warrior. The New York Rangers tried it with a giant named Bob (Killer) Dill. The Rocket KO'd Dill on the ice—and again a few minutes later in the penalty box.

"He's not an unusually strong puncher," said one of Richard's sparring partners, "but he's awfully quick. He gets that first blow in and it hurts."

But the Rocket will best be remembered in five old NHL cities for the pain and suffering he brought to bear with his scoring feats. Though there had been some memorable Montreal teams before Richard's time—teams graced by Howie Morenz, Aurele Joliat and Georges Vezina—the beginning of the Canadien mystique dates to Richard's first full season in 1943-44. The Rocket scored 32 goals that year and the Habs won their first Stanley Cup (and only their fourth overall) since 1931. The next season, Richard became the first player ever to score 50 goals, netting them in *50 games*. By the time he announced his retirement just before the 1960-61 season, he had founded the NHL's 500-goal club, stepping down with 544 goals.

And Moore never remembers the Rocket discussing strategy with his linemates. "We didn't have to because we always *knew* where the other guy would be," he said, "whether we could see him or not. Anyway, hockey is too fast and fluid for X's and O's."

Richard's star always shone brightest in the Stan-

The bloodied face of Maurice (Rocket) Richard (right) following the Canadiens' 1952 playoff victory over Jim Henry and the Boston Bruins was testimony to the extremes opponents took to harness his vast talents.

Montreal's Dickie Moore (12) and the Richard brothers, Henri (16) and Maurice, swarm the Toronto zone during the 1960 Stanley Cup finals.

ley Cup playoffs. Despite the inflated scores of today and the addition of two rounds of preliminary series (there were only semifinal- and final-round series from 1943 through 1967), the Rocket still holds the record for game-winning playoff goals (18) and overtime goals (six), and ranks third in career playoff goals scored (82).

Bill Dineen, a forward with Detroit and Chicago during the 1950s, described the Canadiens as "positively scary. They could beat you in so many ways. And then there was the Rocket—he was always their ace in the hole. You might catch them on an off night during the season. But when the playoffs came along, you knew you were going out there to give your best, but there was that feeling way down that it wasn't going to be good enough."

Dineen witnessed firsthand the beginning of the end of Detroit's empire in 1956. The Red Wings, Stanley Cup champions the previous two years (the last the club would win in a dry spell that extended through the 1980s), were done in by Montreal in the finals in five games and undone by Beliveau, who scored seven goals to set a standing final-series record. In 10 playoff games overall, the graceful center tallied 12 goals, tying Maurice Richard's single-season playoff mark.

Though he was concluding only his third full season, Beliveau already was being hailed as the Rocket's heir apparent—not simply in goal production, but as the pride of French-Canada. "He is the most polished player ever produced," Selke said. "There

are others as effective as he is, but none as smooth and easy."

Beliveau was dignified by hockey standards, exuding coolness, confidence and maturity that belied his youth. Here was one great hockey package to lead by example.

"You could see his effect on this team, this team that featured such great veterans as Rocket Richard and Harvey," Hall of Fame referee Red Storey once said in an interview. "You could see that the Rocket, who never was a great oral communicator with his teammates, was almost glad that someone like Beliveau was there to handle that. Jean spoke to all who surrounded him, he educated and coached his peers, he trained the young kids and worked diligently for the Canadiens from the day he first arrived.

"As far as I'm concerned, Beliveau represents what hockey is all about or should be about. Guys his age, like Moore and Geoffrion, did not seem to resent his leadership ability. They listened just as hard as the other guys."

For sheer artistry, few players have ever matched Beliveau. He was an effortless skater with perfect balance, a clever playmaker who could stickhandle and pass as if the puck were attached to some mechanism in his mind. He had a wicked and accurate shot, and with his extraordinary size for the era (6-3, 205 pounds), he ruled the slot.

"When he has the puck 15 feet out, unchecked, it is almost a sure goal because there is nothing a goal-

The spectacular goaltending of Jacques Plante was a big factor in Montreal's five straight championships in the late 1950s. Plante won the Vezina each season.

keeper can do about it," Terry Sawchuk said. "His slap shot is a bullet on the mark."

Even before he joined the Canadiens, Beliveau was a legend in Quebec. Playing junior hockey for the Quebec Citadels, he packed the city's new arena, Le Colisee, which is known even today as the "House That Beliveau Built." The idolization reached such proportions that the city's seniors team, the Quebec Aces, twice outbid the Canadiens for his talents, keeping "Le Gros Bill" in Quebec City two additional seasons before he finally yielded to the blandishments of Le Club de Hockey Canadien.

Beliveau was a towering figure on the Canadiens for 18 full seasons and 10 Stanley Cups, totaling 507 goals and 1,219 points in his career. He is best remembered by many as the pivot on the most formidable power play in history, centering Olmstead and the Rocket with Harvey and Geoffrion on the points. After Beliveau scored three goals in 44 seconds against Sawchuk and the shorthanded Bruins on November 5, 1955, the league put into effect the following season the rule that permits a player serving a minor penalty to return to the ice when the opposition scores.

"We'd been scoring two goals quite often," Beli-

veau said. "But three goals—that was too much."

Beliveau was nearly as awesome on his regular shifts with Olmstead, an unrelenting, rugged digger, and Geoffrion, an offensive wheel with a terrifying shot. By Beliveau's account, Olmstead's assist record (which Beliveau would eclipse in the 1960-61 season) was not mere happenstance; indeed, few men ever lived who were as unselfish.

"He'd be giving us hell all the time, but what a competitor," Beliveau said. "Sometimes, he'd be taking on two guys for the puck in the corner, so I'd go over to help him. He'd cuss and scream for me to get back in front of the net. 'You can score,' he'd tell me, 'so get out there where you can score. My job's in here to get the puck for you.'"

Said Dickie Moore: "Sometimes Bert could be a pain in the arse. But if you gave him the puck, you always knew you were going to get it back."

Considering Geoffrion's reputation as a gunner, Beliveau believes the line would never have reached the heights it did had it not been for Olmstead's spadework. "Geoff's and my best years were with Bert," he said.

A Canadien for seven full seasons, Olmstead was traded to Toronto after the 1957-58 season—a year in which the other teams, according to one writer,

**High-scoring right wing Bernie Geoffrion (left): his slap shot went boom, boom.
Durable defenseman Doug Harvey (right): the pulse of the early Montreal dynasty.**

realized "a Frankenstein was in their midst." Despite a murderous stretch of injuries to Olmstead, Beliveau, the Rocket (a severed Achilles tendon nearly ended his career) and Plante, the Canadiens won their third successive Cup behind an imposing exhibition of down-the-line strength.

"Our fringe players, the ones who are overshadowed by the stars, gave 100 percent," said Frank Selke Jr., the team's publicist. "Our third line, Phil Goyette, Andre Pronovost and Claude Provost—they aren't exactly great players, but they are one of the hardest-working lines in the league. They'll climb all over you, forecheck and keep you at the other end of the ice."

Such was the talent and depth that these role players had to settle for being superior craftsmen where they might have built legends elsewhere.

Goyette, a master puckhandler and face-off man, did indeed become one of the league's top centers after he was traded to the New York Rangers in 1963. Donnie Marshall, a prolific scorer in the junior and minor league ranks, became a brilliant defensive specialist. Provost, a veritable pest, and Pro-

novost, an aggressive mucker, were relentless checking wingers. Hard-working Marcel Bonin initially replaced Olmstead on the Beliveau line and came close to filling those large boots. In the 1959 playoffs, his 10 goals led all scorers. When a bad ankle hobbled Harvey during the 1958-59 season, ending his four-year monopoly on the Norris Trophy as the NHL's top defenseman, Tom Johnson stepped forward to earn the award.

Beliveau maintains the Canadiens dominated because "we were just a bit faster and quicker. Other teams had great skaters, sure, but as a team we had more."

As a team. To this day, members of the Canadiens dynasty rarely use "I"; almost always, it is "we".

"Because we were always together, we looked after each other," Beliveau said. "If a player was slumping, we'd all try to pick him up. If he couldn't score, we might try to set him up a little more than we usually did. Sure, we had rivalries, and they were good for us. But the rivalries never turned into jealousies."

There were only two players with egos that needed stroking: Geoffrion and Plante.

Geoffrion, a colorful character and popular lock-er room prankster, was nevertheless sensitive to criticism and subject to soaring mood swings depending on his production. "Guys express their frustrations in different ways," Moore said. "Boom was so expressive, he let it all come out."

He was nicknamed "Boom Boom" for launching the first deadly slap shot in hockey. Where goaltenders previously had to contend only with the traditional wrist shots and backhands, Geoffrion drew his stick back much like a golfer and slapped a missile that was harder than anything the league had ever seen—if anyone saw it at all. "I saw him draw his stick back, but I never saw the puck until it bounced off the goal post," one opponent admitted. "It's the first time I never saw the shot I was looking at."

And Boom Boom's pleasingly wild personality was the perfect complement to the shot. "Early in every game I let one go that's not far from the goalkeeper's head," he explained. "That makes them think that all the rest of them are going to be high and it makes it easier for me to score low."

Despite his scoring prowess (393 career goals, 429 assists), the swarthy right winger never achieved the popularity he fully deserved in Montreal. He would pour in 30 goals as the league's Rookie of the Year in 1951-52, and become only the second player (next to the Rocket) ever to score 50 goals, as the NHL scoring leader in the 1960-61 season. But years earlier, when the Rocket's infamous suspension in 1955 cut short his most serious bid for a league scoring championship, Geoffrion edged past the idle star for the title, 75 points to 74. In French-Canada's mind, this was the ultimate in lese majesty, never mind that Geoffrion also was French-Canadian. The Rocket had been usurped and Geoffrion still hasn't been totally absolved.

Plante tended to be a loner on a team of togetherness. His unique and risky style unsettled players and coaches who were products of a conformist age. Early in his career, he had raised eyebrows by *knitting* in the clubhouse, which he said helped him relax and refine his supple hands.

Plante introduced the mask to goaltending and was notorious for roaming far away from the net to handle a stray puck, two innovations that Blake initially resisted. "It annoyed Toe because he didn't think Plante needed to do it," Moore said. "But as we know now, the things he did were needed."

When a teammate scored on him in practice, Plante would keep staring straight ahead, as if the puck hadn't gone in. Moore, chuckling as he recalled Plante's foibles, said, "We used to snarl at him, 'Pick it outta there yourself.' "

Plante revolutionized the position with his forays out of the net and perfected the technique of cutting down a shooter's angle. He pioneered the move behind the net to stop the puck, leaving it for a defenseman or passing off to a teammate along the boards. All told, he won the Vezina Trophy seven

Rocket Richard (left), Jean Beliveau and the Stanley Cup: a match made in heaven.

When Bert Olmstead went into a corner, the puck came out—directly to Beliveau or Geoffrion, his sharp-shooting linemates.

times, compiled a 2.37 goals-against average in a career that spanned 18 seasons (11 with Montreal) and three times posted a mark under 2.00. With those results, any club could live with his idiosyncrasies. "You can afford two prima donnas on a team—but no more," Harvey pointed out.

And it was Harvey—not the Richards or Beliveau or Plante—who many believe was the pulse of the Canadiens. "Doug directed all the traffic for us," Moore said. "Everything started with him."

Said Johnson: "Doug could play the whole game because he controlled the game."

Two decades later, when the Canadiens' "Big Three" defense of Serge Savard, Larry Robinson and Guy Lapointe was being acclaimed the greatest defensive triumvirate ever, Beliveau said: "They are the best three ever on one team. But we had the "Big One"—Doug—and that was even better."

Scotty Bowman, who would coach Harvey years later at St. Louis, was convinced that Harvey, Bobby Orr and Wayne Gretzky possessed a special gift that slowed down the action in their minds. Harvey agreed. "I always knew exactly where everybody was on the ice—I could *feel* them," he said. "I always knew before I got the puck what options I had."

One of the great athletes in Canada's history, Harvey had been a prep football standout at running back and a hard-hitting outfielder for the Ottawa Nationals of the old Class-C Border League. In 1948, he batted .340 and rapped a league-high 16 triples with 24 stolen bases. The next season, he won the league batting title with a .351 mark, adding 10 triples, 14 home runs and 30 steals for good measure. "I think I can hit any kind of pitching," he told a reporter, "but I know that I am a very ordinary fielder." Already a regular on the Canadiens' defense, he conceded that hockey would be his calling "because that is where the money is."

Harvey won the Norris Trophy seven times in his career, second only to Orr's eight awards. Six-foot tall, he played at 180 pounds in his prime but loomed much larger. His powerful shoulders and massive back were supported by deceptively thin legs that never tired. His impassive features, with a turned-up nose between wide-set eyes, seemed to give him perpetual youth.

Besides playing at least 45 minutes a game, Harvey was an invaluable presence in practice and away from the ice. Under Blake, he was free to exercise his rare qualities of leadership. "I used to tease Toe that he was successful because he had one less guy than anybody else to coach," Harvey recalled.

"Doug loved to be around people, and they loved to be around him," Moore said. "When you have a guy like that, who everybody looks up to, you develop a helluva camaraderie. We were always together because we enjoyed it. The strays didn't stay around too long."

It was Blake's belief that the best practice was a scrimmage, and those intersquad games often were more rugged than the real thing. "Because Doug knew the game so well, he spotted everything and told you about it," Moore said. "If you didn't listen, he'd give you a hit you wouldn't forget."

After the Canadiens reached their zenith by winning their fifth straight Cup in 1960, the slow descent began the following September when the Rocket announced his retirement in camp. His absence left a void in the Canadiens' dressing room, where an inscribed war-poem couplet—"To you with failing hands we pass the torch, be yours to hold it high"—was given added meaning.

In the previous five Stanley Cup finals, Les Habitants had conquered all challengers with comparative ease. They were extended to a sixth game only once (in 1958 against Boston), winning three final series in five games and four straight games in 1960, when they blitzed through the playoffs without a loss. In each of the next four seasons, however, the Habs would be bounced out of Stanley Cup contention in the opening playoff round. It was little consolation that they finished first during the regular season three years. Ditto for the Hart trophies, emblematic of the MVP, won by Geoffrion in 1961, Plante in 1962 and Beliveau in 1964, or goaltender Charlie Hodge's Vezina in 1964, or Bobby Rousseau's Calder Trophy as the top rookie in 1962.

One year after the Rocket retired, Harvey was sold to New York, where he became playing coach of the Rangers. It was painful enough without Maurice, their captain since 1956, but without Harvey as well, the magic was gone. Moore played his last game for Montreal in the 1962-63 season. That summer, Plante, Goyette and Marshall were traded to the Rangers. Geoffrion retired at 33 after the 1963-64 season (only to make a comeback with New York after a two-year absence).

Still a strong team—and at times a dominating one—Montreal nevertheless failed in the playoffs with each passing year. The Canadiens would not reach the top again until the 1964-65 season, when the only players who were among the vestiges of the 1950s dynasty were Beliveau, Henri, Provost, Talbot, Hodge and center Ralph Backstrom, who had been voted the NHL's top rookie in 1959.

Selke, who had stepped down after the fourth year of the drought (at 71 years old), was succeeded by perhaps the consummate hockey architect in Sam Pollock, the director of the Montreal farm system for the previous decade. As general manager over the next 14 seasons, Pollock would direct the Canadiens to nine Stanley Cup titles.

The Canadiens of the 1960s did not bring the array of stars into their championship years that the 1950s dynasty had (*only* goaltender Gump Worsley, right wing Yvan Cournoyer, left wing/center Jacques Lemaire and defensemen Jacques Laperriere and Serge Savard would be elected to the Hall of Fame), but they retained an important ethic.

"When you came up through the Montreal organization, you were thoroughly conditioned to their system, a winning system," said Gilles Tremblay, a

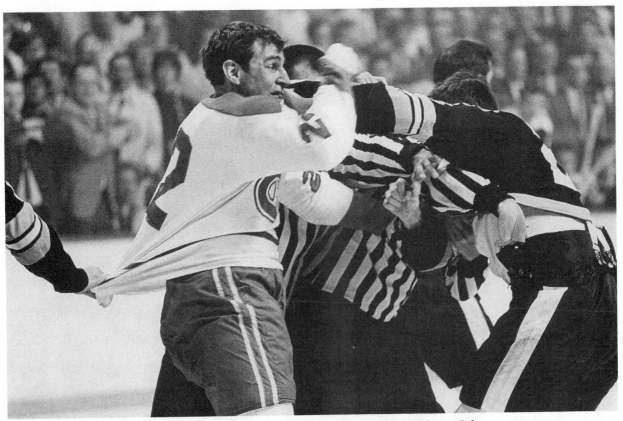

One of the cornerstones of the Canadiens' second dynasty run was right winger John Ferguson (left), a battler who became perhaps the most feared enforcer in the league.

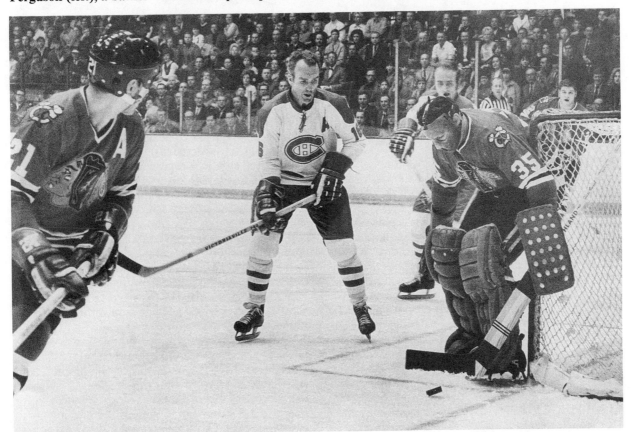

Henri Richard awaits a rebound in the slot as Chicago goalie Tony Esposito, originally a Canadien, steers aside the puck.

Big and beautiful on ice, Beliveau was well established as the pride of the "Flying Frenchmen" by the late 1960s.

fixture on left wing throughout the 1960s. "Sam thinks of how a player will fit into the overall team unit. If he suspects that the player, no matter what his talents, might harm team unity or performance, he gets rid of the guy."

Beliveau confirmed the positive effect of that ideal. "Almost all of us came out of the Canadiens' system," he said, reflecting on the 1950s dynasty. "We may not have played on the same junior teams, but we all had the same style of play. When they brought us together, it was easy to blend in."

But what the Canadiens lacked in their system in the early 1960s was muscle. They went outside the farm to get right wing John Ferguson, who became one of the most feared battlers in league history, and hard-nosed defensemen Ted Harris and Terry Harper. It was only then that Les Habitants began to win back the respect they had commanded in the previous decade, when their top stars could fend for themselves.

"They talk about Beliveau being the inspiration," Boston bad boy Derek Sanderson once said, "but the real drive for that team comes from Ferguson. He's something else."

Twelve seconds into his NHL debut in the 1963-64 season, Ferguson engaged Boston enforcer Ted

Green in a lusty brawl. "All of a sudden," Tremblay said, "we had a lot more room to skate again."

Ferguson became a leader not as a scorer (although he averaged 18 goals per season in an eight-year career with Montreal) but as an aggressor. The Canadiens' smallish forwards had taken a beating during their playoff failures, but Ferguson put tradition back on course by running amok in the postseason in each Stanley Cup championship of the 1960s:

• In the fifth game of the 1965 Cup finals, he beat up Chicago's Eric Nesterenko after the Black Hawks had rallied from a two-game deficit to tie the series. Nesterenko retired to the dressing room to have his face sewn up and the Hawks retreated from the offensive. They lost the game, 6-0, and the Cup to the Canadiens in seven games.

• In 1966, when Ferguson pummeled Toronto's Eddie Shack in the second game of the playoffs, "the chain reaction reflected all down the Maple Leafs' bench," according to one report. Toronto, which had won the Cup in 1962, 1963 and 1964, was swept in four games by the Canadiens, who went on to win their second straight championship.

• One year after Montreal lost the 1967 finals to Toronto, Ferguson stripped the brash, young Bos-

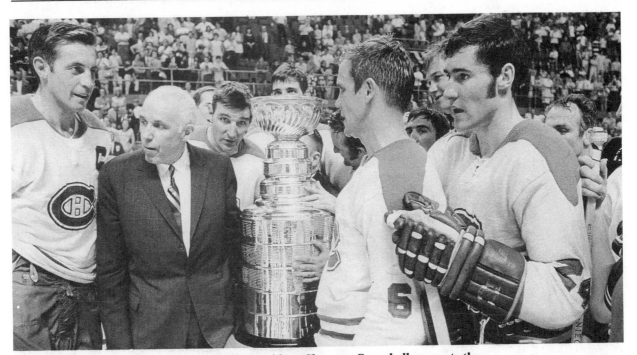

Montreal players gather around as NHL President Clarence Campbell presents the 1969 Stanley Cup—the Canadiens' fourth title in five years.

ton Bruins of their badge of courage—intimidation—in the first game of the 1968 playoffs. He battered a familiar face, Ted Green's, to set the tone for a four-game sweep and an eventual Cup title in the first year of expansion.

● And in the 1969 finals, Ferguson shot all over the ice like flying shrapnel, crashing into St. Louis Blues bodies as he buzzed the net at breakneck speed. The Blues were visibly rattled—and swept in four straight for the second consecutive year.

"We all have our jobs on a hockey team," Cournoyer once explained, "and we respect a player who does his job because he is bringing something special to the team. John was a rough and hard hockey player because the Montreal Canadiens needed a player like that. Without him, and without guys like Terry Harper and Ted Harris on defense, we would not have been as good as we became."

Unlike their forebearers of the 1950s, these Canadiens did not churn out the raw numbers indicative of offensive or defensive perfection. Montreal had led the NHL in both goals scored and fewest goals allowed from 1956 through 1960, but only in the 1965-66 and 1967-68 seasons did this edition lead in either category, both times in fewest goals allowed. Worsley, acquired from New York in the Plante trade, shared the Vezina both years with his backups, Hodge on the early team and young Rogie Vachon on the latter. The closest any Canadien came to a scoring title was second place in 1966, when Rousseau (30 goals, 48 assists) wound up tied with Chicago's Stan Mikita, one point ahead of Beliveau.

What the numbers did not convey was that the sum of Montreal's parts equaled perfect balance. The veterans Beliveau and Henri Richard and Backstrom were the perfect playmaking centers to create

opportunities for such flyers on the wing as Rousseau, Tremblay and Cournoyer. Grinders Claude Larose and Provost kept opponents frustrated with tight checking. Harper, Harris, J.C. Tremblay and Laperriere formed one of the great defensive units in hockey.

"Of all the teams we have had, this is the one that everyone seems to forget," Pollock lamented.

This dynasty was partly the product of two strong rookie classes. Ferguson, Harper, Harris and Laperriere arrived in the 1963-64 season to restore the muscle so badly needed. Laperriere won the Calder Trophy as the NHL's top rookie and two seasons later received the Norris as the top defenseman. And after the 1967 setback to Toronto, defenseman Savard and scoring whiz Lemaire reinforced the team that would win the championship in 1968 and 1969. On the latter Cup team, Savard was voted the Conn Smythe Trophy as the playoff MVP. Lemaire, gifted with a blistering shot, would tally 366 goals and play on eight Cup champions in a 12-year career with the Canadiens.

By 1970, however, cracks were visible in the Canadiens' superstructure. A fifth-place team in the 1969-70 East Division standings, Montreal failed to qualify for the playoffs, breaking an NHL-record string of 21 consecutive postseason appearances (a mark eclipsed by Boston in 1989). Blake had stepped down after the 1968 championship. Age was creeping up on Beliveau, Ferguson and Richard. Worsley was sold to Minnesota, and Gilles Tremblay had already played his last season (in '68-69) due to an asthmatic condition. The Canadiens faced a difficult assignment: rebuilding while trying to remain on top.

"I have to be a realist," Pollock said then. "It's

The Canadiens began reloading in the summer of 1971 for their third dynasty run, hiring Coach Scotty Bowman (above), who would lead the club to five titles.

just not conceivable that we can dominate the league the way we used to."

But as Pollock focused his attention on the task at hand, this "relic" of the 1960s rose up in the 1971 playoffs behind a rookie goaltender/law student with six games of NHL experience to annex Montreal's fifth Stanley Cup title in seven years. Coach Al MacNeil, who had taken over the team in midseason when Claude Ruel resigned, selected 23-year-old goalie Kenneth Wayne Dryden to open the playoffs against the Boston Bruins of Phil Esposito, Bobby Orr, John Bucyk and Ken Hodge, the highest-scoring team in hockey history at the time (with 399 goals). When the playoffs were over, the Canadiens had the Cup and Dryden had been named the playoff MVP.

"The credit goes to the whole team," Esposito said after Montreal's stunning seven-game upset in the first round, "but if one man stood out, it was Dryden."

At 6-foot-4, Dryden was a king-sized man with grand ambitions in life. He was hockey's most intellectual gladiator, a goaltender who could describe his craft as no one ever had. "Hockey is much like the litigation aspects of law," he said. "In both hockey and litigation there are long periods of preparation followed by relatively brief presentations. And then the results are there—graphically. The jury returns its verdict. The red light flashes behind you. The numbers go up on the scoreboard. The only difference is that you can't appeal the decision of a goal judge during a hockey game."

Dryden readily admitted that hockey was only a challenge he felt compelled to meet before he turned to law "for the public interest, the community benefit." When he finally retired to Cambridge, England, to begin that practice, Dryden had posted a career 2.24 goals-against average and won the Vezina five times in seven full seasons. In 1983, he was enshrined in the Hall of Fame.

If the year of 1971 provided the Canadiens with their goaltender of the future, it also gave them a coach nearly the equal of Blake and their next great French-Canadian hero.

In the aftermath of the championship, MacNeil was replaced by Scotty Bowman, a Pollock protege who had managed and scouted for years in the Montreal system before leaving to coach the expansion Blues into three straight Stanley Cup finals. Back with the Canadiens, he would lead them to five *titles* in eight seasons.

On the very same day Bowman was hired, Pol-

With Beliveau lost to retirement after the 1971 Cup title, Guy Lafleur (left) arrived to carry the torch and tradition of Canadien hockey, joining budding superstars in goalie Ken Dryden and defenseman Guy Lapointe.

lock used the first overall pick in the amateur draft to select Guy Lafleur to offset the losses of Beliveau and Ferguson to retirement. Coming off back-to-back 100-goal seasons in juniors, Lafleur was destined to become the most electrifying performer in the NHL and Les Habitants' all-time leading scorer with 1,246 points (518 goals, 728 assists).

That Pollock even had the opportunity to draft Lafleur was due to a shrewd plan that would enable him to build the third tier atop the Canadien dynasty. Back in 1967, Pollock had been the man commissioned by the league to work out the format for the original expansion draft. Cunningly, he also came up with the idea of trading away fringe players in return for future first-round draft picks from those same expansion clubs desperate for a quick fix.

In 1970, Pollock had sent minor leaguer Ernie Hicke to Oakland in exchange for the Seals' No. 1 pick in 1971—in effect, trading Hicke for Lafleur. He engineered similar deals to draft defenseman Larry Robinson in the second round in 1971, left wing Steve Shutt and goalie Michel Larocque in the first round in 1972, left wing Bob Gainey in the first round in 1973, and center Doug Risebrough and

right wing Mario Tremblay in the opening round in 1974, when Montreal had five first-round picks.

By the end of the decade, Montreal was riding roughshod over the league and other clubs were thinking twice before dealing with Pollock. "Pollock doesn't like it when I say this, but the best thing we could do is not phone him for four or five years," said New York Islanders General Manager Bill Torrey. "Then maybe we'd achieve parity. I'm walking proof of the wisdom of not trading No. 1 choices."

Indeed, Pollock had tried to woo the No. 1 pick from Torrey in the 1973 draft. Torrey resisted—and selected defenseman Denis Potvin.

After the Canadiens added yet another Stanley Cup title in 1973, the winds of war began to blow across hockey North America, most noticeably in Philadelphia, where the Flyers were getting their act together as the Broad Street Bullies. Intimidation suddenly became fashionable, and the Flyers shock troops ruled by terror for two seasons, winning Stanley Cup championships in 1974 and 1975. "Canadiens teams always have won with their skating and goals," said Pollock, who refused to join the hit parade. "The reason we didn't win was that we al-

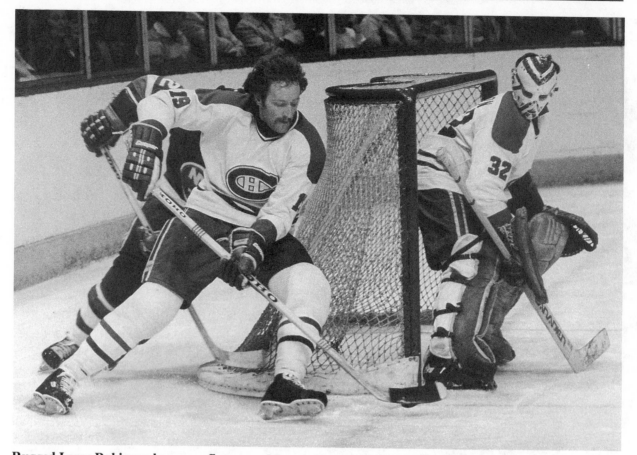

Rugged Larry Robinson became a fixture on Montreal's outstanding defense through the 1980s.

lowed too many goals."

With an eye toward skating and shooting and checking, the Canadiens had been piecing together the juggernaut that would crush the Flyers and their imitators artistically rather than physically. Oh, Montreal had hitters in Gainey, the quintessential defensive forward, Risebrough, the feisty center, and Robinson, the towering Ontario farm boy who would win the Norris Trophy in both 1977 and 1980. And if the Philadelphias and Bostons really wanted to rumble, Montreal could oblige with storm troopers Rick Chartraw and Pierre Bouchard, the son of former captain Butch Bouchard. But this was a team that would sweep four Stanley Cup titles because of its omnipotence. No other club could skate with the Canadiens, score with them or play their kind of defense.

No one epitomized the Montreal tradition of exciting, dynamic hockey more than Lafleur, with his golden mane flying, his graceful speed and the booming slap shot. After three mortal seasons, Lafleur's comet was blazing by the 1974-75 campaign, when he pumped in a team-record 53 goals to post his first of six consecutive 50-goal seasons. The gifted right winger reached his peak with 60 goals in the 1977-78 season, when he won his third straight scoring title and second consecutive Hart Trophy as the league MVP.

"What made him so great was his ability to do

everything at top speed," said Hall of Fame center Bobby Clarke, a longtime nemesis with the Flyers. "There was no fear in him."

When the line of Lafleur, Shutt and 6-foot-5 center Pete Mahovlich (a 30-goal scorer five times with Montreal) gave way to the Lafleur-Lemaire-Shutt pairing in the 1976-77 season, Les Habitants had a trio of sharpshooters that rivaled their two legendary lines of the 1950s. In their first season together, they produced 150 goals, led by Shutt's league-high 60 tallies (a standing record for left wingers).

"Guy did everything so naturally, there was no need for a game plan," Lemaire remembered fondly. "He did things on the ice we had never seen before."

Shutt became a deadly sniper alongside Lafleur, scoring 424 goals in a 13-year career. "He burns and burns and burns for first, the team, and secondly, himself to do well," Shutt said in 1977. "If any guy on the team is floating, he'll hear from the Flower —not loudly, but a little prod in the back."

Playing with passion was second nature to supporting members of the cast like left winger Yvon Lambert, an immovable screen in front of opposing nets; gentlemanly center Doug Jarvis, a tight checker and face-off specialist; left wing Murray Wilson, a pesky "shadow" and perhaps the fastest skater in the league, and veteran right wing Rejean Houle, the No. 1 pick in the 1969 draft.

Canadiens captain Serge Savard hoists the silverware as he leads his teammates around the ice after their 1979 five-game Stanley Cup win over the Rangers.

Savard, Robinson and Lapointe knocked down pucks and bodies in front of Dryden and Larocque, who shared the Vezina in 1977, 1978 and 1979, following Dryden's solo Vezina season in 1976. The "Big Three" defensemen raised the transition game to an art form, swatting pucks into corners or behind the net, then beginning a rush up ice or setting one up with a crisp pass. Brian Engblom, Bill Nyrop, Bouchard and Chartraw contributed nononsense defensive support.

The torch of the 1960s dynasty was carried by Lemaire, Savard and Cournoyer, the captain, who still displayed the bursts of acceleration that earned him the nickname "Roadrunner." He also retained the puck sense that enabled him to net 428 career goals, scoring 32 goals when Montreal began its four-year Cup run in the 1975-76 season, then 25 and 24 the following two years. And in the long career of Cournoyer, no Canadien teams ever won in such convincing fashion.

In this case, the numbers speak for themselves. Montreal's regular-season records from 1975-76 through 1978-79: 58-11-11, 60-8-12, 59-10-11, 52-17-11. The playoff marks: 12-1, 12-2, 12-3, 12-4.

That second championship season bordered on the unthinkable—*only eight losses over an 80-game schedule!* The Canadiens established standing records for most victories, points (132) and fewest defeats (over at least a 70-game schedule), and they outscored the opposition by 216 goals (387-171, or by 2.7 goals per game).

Savard, however, maintains that the times gave this edition an advantage the previous Montreal dynasties didn't enjoy. "There was so much expansion going on that the league wasn't balanced," he said. "There were teams like Colorado and Cleveland that didn't belong. . . ."

After watching the 1976-77 team sweep the Bruins in the Cup finals, 1950s defenseman Tom Johnson, Boston's assistant general manager, pondered the inevitable comparison. "It's impossible to rate teams from different eras because you're talking about the old NHL with six teams and the new NHL with 18 teams," he said.

"However, this Canadiens team has no center as good as Jean Beliveau, no winger as good as Maurice Richard, no one defenseman as good as Doug Harvey, no one goaltender as good as Jacques Plante. But this Canadien team has other things that we didn't have, like great depth and balance. It has every element a team needs, and it's the hardest-working, best-checking great team I've ever seen."

Beliveau, always the diplomat, avoids rating one dynasty superior to another. "Let's just say it would be one hell of a series," he chuckled.

The debate is destined to live on in Montreal, eternal as the flame that lights the torch passed on to each Canadiens team.

PITTSBURGH STEELERS

1974 to 1979

The cornerstone of the vaunted Pittsburgh Steeler machine was Mean Joe Greene, a hard-charging defensive tackle.

A Curtain Shrouds The NFL

By Chuck Finder

January 27, 1969, figured to be just another day in Pittsburgh Steelers infamy. The team called a press conference to announce its new coach. He arrived five hours late.

Same old Steelers.

Through the previous 36 years, Pittsburgh had had 15 head coaches, eight winning teams and no playoff berths. Players had survived player-coaches, co-coaches, tri-coaches, the same coaches twice and one Nixon administration (Coach Mike Nixon went 2-12 and out the door after one season, 1965). Management had showed great acumen in selecting quarterbacks by trading for a creaky Bobby Layne and letting Len Dawson and Johnny Unitas slip away. The franchise became the laughingstock of the National Football League. They were, indeed, the same old Steelers.

It was Art Rooney who had given them their handle. At training camp in Hershey, Pa., in the summer of '41, someone had asked the club owner about his team's new look. "The only thing different is the uniforms," Rooney replied. "It's the same old Steelers."

The name stuck. S.O.S.

So it was on a January day in 1969 that Charles Henry Noll came to the Steelers' rescue, albeit a bit tardy because of flight problems. Chuck Noll, 37, had spent three years on Don Shula's Baltimore staff in the NFL and six before that with Sid Gillman's Los Angeles/San Diego Chargers of the American Football League. He had served seven faithful seasons as a messenger guard for Paul Brown's Cleveland Browns from 1953-59. He knew nothing but winning.

"I just don't believe that any certain area is doomed to have losers," Noll said at his introduction.

"But this is the City of Losers," a skeptic said.

"We," Noll declared, "will change history."

The next day, Noll selected a 6-foot-4, 270-pound defensive tackle from North Texas State by the name of Joe Greene with Pittsburgh's first pick in the draft. The Steelers would not be the same.

"You know," said Art Rooney Jr., harking back to a time when he constituted half of the team's scouting department, "Joe was the cornerstone of the whole thing."

The building began. After Greene came offensive tackle Jon Kolb and defensive end L.C. Greenwood later in the 1969 draft; quarterback Terry Bradshaw and cornerback Mel Blount in 1970; linebacker Jack Ham, defensive linemen Dwight White and Ernie Holmes and safety Mike Wagner in 1971, and running back Franco Harris in 1972. A dab of mortar, a few more bricks—wide receivers Lynn Swann and John Stallworth, linebacker Jack Lambert and center Mike Webster in that mother lode 1974 draft —and Noll had the foundation of his dynasty.

Eight straight seasons the Steelers of the 1970s made the playoffs. Seven times they won the American Football Conference's Central Division. They were 99-44-1 for the decade, and from 1972-79 they went 88-27-1 with a remarkably consistent 50-1 record against teams that finished the regular season below .500. They were 14-4 in the playoffs, 13-2 from 1974-79. They won a record four Super Bowls, thereby evolving from Same Old Steelers into Super Steelers.

"If the truth were known, we were very greedy," said Greene, regretting near misses in 1972 and 1976. "Six Super Bowls. Then we truly would have put some distance in."

Sticking close to the Steelers in football immortality are Vince Lombardi's Green Bay Packers and Shula's Miami Dolphins. The Packers won five NFL titles and the first two Super Bowls. The Dolphins played in three consecutive Super Bowls, winning two and finishing undefeated in 1972. But the Steelers won two with defense, sat out two and retooled, then won two more with offense. Their four championships and pair of back-to-back titles set precedents that have proved difficult to match. After Super Bowl XIV, the last of their championships, Greene was asked if history would deem Pittsburgh a dynasty. Answered Greene: "Wouldn't you say that four out of six would qualify us for that?"

Glory days continued for the Super Steelers a decade afterward. Greene, the leader from the start, in 1987 became the first member of the four championship teams enshrined in the Pro Football Hall of Fame. Ham went in a year later, telling a crowd laden with Pittsburghers, "I hope all of you remember the road to Canton." Bradshaw and Blount followed in 1989. "Down the road there will be 10, 12 in the Hall of Fame, I imagine," said Steve Furness, a defensive tackle who relieved Greene and later started alongside him. "Who knows?"

The Steelers of the 1970s had such a multitude of stars and stories: Rooney, the cigar-chomping owner who bought the club in 1933 ... Noll, the connoisseur of fine wines and football players ... Greene, Bradshaw, the 1971 draft, Harris ... the Immaculate Reception ... the 1974 draft ... the Steel Curtain ... the Spirit of '76 ... Rocky Bleier, war veteran ... Bradshaw and Swann ... Bradshaw and Stallworth.... They made the Steelers super. They dominated a decade.

Legend has it that Rooney, known simply as the Chief, financed the team with winnings from a racetrack, where he was adept at handicapping the horses. He hit an even bigger jackpot in 1936 after a

Art Rooney, the cigar-chomping owner of the Pittsburgh Steelers.

successful weekend at two New York tracks. A quarter of a million dollars went pretty far during the Depression.

The Steelers did not. The first four seasons the Chief hired Jap Douds, then Luby DiMelio, then Joe Bach to coach the team originally dubbed the Pirates, after the city's baseball club. He fired Bach to hire Johnny Blood, the player/coach/wild man, and he rued that move until his death in August 1988. But there were other blunders.

Rooney drafted Byron (Whizzer) White in 1938, made him the league's highest-paid player for one season and then let him leave for Oxford and later the biggest bench of all, the U.S. Supreme Court. To his friend George Halas of the Chicago Bears he traded a first-round draft choice that became Hall of Fame quarterback Sid Luckman; in return he got end Edgar (Eggs) Manske, who lasted one season. His first pick in the 1946 draft was Army's Doc Blanchard, but Uncle Sam had first dibs on the Heisman Trophy winner and Blanchard enjoyed an impressive career in the Air Force. Rooney brought back Bach as coach in 1952, and that lasted two seasons. He next brought back Walt Kiesling, who had initially coached from 1939-44, and Kiesling released Unitas before seeing him play an exhibition. Two years later Rooney's No. 1 draft pick was Dawson, who spent three years on the bench before being traded. He later became a star in Kansas City, while Unitas did the same in Baltimore; both are in the Hall of Fame. During that time, the Steelers were stuck with such eminently forgettable quarterbacks as Rudy Bukich, Ed Brown, Ron Smith, Kent Nix and Dick Shiner.

It took the Chief two generations for his original investment to pay off.

It took Chuck Noll.

"Chuck put it together," said Andy Russell, the veteran linebacker who experienced a winning season in 1963 and not again until nine years later. "He's got a good eye for talent, and he brought us together with the proper amount of praise and the proper amount of criticism."

Noll had learned to be a devotee of talent, particularly big running backs, from winning four conference and two NFL championships with Cleveland. He had studied defense with the Chargers, who in a six-year span participated in five division titles and one AFL championship. He had gleaned much about handling players in Baltimore, where the team lost a scant seven regular-season games in three years and reached the Super Bowl. The Steelers, after Penn State Coach Joe Paterno turned them down, offered Noll the opportunity to lead them from the doldrums.

"The Rooneys convinced me that they had one goal—a winner—and they were willing to pay the price to produce one," Noll reflected.

The day after he arrived, Noll proceeded to assemble a team. He and the Rooney sons—Dan, a vice president, and Art Jr., the director of player personnel—had agreed to a philosophy of procuring the best available athlete. They also had agreed that Noll and his assistants would have the final say on selections. Hence, they started by plucking some real plums: Mean Joe Greene from the Mean Green; Kolb, the Oklahoma State center, and Greenwood from Arkansas AM&N.

The new kids won Noll's opening game in Pitt Stadium—"I thought we were on our way to the Super Bowl," Greenwood said—and lost the next 13. That winter, the Steelers swept out Louisiana. They drafted Bradshaw from Louisiana Tech and Blount from Southern University in Baton Rouge. Noll hired Lou Riecke, a guy in the lumber business in New Orleans, to teach the players to lift weights. In those days, a strength coach was an innovation.

Noll prodded, praised and criticized the Steelers to a 5-9 record in 1970. The rookie Bradshaw threw four times as many interceptions (24) as touchdowns (six) and completed only 38.1 percent of his passes. The defense gave up 20 or more points in six of the last nine games. Still, recalled Bleier, back by then from Vietnam: " '70 was a unique year for the franchise. '70 was like a break, a breaking away from old tradition. Three Rivers Stadium. New facilities. New head coach. It was almost like a cutting of the past."

"Weapons," Noll pleaded at the draft table in 1971. "Weapons." The Steelers struck upon a stockpile. They selected Grambling wide receiver Frank Lewis in round one, Penn State's Ham in round

Dynasty Data

Regular Season Yearly Record
1974-1979

Season	W	L	T	Pct.	Avg. Score Pitt.-Opp.	Place	Coach
1974	10	3	1	.750	22-14	1	Chuck Noll
1975	12	2	0	.857	27-12	1	Chuck Noll
1976	10	4	0	.714	24-10	1†	Chuck Noll
1977	9	5	0	.643	20-17	1	Chuck Noll
1978	14	2	0	.875	22-12	1	Chuck Noll
1979	12	4	0	.750	26-16	1	Chuck Noll
Total	67	20	1	.767	24-14		

†Tied for position.

Playoffs

Season	AFC Playoff	AFC Championship	Super Bowl	Total Playoff Record
1974	32-14 Buffalo	24-13 Oak.	16-6 Minn.*	3-0
1975	28-10 Balt.	16-10 Oak.*	21-17 Dal.*	3-0
1976	40-14 Balt.	7-24 Oak.		1-1
1977	21-34 Denver			0-1
1978	33-10 Denver	34-5 Hous.*	35-31 Dal.*	3-0
1979	34-14 Miami	27-13 Hous.*	31-19 L.A.*	3-0
Total				13-2

*Game played in January of following year.

Additional Data

Best Year—1978 (14-2-0).
Worst Year—1977 (9-5-0).
Most Lopsided Victory—45-0 over Kansas City, 1976.
Most Lopsided Defeat—35-7 to San Diego, 1979.
Most Consecutive Regular-Season Victories—11 games from Oct. 5 through Dec. 13, 1975.
Most Consecutive Regular-Season Defeats—3 games from Sept. 26 through Oct. 10, 1976.
Shutouts—The Steelers held opponents scoreless in 10 games..
Times Shut Out—The Steelers were shut out only once during their dynasty years—by Oakland in 1974.

After almost four decades of frustration, Rooney found the man who could turn his Steelers into winners: Chuck Noll.

two, Southern Cal guard/tackle Gerry Mullins and East Texas State's White in round four, Kansas tight end Larry Brown in round five, Texas Southern's Holmes in round eight and Wagner in round 11.

"We gambled a little bit, and it paid off," Rooney Jr. said of Wagner, a two-time Pro Bowl safety who missed much of his senior season at Western Illinois. "I'd like to say it was a brilliant move."

In one swoop, the Steelers got seven starters to go with five from the previous two drafts. A defensive front four—Greene and Holmes on the inside with Greenwood and White on the ends—was in place for the better part of a decade. Russell and Ham manned the outside linebacker positions. Wagner and 1971 free-agent safety Glen Edwards joined Blount in the hard-hitting secondary. They pieced an offense around Bradshaw. The Steelers finished the year seven points shy of 8-6, but just the same improved to 6-8.

"I thought that (1971) draft was the one that made us a playoff football team," Rooney Jr. said. "The '74 draft was the one that really helped us to the Super Bowl. But once the '71 players got in there, we could play with the good teams."

The Steelers' surge coincided with the 1972 arrival of Harris, a first-round pick from Penn State. A smooth arrival, it was not. His contract negotiations dragged. Once he signed, he lumbered through practices.

"Really, he started off kind of poorly," said Furness, a fifth-rounder from Rhode Island in that class of '72. "I think they were kind of worried about him. He wasn't really in shape and hadn't shown that he deserved to be there."

Harris started only one of the first five games of the season. Suddenly, the blocking back for Lydell Mitchell at Penn State began churning up yardage in the Steelers' trapping offense. He equaled the NFL mark of Jim Brown, Noll's former teammate, with six straight 100-yard rushing games. His star glimmered.

In the meantime, Bradshaw was winging them to victory in the final 1:06 at St. Louis. The defense was sacking New England's Jim Plunkett six times. ("I tell you," Plunkett remarked, "that pass rush of theirs is something else.") Minnesota was driving inside the Steelers' 5-yard line three times and getting rebuffed each time. There started a string of home sellouts that would stretch for 16 years. Up popped the fan clubs: placekicker Roy Gerela's Gorillas, Ham's "Dobre Shunka" (Polish for "Great Ham") and, of course, Franco's Italian Army. It became quite the rage to support the third of nine children of American Army Sgt. Cad Harris and his Italian World War II bride, Gina.

In the end, when the 6-2, 230-pound rookie rumbled to 1,055 total yards and Frank Sinatra became an honorary Franco's army man and the Steelers clinched their first-ever title with a 24-2 spanking of San Diego, White turned to no one in particular, smiled and said, "Same old Steelers." The defense, at first called "The Body Snatchers," yielded five

Another key to the rise of the Steelers was quarterback Terry Bradshaw, pictured above (left) with Noll and backup quarterback Terry Hanratty in 1971.

points in the last three games. The team won 11 times, the most in franchise history, and lost three. The House of Rooney was righted in four short years. Yet the Chief, who had waited 40 years for his team's first division championship, missed its glowing moment.

The Oakland Raiders invaded Three Rivers Stadium on December 23 for the first playoff game in Steelers history. This magical 1972 season had begun there, with the Raiders and a 34-28 Steelers upset made possible by a blocked punt, two interceptions and a fumbled punt. One Pittsburgh newspaperman wrote after that opener, "The longest prayer vigil in the history of football may have ended yesterday." Three months later, with 22 seconds left, Oakland protecting a 7-6 lead and the Steelers 60 yards from the end zone on fourth and 10, the football gods finally smiled on Pittsburgh. How else to explain the Immaculate Reception?

Bradshaw scrambled to avoid the Oakland rush and heaved a pass down the middle of the field. The ball caromed off Raiders safety Jack Tatum and Steelers running back Frenchy Fuqua when all three collided at the Oakland 35-yard line. Harris, who had left his blocking assignment for an improvised pattern, grabbed the fluttering ball just before it hit the ground at the Oakland 42 and darted down the left sideline to the end zone. The officials

huddled, consulted with NFL supervisor of officials Art McNally, who was watching the game from the press box, and ruled the play a touchdown.

Rooney never saw it unfold. When those 22 seconds remained, he headed for the elevator. Holding the door for him was Pirates baseball announcer Bob Prince, who a dozen years before had similarly gone to the locker room prematurely and missed Bill Mazeroski's World Series-winning home run.

At least there was no doubt about Maz's homer. The Immaculate Reception was another story. The Raiders contended that the ball had bounced off Fuqua's shoulder pads and that Tatum never touched it, thus making the pass incomplete because two offensive players could not touch a pass in succession. Asked afterward if he had touched the ball, which would have negated his teammate's catch and game-winning touchdown, Fuqua said, "I'm not chopping down any cherry trees, but . . . no comment." Said Tatum: "I didn't hit the ball."

"A miracle sent from heaven," Bradshaw said.

That victory propelled the Steelers into the AFC championship game against the undefeated Miami Dolphins on New Year's Eve in balmy 60-degree temperatures in Pittsburgh. But the Steelers were cool to Larry Seiple in the second quarter, turning their backs on the Miami punter to cover downfield. So, the alert Seiple jogged half the distance of

Pittsburgh running back Frenchy Fuqua had style, both on and off the football field.

Pittsburgh vs. Most Frequent Opponents

(5 or More Regular-Season Games)

Opponent	W	L	T	Pct.	Avg. Score Pitt.-Opp.
Kansas City	5	0	0	1.000	33-11
Cleveland	11	1	0	.917	30-18
Cincinnati	9	3	0	.750	20-13
Denver	3	1	1	.700	25-18
Houston	8	4	0	.667	21-13

the field to set up Miami's first touchdown in a 21-17 Dolphin triumph. The Steelers' bitterness lingered long after.

"We should have beaten the Dolphins," Wagner said. "Not to take anything away from Miami, but if we played them five times, we would win four. In my mind, that was one of our better teams. I really think '72 was a great year. Everything started to click. Cohesion came, and we started winning."

Said Bleier: "We could have gone to the Super Bowl. But I think our problem was we had not jelled together, knowing how to win."

1973 did nothing to bring them closer. In March, Holmes suffered a nervous breakdown and unloaded a shotgun and a pistol at trucks along the Ohio Turnpike, wounding the pilot of a police helicopter. For his sentence, he spent two months in a psychiatric hospital. A quarterback controversy disrupted the Steelers during the season, and Bradshaw managed only 1,183 yards passing. Hobbled by injuries, Harris rushed for 698 yards on the same number of carries as his rookie year. The Steelers dropped three consecutive games near the end of the season. They qualified for the playoffs as the AFC wild-card team with a 10-4 record but lost their first game to Oakland, a team they had beaten in their three previous meetings. "I'd hate to think we got fat," Greene said.

Not hardly. This was a young team—just six players were left from the days before Noll arrived, and only six players on the 1974 roster were older than 28. Maybe they needed time.

A 1974 players strike, which disrupted most of the exhibition season, gave a bumper crop of rookies just that. By the start of the season, first-year players abounded in Steeler uniforms. The flashy Swann from USC returned punts. The wild Lambert, whom they had seen diving on cinders in practice at Kent State, started at middle linebacker. Wisconsin's Webster backed up veteran Ray Mansfield at center and handled the snapping duties on kicks and punts. The dependable Stallworth from Alabama A&M and free-agent find Donnie Shell, the safety who had toiled at linebacker at South Carolina State, dazzled on special teams.

The new talent notwithstanding, hard times followed. Noll benched Bradshaw in favor of lean Joe Gilliam, who started the first six games, and local hero Terry Hanratty, a native western Pennsylvanian who had been drafted in 1969, a year before Bradshaw. One newspaper published a quarterback poll and Bradshaw won, although the other vote-getters included Greene, the team's radio announcer, the retired Layne and Linda Lovelace.

Bradshaw returned in the seventh game and the Steelers went on to win six of their last eight contests and clinch the division title with a 10-3-1 record. Noll, normally reserved, responded: "What's this champagne bit? We want rings."

The Steel Curtain was working on that. Pittsburgh's defense ranked first in the league against the pass and sixth against the run while permitting

By the middle of the 1970s, there was no doubt that Terry Bradshaw was the man in charge of Pittsburgh's offense.

the second fewest points in 1974. Greenwood, Greene, Holmes and White—alias Hollywood Bags, Mean Joe, Fats and Mad Dog—spearheaded a unit that registered a league-leading 52 sacks. The stunt 4-3 defense thrived on its linemen crisscrossing and rushing and terrorizing. That unit was so awesome that Wagner does not remember making a tackle on a running play the first five games of the season.

The Steel Curtain held O.J. Simpson to 49 yards rushing in a 32-14 triumph over Buffalo in the first round of the playoffs. Then, Greene recollected, the defense really got motivated.

"I think the turning point of the team was that week (before the AFC championship game against Oakland)," Greene said. "Chuck Noll gave an outstanding talk the Wednesday of that week. He was saying something like: 'Well, some people think the Super Bowl was played this past week and the two best teams in football played in it (Miami and Oakland). I want to tell you something. The best team in football is sitting in this room.'

"That right there won the game. It gave us the mindset, the attitude. That was the turning point of the whole thing."

The Steelers trailed, 10-3, after three quarters in Oakland, but they turned two interceptions of Ken Stabler into touchdowns and a 24-13 triumph. The Raiders dented the defense for only 29 yards on 21 carries. "You have to go to the air on us," Greenwood said. "We'll beat you. We'll bend some. We never break."

That also went for Minnesota in Super Bowl IX. "You guys are in for a long day," Greene told Vikings defensive tackle Alan Page in the tunnel beforehand. The Curtain came down hard on Minnesota: It intercepted three passes and yielded just nine first downs, 119 total yards and 17 yards rushing on 21 carries. Running back Chuck Foreman became so riled at one point he said, "Come on, you mothers, give us a yard." The Vikings' only score came on a blocked punt.

Harris was the offensive star for Pittsburgh, romping to a Super Bowl-record 158 yards on 34 tries. The Steelers secured the 16-6 victory when Bradshaw rifled a four-yard touchdown pass to Brown with just over three minutes left. At that point, Page threw his elbow pads in the air and said to the opposing guard, "Hell, (Jim) Clack, I'm all through."

The Chief finally hoisted a championship trophy. The Super Bowl roster numbered 14 players in their first year and 35 age 26 or younger. There was more to come.

The Steelers won 12 of 14 games in 1975, but

The Steelers tapped Penn State to draft big back Franco Harris, pictured above (32) following a Jim Clack block in 1977.

1974 Steelers (left to right) Joe Gilliam, Frank Lewis and Ron Shanklin.

Big, steady Mike Webster arrived in 1974 to anchor the Steeler offensive line.

those two losses stuck in Greene's craw. He wanted an undefeated season. "I think the best team was probably '75, and I didn't get a chance to play," said Greene, who missed virtually half of the season with a variety of injuries. "I thought I was an important part of the team, but they didn't even need me. The easiest was that second time. There was a charge. We knew from day one where we were going."

Still, the Steelers tended to lollygag, to wait until late to seal victories. "The kind of team that would drive coaches crazy," Wagner said. "We played games on the back of our heels until it got to the fourth quarter."

Although Harris gained a team-record 1,246 yards and Bradshaw passed for 2,055 yards and 18 touchdowns, it was the defense that lifted the Steelers. Ham, Lambert and Russell were voted All-Pro linebackers. Blount was named the team's most valuable player and the NFL Defensive Player of the Year for his league-leading 11 interceptions. Time magazine profiled the front four.

The Curtain yielded 154 yards in a 28-10 defeat of Baltimore in the first round of the playoffs. It set up all of the Steelers' points and turned away the Raiders nine of the 11 times they crossed midfield in the conference championship, a 16-10 Pittsburgh

victory. And it stoked the Steelers against Dallas in Super Bowl X, which came as no surprise to quarterback Fran Tarkenton of Minnesota.

"Their defense is the most dominating in football," said Tarkenton, who had been harassed by the Curtain in the previous Super Bowl. "It is also the most frustrating."

The Cowboys didn't need to stir up the Steelers any more, but they did just that when Dallas safety Cliff Harris patted Gerela on the helmet after a botched field goal in the third quarter and said, "I'm glad you missed that." Lambert shoved Harris and a fracas ensued. The Steelers were losing, 10-7, but Lambert's outrage inspired the Steelers, who tallied a safety, two field goals and a touchdown in the fourth quarter to win, 21-17.

"Lambert was the fellow who held us together when things weren't going good," Greene said afterward. "He spearheaded us. He made the licks that got us going."

By angering Lambert, Cliff Harris managed to provoke key Steelers on both sides of the ball. In the AFC title game two weeks before, Swann had suffered a concussion that doctors feared was one hit away from brain damage, and Harris, upon learning that Swann still might play, said: "I'm not going to hurt anyone intentionally. But getting hit again while he's running a pass route must be in the back of Swann's mind. I know it would be in the back of my mind."

That was all Swann needed to hear. "He was trying to intimidate me," the receiver told reporters. "He said I'd be afraid out there. He needn't worry. He doesn't know Lynn Swann. He can't scare me or the team. I said to myself, 'The hell with it, I'm gonna play.'"

Did he ever. Swann caught four passes for 161 yards, including a 64-yard touchdown for Pittsburgh's final score, and was named the Super Bowl MVP. His juggling, sprawling, 53-yard catch over Dallas' Mark Washington became a freeze-frame of football lore. That day marked the start of a surge by the Steeler offense. "We had an abundance of talent," Swann said. "We're talking superior."

Yet here began the emotional problems for these superior Steelers. Holmes was arrested in February 1976 with 250 milligrams of cocaine in his possession. In June, the team waived Gilliam, the former starter, and shortly thereafter he was arrested on drug and weapons charges. In July, the Steelers' game with the College All-Stars got called on account of rain before the end of the third quarter. They released Hanratty late in training camp, leaving rookie Mike Kruczek as the backup. Oakland beat them in the opener, 31-28, and safety George Atkinson beat Swann about the helmet and face, giving Swann a mild concussion. This prompted Noll the next day to launch into a discourse about "football with the intent to maim" and a "criminal element" in the NFL. Atkinson sued Noll for $3 million.

The season unraveled from there. The Steelers

The brightest star in Pittsburgh's outstanding receiving corps was Lynn Swann, who played with a grace and style befitting his last name.

beat Cleveland, then lost two more. After Joe (Turkey) Jones tried to drive Bradshaw headfirst into the Municipal Stadium turf during a Cleveland triumph, the Steelers were 1-4. And in trouble. Bradshaw somehow suffered merely a sprained neck. ("Now," said then-wife JoJo Starbuck, "he knows he can't break his neck.") Kruczek replaced him.

What happened next would long boggle minds and later move Rooney to brand this 1976 team the Steelers' best ever. The Curtain arose and the Steelers won nine straight games. The defense registered shutouts in five of those and allowed only two touchdowns during the winning streak. This was the defense at its most potent. Funny thing: It often acted on its own.

Lambert at times could not read the signals from the sideline or would angrily stop looking if coaches dallied. He would tell the defense to ad-lib or repeat the previous formation. Whatever, Jack Splat was in charge.

"We'd be in the middle of a drive and Lambert would chew everybody's ass off in the huddle," Furness recalled. "You'd look at him, there'd be blood all over the place, he'd be dripping."

Said Wagner: "We had real interesting huddles. Lambert would be going wild. Edwards and Dwight White would be yelling at somebody. L.C. would be cackling. Joe would just be listening. And Jack Ham would just be smiling. You wondered how we ever got anything done."

They ravaged opposing offenses is how, giving up an average of 183.2 yards per game and little more than three yards per play in the last nine games. "What the defense did in those nine games should go down in the record books," said Bleier, who combined with Harris to become the second pair of teammates to rush for 1,000-plus yards each in the same season.

But they all needed an assist from Oakland to reach the playoffs, and the Raiders obliged a week before the regular-season finale by beating Cincinnati, which had led Pittsburgh by a game in the standings. Thus the Steelers won another division title. Bleier—himself a tale of triumph, having overcome a grenade explosion in Vietnam that mangled his right foot—said: "The greatest comeback story this football league has ever known, that's what it will be."

Swann (left) embraces fellow receiver John Stallworth after another Steeler touchdown.

Pittsburgh back Rocky Bleier with Raider safety George Atkinson, who sued Noll for $3 million.

Alas, it was not meant to be. While trouncing host Baltimore, 40-14, in a first-round playoff game, the Steelers saw Fuqua pull a calf muscle, Harris reinjure his ribs, Bleier bruise his big toe and even Gerela get hurt. To cap this day, a plane crashed into the upper deck of Memorial Stadium shortly after the game. "I thought it was a kamikaze pilot from Oakland," Mansfield joked at the time. Said Noll, in all seriousness, "It's not pleasant when you lose your whole football team."

The Steelers returned to Oakland for the AFC championship game with one healthy running back. Bradshaw, who had started only three of Pittsburgh's last nine regular-season games but had been a stunning 14 of 18 against Baltimore, misfired on 21 of 35 pass attempts and tried to elude the Raiders' blitz all game. "I know what it feels like to fight a war without weapons," Noll remarked. Oakland grabbed a 24-7 victory and added a Super Bowl conquest.

"It was the Raiders' time," Greene said. "It was fate. It was fate."

If the Steelers thought that was bad, 1977 was worse. Noll started the year in court with the At-

kinson case. (He was absolved.) Both Bradshaw and Kruczek sustained injuries against Houston in the fourth week, leaving rookie defensive back Tony Dungy to play quarterback, his college position. Bradshaw returned the next week and played with a cast on his broken wrist. Cornerback Jimmy Allen retired and unretired over a contract dispute. Edwards similarly went AWOL. Wagner missed much of the year with a neck ailment. Even Noll did not escape injury; he slipped on a Cincinnati sidewalk and broke his left arm.

The Steelers' one bit of 1977 luck came when Houston toppled Cincinnati in the season finale and propelled them to another division title with a less-than-stellar 9-5 record. The grateful Steelers sent each Oiler a new $50 briefcase. Case closed: In Denver, one fumble, one blocked punt and three interceptions led to a 34-21 Broncos playoff defeat of Pittsburgh. So frustrating was this game, this season, that Greene punched Denver lineman Paul Howard in the first half. Some heralded this as the end of the Steelers' era.

Then the NFL intervened. The league altered the rules to restrict the mugging of receivers and to per-

Two wild and crazy members of the Steel Curtain defense: intimidating linebacker Jack Lambert (left) and lineman Ernie Holmes.

End L.C. Greenwood and his Steeler linemates made life miserable for opposing quarterbacks, such as Seattle's Jim Zorn.

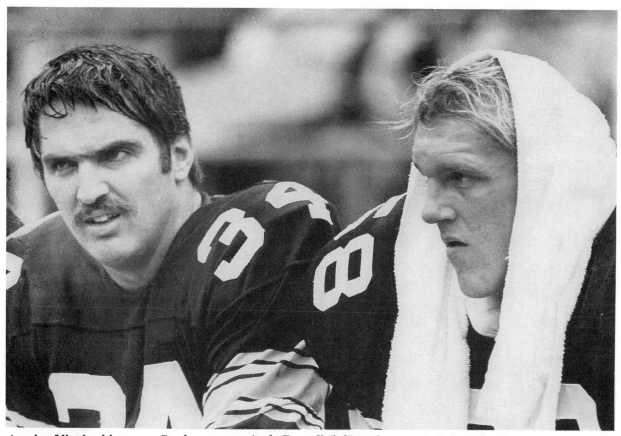

A pair of linebacking aces: Steeler veteran Andy Russell (left) and young Jack Lambert in 1976.

mit offensive linemen to extend their arms and open their hands when pass blocking. The Steelers saw this as an attempt to undercut their defense. No more could Blount bash receivers during patterns. No more could the front four easily pull stunts and dash past linemen. Ironically, in so changing the rules, the NFL removed the shackles from the Steeler offense. "We were the ones they were trying to hurt," Greene said, "and we were the ones who benefited the most."

Bradshaw completed 14 of 19 passes in the 1978 opener at Buffalo. He used a high school gadget play, the flea flicker, to beat Cleveland in overtime. The Steelers won their first seven games, with no opponent coming closer than a touchdown. Harris rushed for 1,082 yards, his fifth of sixth straight 1,000-yard seasons, but the once-vaunted Steelers' rushing attack ranked ninth out of 14 teams in the AFC. Instead, the Steelers came to pass. Bradshaw, considered raw (read: dumb) when he left Louisiana Tech eight years earlier, tossed 28 touchdown passes, topped the AFC in quarterback rating and was named All-Pro for the first time. Swann caught 61 passes and became a second-time All-Pro. A 215-pound tight end, Randy Grossman, replaced the injured Bennie Cunningham at midseason and reeled in 37 passes. Bradshaw was protected by a strong line anchored by Webster, another All-Pro, and featuring Mullins and veteran Sam Davis at guard, Kolb and Ray Pinney (who replaced the injured

Brown) at tackle. The team went 14-2, posting the league's best record in the first year of the 16-game schedule.

The Steelers appeared in order for another Super Bowl run. Allen, the 1977 contract malcontent, had been traded in July. Lewis was shuffled off to Buffalo to make room for Swann and Stallworth. The unpredictable Holmes was shipped to Tampa Bay and replaced by Furness. The roster contained 22 players not present for Super Bowl X. But many of the players who had lifted Pittsburgh to its previous Super Bowl glory remained, including Bradshaw, Harris, Bleier, Swann, Stallworth, Kolb and Mullins on offense and Greenwood, Greene, Ham, Lambert, Blount and Wagner on defense.

In the playoff opener, the offense gained 425 yards and a 33-10 triumph over Denver. In the cold and rain at Three Rivers Stadium a week later, the home team scored 31 first-half points and slid to a 34-5 victory over Houston. The Steelers packed their Terrible Towels—Swann even waved one of the black-and-gold rags on the sideline—and headed for Miami to play Dallas again in Super Bowl XIII.

Bradshaw became the focus of the first Super Bowl rematch. Dallas linebacker Thomas (Hollywood) Henderson put him there, criticizing him all week. Henderson said Bradshaw could not spell "cat" if you spotted him the first two letters and added, "Somebody had to die for him to get the

Linebacker Jack Ham, shown intercepting a Raider pass in 1974, was another key to Pittsburgh's outstanding defenses of the middle and late '70s.

Cornerback Mel Blount (47) was a hard hitter and the longtime leader of the Steelers' classy secondary.

starting job." Real dumb, this Bradshaw. He attempted third-down passes against a run-containing Dallas defense 13 times and produced two touchdowns and five first downs. He also passed for 253 yards by halftime and finished with 318 yards and four touchdowns, both Super Bowl records. The game's MVP got a measure of help from the defense, which had five sacks, two fumble recoveries, one interception and Cowboy tight end Jackie Smith's dropped pass in the end zone. The result was a 35-31 Pittsburgh triumph that made the Steelers the first team to win three Super Bowls—all quarterbacked by Bradshaw. Wrote one newspaperman afterward, "Li'l Abner Bradshaw is dead."

"Crazy man" was how Greene later described the quarterback. Bradshaw almost always played with pain. A hamstring operation in 1970. A separated shoulder in 1973. Rib injuries too numerous to mention. A concussion in Super Bowl X while throwing the game-winning touchdown to Swann. The sprained neck and wrist injuries in 1976. The broken wrist in 1977. A broken nose and a pulled abdominal muscle for 10 weeks in 1978.

In the 1979 opener, Bradshaw left the game in the second quarter with a sprained toe but came back in the second half to lead the Steelers over New England in overtime. Two weeks later he was carried off the field in St. Louis on a stretcher before halftime, only to return and lead Pittsburgh to another victory. Paul Zimmerman of Sports Illustrated wrote that year, "... Man, if Terry Bradshaw ain't limping and bleeding, the argument hasn't even started." Against Dallas at midseason, in a game billed as Super Bowl XIII½, the 6-3, 215-pound quarterback survived all kinds of abuse to lead the Steelers, 14-3. Said Swann: "He was rubbing his arm. He was limping, and a little blood was coming from his mouth. But I wasn't worried. I only pay attention when he looks real bad."

What a season it was. Bradshaw passed for 311 yards and four touchdowns in a 38-7 victory over Washington despite suffering from an upset stomach and dizziness that caused him to miss most of the second half. A week later he had 232 yards, three touchdowns and back spasms against Kansas City, which he called "the worst game I've played all year." Pittsburgh won by 27 points. After San Diego Coach Don Coryell called the 1979 Steelers the "best team of all time," the Chargers trashed the Steelers, 35-7. Noll responded by putting his team through one of his usual post-defeat hell weeks. "It was like, pity the team that plays the Steelers after they lose," Furness said. The unfortunate victim was Cleveland, which saw Bradshaw hit 30 of 44 passes for 364 yards as Pittsburgh won in overtime. The Steelers cruised to a 12-4 record and their sixth consecutive Central Division crown. The mantel had a smidgen of room left on it.

In the battle for Team of the Decade, the Steelers beat the Dolphins, 34-14, in their first playoff game. The defense held Miami to 25 yards on 22 rushes, rekindling memories of its 1974 charge.

The Curtain held Houston's Earl Campbell to 15 yards on 17 carries a week later in the battle for the conference championship. After one tackle, Campbell mimicked the famous commercial by asking Greene if he would like to have a Coke. The Steelers managed a smile, although they needed another group of huddling officials—a la 1972—to rule that Houston's Mike Renfro didn't have possession of a Dan Pastorini pass inbounds in the end zone. "When I go," Oilers Coach Bum Phillips said after this 27-13 Steelers victory, "I want a P.S. on my tombstone that says, 'He'd have lived a hell of a lot longer if he hadn't had to play Pittsburgh six times in two years.'"

With Swann attracting double coverage despite nursing injuries that year, Stallworth worked free to be the Steelers' leading receiver with 70 catches for 1,183 yards. He was a rangy receiver whom Noll had coveted as far back as 1974, when the coach wanted to draft him in the first round. The Steelers chose Swann instead. Thanks to a Senior Bowl coach who hid Stallworth's abilities by moving him to the secondary for the game, Stallworth lingered until the fourth round. The Steelers jumped, knowing he would star. "Noll felt that we had gotten two first-round picks when Stallworth was still there," Rooney Jr. said.

Stallworth did not possess the grace of Swann, of whom Greene said, "If the ball was in the air, it belonged to him." Rather, Stallworth was dependable, durable, always making that catch over the middle, always there on third down. He got much less publicity than Swann, but that never seemed to bother him. "The rivalry doesn't get to the point where it's a jealousy-type thing," he said. "I think we have big egos, but we're able to subdue them a little bit for the team effort."

At the close of the decade, his moment arrived. Super Bowls X and XIII belonged to an extent to Bradshaw and Swann; Super Bowl XIV was all Bradshaw and Stallworth.

They teamed three times for 121 yards and one touchdown, that coming with the Steelers behind the Rams, 19-17. Noll sent in a deep post pattern to Stallworth as a third-down play. The 60 Slot Hook and Go earned them a 73-yard touchdown pass and the respect of Los Angeles cornerback Rod Perry, who said afterward, "Haven't you ever seen a perfect play?"

As usual, Lambert was exhorting the defense to greatness. Even more important than a key interception he made late in the game was the tongue-lashing he gave his teammates late in the first half. "He bellowed so loud," Shell said, "that I got kind of scared. I don't recall what he said, but I can tell you I didn't say anything." Said Lambert: "I did go into a tirade, but I was very concerned the way the defense was playing. It seemed to me that we didn't have the necessary intensity. We weren't flying around the field the way we should have."

The Steelers perked up, recovered from a 13-10 halftime deficit and scored 21 second-half points to win, 31-19. Bradshaw finished with 14 completions on 21 attempts for 309 yards, two touchdowns and another MVP honor. Stallworth likewise found hero status. The first-time All-Pro was one of 21 Steelers (including defensive back J.T. Thomas, who was sidelined with a blood disorder in 1978) to savor all four Super Bowl triumphs.

"Winning a fourth Super Bowl should put us in a special category," Blount told reporters afterward. "I think this is the best team ever assembled. They talk about Vince Lombardi, but I think the Chuck Noll era is even greater."

It certainly was becoming familiar. The presentation ceremony was so routine, NFL Commissioner Pete Rozelle handed the last Vince Lombardi Trophy to Rooney and said, "We have to stop meeting like this." Greene had an idea: "One for the thumb."

But this game rang in a new decade. The thumb would go bare.

"We lost our confidence and attitude edge," Greene said of the 1980s, which the Steelers started with 9-7 and 8-8 records. "When things started to go bad—the long runs, the long bombs—people started getting big plays on us. It was the beginning of the end."

The last remnants of the Steel Curtain front, Greene and Greenwood, retired in 1981. Ham and Swann left in 1982, Blount and Bradshaw in 1983. Harris remained a Steeler through the 1983 season and closed out his career with Seattle in 1984. Stallworth lasted until 1987. Webster retired after the '88 season, went to Kansas City as an assistant coach and then unretired, saying he'd rather play for the Chiefs instead.

Pittsburgh had its fun. The City of Losers gave way to the City of Champions. The 'Burgh brought home world championships in baseball and football in 1979. It grew accustomed to victory parades. Folks relived these times a decade after *their* decade, when the Steelers started to dominate the Hall of Fame as well. "We had such a great football team," Bradshaw said upon making it four Steelers in three years in 1989, "just pick a number, pick a name, they should be in there."

Said Greene: "I don't think anyone could have accused us of being hotdogs. I think that has something to do with our run, that we were on the brink from '72 to '79. We were dangerous. Sometimes lethal. But we were always dangerous."

They were, for most of a decade, the same old Steelers—Super.

Bradshaw makes it very plain who's No. 1 after the Steelers' Super Bowl IX victory over Minnesota in 1975.

BROOKLYN DODGERS 1947 to 1956

Jackie Robinson and his boss, Walter O'Malley, in 1956, the Dodgers' second-to-last season in Brooklyn.

The Bums: Lovable And Lethal

By Joe Gergen

On a Wednesday afternoon in October 1956, the Brooklyn Dodgers made their final appearance in a World Series. Their lineup for Game 7 against the New York Yankees included four players destined for enshrinement in the Baseball Hall of Fame, a onetime National League batting champion, a former Rookie of the Year and one of the best first basemen in history. Plus, the starting pitcher was a man who would win both the Cy Young Award and Most Valuable Player honors for his efforts that season.

Not unexpectedly, the Dodgers lost.

In the course of a decade, they won more than 61 percent of their games. They also captured six National League pennants in that time frame, lost a seventh in the bottom of the ninth inning of the concluding game of a remarkable playoff series against the New York Giants and were denied a chance to compete in another pennant playoff because of a 10-inning defeat on the final day of the regular season. They would have been regarded as the dominant team in all baseball but for one small detail: Their timing was terrible.

At the pinnacle of their glory, which ran from 1947 through 1956, the Brooklyn Dodgers shared the local and national stage with the New York Yankees. While the Dodgers were winning their six flags, the Yankees compiled eight first-place finishes in 10 years in the American League and won more than 63 percent of their games. Each time the Dodgers advanced to the World Series, the Yankees were there to meet them. On all but one occasion, the Dodgers lost.

It was part of the Brooklyn club's charm. Perhaps no baseball team in history broke more hearts. No matter. They would be repaired in time for the following season because Dodger fans of the post-World War II era lived on a diet of hope and promise. Their rallying cry was a simple one: Wait 'Til Next Year.

"A whole country was stirred by (their) high deeds and thwarted longings...," wrote Roger Kahn in the introduction to "The Boys of Summer," his book about the team and its times. "The team was awesomely good and yet defeated. Their skills lifted everyman's spirit and their defeat joined them with everyman's existence, a national team, with a country in thrall, irresistible and unable to beat the Yankees."

That's not entirely accurate. The Brooklyn Dodgers, much to their own surprise, did defeat the Yankees in the 1955 World Series. It was a singular moment. The Bums, as they were fondly known throughout the Borough of Churches, traditionally stumbled on the final step, perhaps explaining why they were the subject of more books, more poetry, more songs and more passion than any baseball team in history.

Some of their losses were excruciating, none more so than the third game of the 1951 playoffs when the Giants rallied in their final at-bat to stun the Dodgers, 5-4, on Bobby Thomson's three-run homer. Once, Brooklyn was a perfect loser, victimized by Don Larsen's improbable feat of retiring all 27 batters he faced in Game 5 of the 1956 fall classic. Even then, however, the Dodgers rallied to win Game 6 in 10 innings, forcing a seventh game on October 10. It would be the last World Series game staged at cozy, historic Ebbets Field.

This was the Dodgers' batting order, as presented by captain Pee Wee Reese:

Jim Gilliam, 2b
Reese, ss
Duke Snider, cf
Jackie Robinson, 3b
Gil Hodges, 1b
Sandy Amoros, lf
Carl Furillo, rf
Roy Campanella, c
Don Newcombe, p.

From that group, Reese, Snider, Robinson and Campanella would be inducted into the Hall of Fame at Cooperstown, N.Y. Furillo had won a batting title in 1953, the same year Gilliam had been selected as the league's premier rookie. Hodges was a feared slugger and a nimble first baseman. Newcombe had just completed a 27-7 campaign, for which he would be honored as the league's outstanding pitcher and MVP.

The stage was set for a last hurrah by the franchise, whose majority owner—upset that a new and larger ball park was not on the drawing board in Brooklyn—was casting covetous glances at the West Coast, a potential gold mine. The Dodgers had the momentum and the home-field advantage. And the Yankees were entrusting the game to Johnny Kucks, a 23-year-old righthander making his first Series start.

What happened—Kucks tossed a three-hit shutout and the Yanks' Bill Skowron smashed a bases-loaded home run in a 9-0 New York triumph—can't be construed as an upset, not in light of the Yankees' mastery over the Dodgers. In Brooklyn, it was viewed as another grave disappointment but temporary in nature. The real tragedy was a year away.

In retrospect, the attempted trade of Robinson after the 1956 season was the signal for the end of an extraordinary era. For the 10 years that he appeared in a Dodgers' uniform, he was the most significant figure in baseball—the man who broke the

The foundation for the Dodgers' N.L. dynasty was poured by Larry MacPhail (left) and strengthened by Manager Leo Durocher.

Dynasty Data
Yearly Record
1947-1956

Year	W	L	Pct.	GA(+)/GB	Place	Manager
1947	94	60	.610	+ 5	1st	C. Sukeforth
						B. Shotton
1948	84	70	.545	7½	3rd	L. Durocher
						B. Shotton
1949	97	57	.630	+ 1	1st	B. Shotton
1950	89	65	.578	2	2nd	B. Shotton
1951	97	60	.618	1	2nd	C. Dressen
1952	96	57	.627	+ 4½	1st	C. Dressen
1953	105	49	.682	+13	1st	C. Dressen
1954	92	62	.597	5	2nd	W. Alston
1955	98	55	.641	+13½	1st	W. Alston
1956	93	61	.604	+ 1	1st	W. Alston
Total	945	596	.613			
Under Sukeforth	2	0	1.000			
Under Shotton	326	215	.603			
Under Durocher	36	37	.493			
Under Dressen	298	166	.642			
Under Alston	283	178	.614			

Additional Data
Best Record—1953 (105-49).
Worst Record—1948 (84-70).
Longest Winning Streak—13 games, July 21 through July 31, 1947; August 7 through August 20, 1953.
Longest Losing Streak—8 games, May 15 through May 23, 1948.
Best Record vs. One Opponent, Season—20-2 vs. Pittsburgh, 1953.
Worst Record vs. One Opponent, Season—8-14 vs. Boston, 1948; 8-14 vs. New York, 1952.

color line—as well as the Brooklyn team's driving force. He was 37 years old and clearly beyond his prime when Walter O'Malley decided to move Robinson.

What antagonized the public was O'Malley's decision to deal the former star to the team's crosstown rivals, the hated Giants. Robinson had decided to quit baseball, however, although news of that decision was not disclosed until well after the trade because Jackie had a longstanding agreement to announce his retirement plans in a magazine story.

The presence of Robinson and so many great players in Brooklyn after the war was credited to a man who shared in only two of those six pennants. He was Branch Rickey, a former major league catcher and manager who found his true calling in the front office. A college graduate, a lawyer and a man of deep religious conviction, Rickey was generous with words (he favored those with polysyllables) and tight with a buck.

He came to Brooklyn in October 1942 after practically inventing the farm system while in the employ of the Cardinals. At St. Louis, he supervised a chain of 32 minor league teams that fed the major league club with an unbroken line of talent. His genius was in recognizing that talent and supervising its development.

The organization he joined in Brooklyn had been in tatters before the arrival of Larry MacPhail. In five years under the direction of the tempestuous MacPhail, the Dodgers had installed lights, tripled their attendance and climbed from the depths of the National League to contending status. They finished second in 1940, claimed their first pennant in 21 years in 1941 and won a club-record 104 games in 1942, only to finish two games behind Rickey's Cardinals.

Looking for new worlds to conquer, the restless MacPhail joined the war effort in Washington. The Dodgers' directors gladly offered the position of commanding officer to Rickey, who had come to a parting of the ways with Cardinals Owner Sam Breadon. Whereas MacPhail had revitalized the Brooklyn club with promotions, slick trades and inexpensive acquisitions, Rickey went to work expanding the farm system.

In his eight seasons on the job, the man created the foundation for success that lasted decades beyond his departure. During his tenure, the Dodgers signed the nucleus of their 1950s championship teams, established a training base in Vero Beach, Fla., that became the model for all baseball and drilled players throughout the organization in what became known as "the Dodger way." In personal style, he owed more to the 19th Century than the 20th; from a baseball standpoint, he was a man of remarkable vision.

Tom Meany dubbed Rickey "the Mahatma" because he fit John Gunther's description of Mohandas K. Gandhi—"a combination of God, your own father and Tammany Hall." He spewed cigar smoke and literary quotations in equal volume. He de-

The indomitable Branch Rickey (right) replaced MacPhail after the 1942 season, installed shortstop Pee Wee Reese (left) as team captain and molded the Dodgers into big winners.

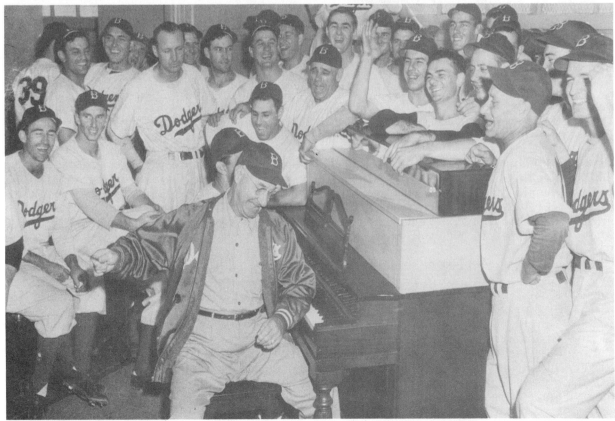

The Dodgers, under the direction of Burt Shotton (front center), sing up a storm after clinching the 1947 National League pennant, their first since 1941 and second since 1920.

Dodger veteran Cookie Lavagetto is escorted to safety after ruining Yankee pitcher Bill Bevens' no-hit bid with a game-winning pinch double in Game 4 of the 1947 Series.

clined to attend baseball games on the Sabbath, fulfilling a promise he had made to his mother, and made no public statement stronger than "Judas Priest." Yet, strong, gifted athletes quaked in approaching him for a raise and emerged grateful when their salaries for the following season had not been reduced.

"He'd say," pitcher Carl Erskine recalled, " 'Well, son, you had a nice year. We're going to let you come back.' And you'd end up thanking him."

Even if he had accomplished nothing else in baseball, however, Rickey would have won everlasting acclaim for addressing a terrible wrong. Signing Robinson to a contract was not an impulsive act. Rickey had long ago decided the black man deserved a place in organized ball. He awaited only the right time and place to carry out his plan.

It was in postwar Brooklyn that he made the decision that would open the game to millions of Americans, that would make baseball truly the na-

tional pastime. He knew the first black player in modern big-league history had to be a special person, a man of strong mind as well as sound body. The chosen would be subject to vile abuse and he had to succeed despite experiencing verbal taunts, physical intimidation and the loneliness of a pioneer.

Jack Roosevelt Robinson had the qualities Rickey sought. He was a superb athlete who had excelled in football, basketball and track as well. Snider, a Californian, remembered him as a star at Pasadena Junior College who left a game between innings to win a long-jump competition in his baseball uniform and spikes. Robinson later continued his education at UCLA. And he had served as a lieutenant in the U.S. Army, always standing up for his rights and those of his race.

Rickey started getting reports on Robinson shortly after he began playing for the Kansas City Monarchs in the Negro leagues in 1945. His scouts had

When ecstatic Brooklyn fans celebrated the Dodgers' 1947 N.L. pennant, little did they realize the World Series frustrations that lay just around the corner.

been checking the physical and moral attributes of dozens of players, ostensibly for the purpose of stocking an all-black team Rickey said he planned to sponsor in Ebbets Field while the Dodgers were on the road. Robinson's character was as formidable as his speed.

Finally, Rickey arranged for his chief scout, Clyde Sukeforth, to visit Robinson in Chicago and to bring him to Brooklyn for an interview. Rickey and Robinson first laid eyes on each other in Rickey's office on August 28, 1945. The meeting lasted nearly three hours and Rickey did most of the talking.

"I knew this wasn't for the Brooklyn Brown Dodgers," recalled Sukeforth, the third man in the room. "Who could describe Rickey? In substance, he said, 'I need more than a great ball player. I need a man who can carry the flag for his race, turn the other cheek. If I get a firebrand who comes up swinging after a collision at second base, it could set

the cause back 20 years.'

"The thing that I think sold Rickey was Jackie thought about it two or three minutes. Then he said, 'I think I can do it your way. If you want to take the chance, I can promise you there will be no incidents.'"

Satisfied he had the right man, Rickey waited until the end of the season and then signed Robinson to a contract with the Montreal Royals, a Triple-A farm club of the Dodgers in the International League. The announcement was made in Montreal on October 23.

While Robinson was winning a batting title and leading the Royals to a championship in 1946, the parent club was enjoying unexpected prosperity. On Rickey's timetable, the Dodgers would begin to blossom two years after the war. "After that," he declared, "I envision pennants, pennants, pennants."

The Dodgers almost arrived ahead of schedule in

Four key Dodgers after a 1949 regular-season victory: (left to right) Don Newcombe, Roy Campanella (standing), Shotton and Carl Furillo.

'46, earning a first-place tie with the favored Cardinals after 154 games. But St. Louis won the first pennant playoff in big-league history, a best-of-three affair, in two games. That served to whet the appetite for 1947.

Technically, Robinson still was Montreal property when he reported to training camp in Havana, Cuba, a site Rickey had chosen because it offered the prospect of less racial tension than the Deep South. As it developed, the furor that grew around the Dodgers that spring involved not Robinson but the manager, Leo Durocher. A controversial character throughout his career, the Lip was suspended for the season by Commissioner Happy Chandler for conduct detrimental to baseball. Specifically, he had been associating with known gamblers and other citizens of ill repute.

The announcement that Robinson's contract had

been purchased by the Dodgers was almost lost in the outcry over Durocher's fate, made public the previous day. A shortstop with the Monarchs and a second baseman at Montreal, Robinson opened the National League season at first base. Sukeforth, the same man who had brought Robinson to Brooklyn for his interview with Rickey, was the acting manager on opening day. Burt Shotton, a longtime Rickey crony from St. Louis, became interim manager for the season upon his arrival in New York.

Robinson's acceptance was not immediate, even among his teammates. During spring training, while he still was wearing a Montreal uniform, several Dodgers who had been raised in the South—most prominently Dixie Walker, the most popular player on the team—passed around a petition stating that they did not want to be on the same team with a black man. Rickey called the ringleaders into

Brooklyn's colorful and inviting Ebbets Field (above) had personality and charm as well as its own "Sym-Phony Band."

The Dodgers fell hard in 1950, when Philadelphia beat them in the season finale to capture the pennant. Leaving the field (left to right) are infielder Wayne Belardi, Robinson and Furillo.

his hotel room and lectured them on truth, justice and the American way. Clubhouse opposition waned.

Elsewhere, however, it escalated. Robinson received hate mail, including death threats, from out of town. He was vilified so badly by Ben Chapman that National League President Ford Frick ordered the Philadelphia manager to curb his tongue. According to a story in the New York Herald Tribune, the Cardinals threatened a strike in their first series against the Dodgers, only to have the planned rebellion broken by the actions of Frick and Breadon. The story, however, was not substantiated.

By some accounts, Robinson was spiked four times against the Cardinals that season. He was the target of more knockdown pitches than any player in baseball and constantly challenged on the basepaths, where his quickness and aggressiveness electrified the sport. And in some cities he had to stay in separate quarters from his teammates.

It was Reese who first reached out to Robinson. Although the shortstop grew up in Louisville, Ky.,

he had declined to sign the Southerners' petition. "I just got out of the service after three years," he told Walker. "I don't care if this man is black, blue or what the hell color he is. I have to play baseball."

The Kentuckian didn't have to befriend Robinson. But one day, when the bench-jockeying was particularly rough, Reese walked over to Robinson on the field, put his arm around the rookie's shoulders and stared into the opposing dugout. The message was clear.

Reese said he had put himself in Robinson's place. "I tried to think what it would be like for me breaking into a black league," he said. "I don't know how he did it without saying anything for two years. They threw at him quite a bit. But it was what they yelled at him. You knew he was an aggressive person just by the way he played and it had to be tearing at his guts."

The Dodgers were drawn together in their effort. It didn't lessen anyone's enthusiasm that Robinson was an exceptional talent. Playing an unfamiliar position, scorned by opponents, he nevertheless

The Dodgers' 1952 All-Star contingent: (left to right) Furillo, Robinson, Campanella, Reese, Duke Snider, Preacher Roe and Gil Hodges.

batted .297, stole a league-leading 29 bases and scored 125 runs. His fierce competitive nature found favor among Walker, Reese, Eddie Stanky, Pete Reiser and other veterans.

No September heroics were required. The Dodgers moved into first place to stay in early July and cruised home five games ahead of the Cardinals. The World Series, which lasted seven games, gained renown for a stunning turnaround and a great catch. Of course, the Yankees won.

Game 4 was one for the memory banks. Bill Bevens, a sore-armed righthander for the Yankees, went into the ninth inning needing only three outs to post the first no-hitter in Series history. He got one out, then walked Furillo, the potential tying run. Spider Jorgensen then fouled out. At this juncture, fleet Al Gionfriddo was sent in to run for Furillo and, with Reiser at the plate as a pinch-hitter for reliever Hugh Casey, Gionfriddo stole second base. After issuing an intentional walk to Reiser, his 10th pass of the game, and watching Eddie Miksis pinch-run at first base, Bevens then threw a fastball

on the outside corner to Cookie Lavagetto, another pinch-hitter. Lavagetto, 34 and in his final major league season, lined the ball off the right-field fence, driving in the second and third runs in the Dodgers' implausible 3-2 victory.

Brooklyn tied the Series at three games apiece with an 8-6 victory in Game 6, thanks largely to a dazzling catch by the 5-foot-6 Gionfriddo of Joe DiMaggio's long sixth-inning drive with two men on base. The Dodgers took an early lead in the deciding game, but Yankees relief ace Joe Page shut them down on one hit over the final five innings and the Yankees won handily, 5-2.

After the season, Rickey traded the popular Walker and pitchers Hal Gregg and Vic Lombardi to Pittsburgh. He wasn't capitulating to racial harmony as much as he was obeying one of his own dictums: Better to trade a player a year too early than a year too late. Walker was 37.

In exchange, the Dodgers received shortstop Billy Cox, pitcher Preacher Roe and utility infielder Gene Mauch. Cox rarely hit for an average, the way he

After a two-year absence from the World Series, the Dodgers were National League kingpins again in 1952.

did in Pittsburgh, but he became the most spectacular third baseman in the major leagues. Roe, a 32-year-old who didn't throw very hard, experimented with a spitball. He compiled a 7-23 record in his final two years with the Pirates; at Brooklyn, he won 93 and lost 37.

There were other changes in 1948. Hodges was shifted from backup catcher to first base, where he excelled. Robinson moved to his natural position, second base, replacing Stanky, who had been traded to Boston. Campanella, who started the year in Brooklyn before being sent down in mid-May, was promoted from St. Paul halfway through the season and became the Dodgers' starting catcher and third black performer (Dan Bankhead pitched in four games for the Dodgers in '47).

The talent was excellent but the pitching was disappointing and the chemistry wasn't right. Rickey decided that the problem was Durocher, who had resumed managing after his one-year suspension. Just after the All-Star Game break, the Mahatma released Durocher, who was signed immediately by the Giants, adding fuel to the rivalry. Shotton

moved back into the manager's office, although he never did bother changing out of his street clothes.

Although the Dodgers finished well back in third place, Rickey was busy working on the future. He had obtained a long-term lease on a former naval air base in Indian River County, Fla., a place so extensive it could house all the organization's farm clubs as well as the big-league team. Thus was born Dodgertown, which opened in '48 and went into full operation in the spring of 1949.

Rickey personally presided over Dodgertown. He delivered half-hour lectures every day during the first week of spring training. Using a chalkboard, he gave detailed instructions on cutoff plays, relays, bunt situations and squeeze plays. And he tested the players on the material.

That year the Dodgers fielded their strongest team in Rickey's stewardship. The smooth, powerful Snider took over in center field at the age of 22, bumping the strong-armed Furillo to right. Five regulars batted .285 or better, topped by Robinson's league-leading .342 average. Jackie also scored 122 runs, drove in 124 and stole an N.L.-high 37 bases in earning Most Valuable Player honors. The Dodgers edged the Cardinals by a game by beating the Phillies in the final game of the season and were honored in a huge parade through Brooklyn the day *before* the World Series began.

At the very least, civic leaders showed foresight. Any thoughts the Dodgers might have had about reversing history—they had lost in all four of their previous Series appearances (1916, 1920, 1941 and 1947)—evaporated in the first game. Newcombe, Rookie of the Year in the National League, was masterful. Allie Reynolds, the Yankees' Super Chief, was superb. Tommy Henrich provided the margin of victory when he led off the home ninth with a drive into the right-field seats at Yankee Stadium.

Remarkably, the second game also was decided by a 1-0 count, with Roe outdueling Vic Raschi and the Dodgers leaving the Bronx with a split by virtue of a Robinson double and a Hodges single. But the Yankees won the next three games at Ebbets Field, clinching their 12th Series triumph with a 10-6 romp behind Raschi and Page.

The Dodgers would sit out the next two fall classics, but they went down kicking and fighting. After trailing the Phillies by nine games with two weeks to play in the 1950 season, they closed fast. Only one game separated the teams when they met in the season finale at Ebbets Field. A Dodger victory would necessitate a best-of-three playoff series.

Newcombe and Robin Roberts, the premier starter for the team that was known as the Whiz Kids, dueled into the ninth inning. The Dodgers, who had tied the score at 1-1 in the sixth inning when Reese's drive to right field stuck in the screen above the wall for a home run, threatened in the home ninth.

Outfielder Cal Abrams drew a leadoff walk and reached second on Reese's single. Snider then followed with a line single to center field that reached Richie Ashburn, playing shallow because it was a bunt situation, on a quick hop. Although it was a no-out situation and Abrams did not get a good jump off second, third-base coach Milt Stock waved the runner home. He was out by a wide margin.

Both Reese and Snider took an extra base on the play but Roberts, after walking Robinson intentionally, retired Furillo and Hodges. Then Dick Sisler, son of Hall of Famer George Sisler (who was a Dodger batting instructor), hit a three-run homer in the 10th for a 4-1 Philadelphia victory.

Stunned by that outcome, Brooklyn fans were flabbergasted three weeks later when Rickey resigned as president of the ball club. He had lost a power struggle with partner Walter O'Malley and was selling his share of the Dodgers, at a considerable profit. John Galbreath, a longtime Ohio acquaintance, had bought the Pittsburgh Pirates and Rickey was heading for a new frontier.

Although Shotton had won two pennants in three full seasons as Brooklyn's manager, he was too much Rickey's man to stay. Taking on the title of president, O'Malley turned over Rickey's old

Snider (left) and third baseman Billy Cox felt good after a Game 5 victory, but the Dodgers lost again to the Yankees in a seven-game 1952 Series.

general-manager duties to E.J. (Buzzie) Bavasi and named Chuck Dressen as the club's new skipper. Dressen, one of Durocher's former coaches and card partners, was a tough and cocky bantam who once had played quarterback for George Halas' Decatur Staleys, forerunners of the Chicago Bears.

Dressen had remarkable recall and utter confidence in his strategic ability, which he was not averse to sharing with the players and the press. "Keep 'em close," he once advised a pitcher, "until I think of something." He did some very heavy thinking in 1951 and, as a result, Brooklyn boasted a 13½-game lead after winning the first game of an

Dodgers vs. N.L.			
1947-1956			
Opponent	W	L	Pct.
Pittsburgh	150	70	.682
Cincinnati	147	73	.668
Chicago	138	81	.630
St. Louis	133	87	.605
Philadelphia	132	88	.600
New York	124	99	.556
Boston-Milwaukee*	121	98	.553
*73-58 (.557) vs. Boston; 48-40 (.545) vs. Milwaukee.			

The Dodgers and Manager Chuck Dressen (above right) were primed for a run at the 1953 pennant with a pitching staff that included (above, left to right) Carl Erskine, Billy Loes and Joe Black. Offensive punch was provided by (below, left to right) Jim Gilliam, Reese, Snider and Robinson.

August 11 doubleheader.

If truth be told, he wasn't the only contributor to the Dodgers' remarkable play. Bolstered by a June trade that brought old-pro Andy Pafko from the Chicago Cubs to fill the club's lone weakness in left field, the Dodgers were blasting the race wide open. Hodges (40 home runs by season's end), Campanella and Snider all would drive in more than 100 runs in '51. Newcombe and Roe each would become 20-game winners. The outspoken Dressen was so confident he proclaimed of the second-place team, "The Giants is dead."

But the Giants, energized by a rookie named Willie Mays, were very much alive. Starting August 12, Durocher's club won 16 games in succession and sliced eight games off Brooklyn's lead. After games of September 20, the Dodgers (92-52) led the Giants (89-58) by 4½ games and someone figured that the reeling Dodgers still needed to win only five of their last 10 games to close out the Polo Grounders even if the Giants won all their remaining games. Well, the Giants did win all seven of their remaining games; Brooklyn, meanwhile, finished 4-6. The Dodgers, in fact, needed a victory on the final day of the regular season just to force a playoff.

New York's victory in Boston had been over for some time as the Dodgers, down 6-1 at one point, rallied to tie the Phillies, 8-8, and send the game into extra innings. In the 12th, with the bases loaded and two out, the Phils' Eddie Waitkus crackled a low line drive toward right-center. Somehow, Robinson speared it with a magnificent dive and held on for the third out despite a hard landing. The great clutch player then homered off Roberts in the 14th for Brooklyn's margin of victory. Alas, it was only a reprieve.

In the first playoff game the following day, the Giants defeated Ralph Branca, 3-1, at Ebbets Field with the help of a home run by Bobby Thomson. Clem Labine, a strong rookie on a tired Brooklyn staff, then shut out the Giants, 10-0, at the Polo Grounds. In the third game, perhaps the most famous game in baseball history, the Dodgers carried a 4-1 lead into the bottom of the ninth.

Then Newcombe, who had been magnificent, tired. Alvin Dark and Don Mueller singled before Big Newk retired Monte Irvin on a popup. Whitey Lockman's double cut the deficit to 4-2 and drove Newcombe to the showers. Dressen called the bullpen. Labine had tried to throw earlier but was predictably stiff. Carl Erskine had just bounced a curve in the dirt.

"How about Branca?" Dressen asked.

"He's throwing hard," reported Sukeforth, the coach in the bullpen.

So Ralph Branca, a 21-game winner four years earlier, walked to his destiny and another meeting with Bobby Thomson. Branca threw a fastball for a strike. His next pitch, also a fastball, was high and tight. Thomson drove it into the left-field stands, completing "The Miracle of Coogan's Bluff." Branca trudged to the center-field clubhouse, put his

head between his legs and moaned, "Why me? Why me?"

And why the Dodgers? Yet, they rebounded strongly in 1952 despite losing Newcombe, their most dependable pitcher, to the U.S. Army. Roe's victories were halved from 22 to 11 and Branca slipped from 13 to four. The beleaguered staff was propped up by Erskine, rookie Joe Black and youngster Billy Loes.

Erskine was something of a minor folk hero from the day he reported from the Texas League in the midst of the 1948 season. Walking into the rotunda of Ebbets Field with his Fort Worth Cats equipment bag, he overhead a fan say, "Dere's Oiskin from Fort Woit." Comedian Phil Foster, a Brooklynite, worked "Oiskin" into his act. "He did more for me than my curveball," Erskine decided.

But Oisk, the abbreviated nickname by which he was eventually known, did plenty for the Dodgers. In 1952, he won 14 games, pitched 10 complete games and tossed a no-hitter against the Chicago Cubs. Black, primarily a starter for Montreal and St. Paul in 1951, gave the Dodgers a presence in the bullpen. He made 54 relief appearances and finished with a 15-4 record and a 2.15 earned-run average. Furthermore, he became the third Brooklyn player in six years to be selected Rookie of the Year. Loes, who had made 10 appearances with Brooklyn in 1950 before entering the service, won 13 games.

The Dodgers won the pennant by 4½ games over the Giants. And with Black (turned into a starter at season's end), Roe and Erskine each winning one game, Brooklyn took a 3-2 lead over the Yankees in the World Series. The final two games were scheduled for Ebbets Field. Would this be next year?

Snider homered twice in Game 6, but with the bases empty, and New York's Vic Raschi, with relief help from Reynolds, evened the Series with a 3-2 victory. For the third time in the Series and the fifth time all year, Black was selected for starting duty as Brooklyn prepared for decisive Game 7. He was knocked out in the sixth when the Yankees broke a 2-2 tie. Trailing 4-2 in the seventh, the Dodgers loaded the bases with one out. Lefthander Bob Kuzava retired Snider on a popup, then ran the count to 3-2 on Robinson.

The Dodgers' cleanup hitter lifted a little popup near the mound. Kuzava never moved. First baseman Joe Collins lost sight of the ball. As the would-be tying run crossed home plate, Billy Martin raced from his position at second base to make the catch at his knees. Kuzava was untouchable in the eighth and ninth innings and another opportunity for Brooklyn had come to naught.

In the course of that Series, Hodges endured a ghastly slump. The strong first baseman, who had hit 32 homers and driven in more than 100 runs for the fourth consecutive season, went hitless in 21 at-bats. Instead of turning on him, however, the fans treated him with a sympathy reserved for a sick relative.

When the slump persisted the following spring,

Catcher Campanella, winning pitcher Johnny Podres (right) and Don Hoak converge as the Dodgers finally win the big one: a seven-game 1955 decision over the Yankees.

The best team in *both* leagues.

A pair of happy Walters: Dodgers Owner O'Malley (left) and Manager Alston after the 1955 victory.

Hodges received hundreds of letters of advice, good-luck charms and religious symbols. Finally, Dressen benched the slugger. On an unusually warm Sunday in May 1953, the pastor at Hodges' church announced to the congregation: "It's too hot for a sermon. So today I want you all to go home, keep the Ten Commandments and say a prayer for Gil Hodges."

Hodges, batting .181 with one home run and five RBIs through May 23, went on a 34-for-78 batting spree (.436) from May 24 through June 12. Over that three-week stretch, he pounded eight homers and knocked in 32 runs.

It proved to be an exceptional season not only for Hodges, who batted .302 with 122 RBIs, but also for the team. With Pafko dealt to Milwaukee, Robinson moved to left field, making room at second base for Jim Gilliam, who drew 100 bases on balls, hit an N.L.-leading 17 triples and was selected Rookie of the Year. Reese stole 22 bases. Snider hit 42 home runs, Campanella 41. The Dodgers won 105 games, 13 more than the second-place Braves, and clinched the pennant on September 12, the earliest date in league history.

They were in their glory that year. Campanella would walk into the clubhouse with a cigar between his teeth and proclaim, "Same team that won yesterday gonna win today." Reese would linger over a game in his captain's chair, wordlessly suggesting that others stay as well. "Rush out of the clubhouse and you rush out of baseball," he'd say.

The fans were in no more of a hurry to leave than the players, for Ebbets Field was a place of exotic sounds and wondrous sights. You never knew what you might see or hear there, and the stands were

Fresh from their 1955 triumph, the Dodgers won the pennant again in '56. Celebrating the clinching (above, left to right) are Don Bessent, Newcombe, Sandy Amoros and Snider. The joyous trio below consists of (left to right) Alston, O'Malley and Reese.

Amoros, a Dodger hero in the 1955 Series, enjoys a victory cigar after Brooklyn's 1956 pennant clincher.

One of Brooklyn's top power sources through its glory years was big first baseman Hodges, pictured above after a 1956 Series homer.

sloped so close to the field that the customers felt they could join in the game at any time.

Certainly, no other major league park had a house band to match the Dodger Sym-phony, a group of zealots who irritated opponents by banging on instruments to celebrate a strikeout or other malfeasance. And no park had anything to rival the great right-field wall, which featured a high wire screen and a huge scoreboard, creating a bizarre series of angles that befuddled visiting outfielders. At the base of the scoreboard was a narrow sign offering free merchandise at Abe Stark's clothing store to any man who connected with the advertisement on the fly. "Hit sign, win suit," it proclaimed.

Furillo, with an intimate knowledge of every ricochet and column, reigned majestically over that wall. He also protected the inventory for Stark, who won the New York City Council presidency with the help of the publicity generated by the sign (and later, after the Dodgers had left Brooklyn, was elected borough president). "What a brilliant promotion," Erskine marveled. "Buy the space and put Carl in front of it. He saved Abe so many suits."

That was precisely the argument put forth by Furillo, through an emissary, to the clothier. He thought it would be a nice gesture for Stark to present his defender with at least one suit. Alas, Stark shared a trait with Rickey. He sent Furillo a pair of slacks.

In a September series at the Polo Grounds, Furillo was hit by a pitch, a not-unfamiliar tactic. When he got to first base, he glared into the Giants' dugout and saw Durocher, whom he despised, make a gesture. He started for the manager, who rose to meet him, and fought his way through a phalanx of players to clamp a headlock on his enemy.

"It was the only time I ever felt sorry for Leo," Snider recalled. "I thought he was going to die."

Standing nearby as the ruckus developed was Babe Pinelli, among the most mild-mannered of umpires. Umpires liked Durocher even less than opponents. "Kill him, Carl, kill him," Pinelli was yelling. As it turned out, Durocher survived and Furillo suffered a broken bone in his hand. That shelved him for the rest of the regular season and preserved his average at .344, good enough for the N.L. batting title.

If it seemed that almost everything that happened to the Dodgers in '53 was positive, the mood was shattered in the first inning of the first game of the World Series. Erskine, a 20-game winner, was raked for four runs, three scoring on Martin's triple, and the Yankees rolled to a 9-5 victory. Oisk came back in Game 3 to set a Series record with 14 strikeouts in a 3-2 victory. But New York won in six games as Martin, the fielding star a year earlier, collected 12 hits, including the game-winner in the ninth inning of the deciding contest.

More bad news followed. Fresh on the heels of that disappointment, Dressen decided he wanted more than the standard one-year contract offered by the Dodgers. His wife even composed a letter to O'Malley, outlining her husband's request. At a press conference, O'Malley wished Dressen well in his future endeavors. The club policy was written in stone.

The Dodgers reached into their minor league system and brought forth Walter Alston, a man so anonymous that he quickly was dubbed Walter Who? He was not very popular among the veterans in 1954, although that doesn't entirely explain why the Dodgers won 13 fewer games than the previous year. Pitching had something to do with it. And the Giants, with Mays back from the Army, won the pennant by five games.

A year later, Alston was more relaxed and confident. And the Dodgers made his managerial job easier. They won their first 10 games, lost one, then won 12 of the next 13. After the 55-22 first half, they coasted home 13½ games ahead of the Braves.

With the team riding high, management staged Pee Wee Reese Night on July 22, 1955. The captain received a new car, among many gifts, and it took 50 minutes to read the list of presents that Reese was getting. But the most moving tribute occurred after the fifth inning when the lights were turned out and customers lit matches and cigarette lighters. Together, 33,003 fans sang "Happy Birthday" to Harold Henry Reese, who was to turn 36 the next day.

"When I came to Brooklyn in 1940 (after being purchased from the Louisville club of the American Association), I was a scared kid," Reese told the throng. "To tell you the truth, I'm twice as scared right now."

That Pee Wee was the most respected of Dodgers was proven again and again, sometimes under unexpected circumstances. Reese, Snider, Erskine and Rube Walker, the backup catcher, lived in the same neighborhood and would car-pool to games against the Giants at the Polo Grounds. They were speeding up the West Side Highway one night, with Reese at the wheel, when they were stopped by a motorcycle officer. "OK, captain, let's see you do your stuff," needled Snider from the passenger's seat as the policeman approached.

He asked for a driver's license and stared at it for a moment. "Where do you work, Mr. Reese?" he asked.

"I work for the Dodgers."

"You're not Pee Wee Reese, are you? I'm a great fan."

"Yes, I am, officer. We're on our way to the Polo Grounds."

"Well, better slow it down, fellas. There are some guys up ahead who might nail you." And he handed Reese back his license.

"On the very next night," Erskine recalled, "Duke was driving his Pontiac wagon and he's stopped at nearly the same spot by a different cop. Pee Wee says, 'OK, Duke, your turn.' Now Duke is more impulsive. When the policeman looks inside, he says, 'I'm Duke Snider of the Dodgers, officer, and this is Pee Wee Reese, Carl Erskine and Rube Walker. We're headed for the Polo Grounds and we don't want to be late.'

"The cop cuts him off. 'I don't like baseball,' he says. Now Duke gets ticked. 'I don't like cops,' he says. 'Give me the ticket.' And that's what he did."

Reese, Snider, Hodges, Furillo and Campanella all had big years in '55, with the catcher winning his third MVP award. Newcombe not only compiled a 20-5 record but the 6-foot-4 pitcher also hit seven home runs and batted an astonishing .359.

Still, the usual pattern appeared to be forming in the World Series when the Yankees won the first two games. The Dodgers scored 21 runs in winning the next three games at Ebbets Field to take a 3-2 lead—but they had been there before. And when New York shelled Karl Spooner, a late-season sensation the previous year, in the first inning of Game 6 and rolled to a 5-1 victory, it seemed history was about to repeat itself.

The antidote was Johnny Podres, a heretofore undistinguished lefthanded pitcher from the New York orchard country around Lake Champlain. Podres had only a 9-10 record during the regular season, but the 23-year-old had gone the distance while winning Game 3. He was fearless and had a nice changeup. After 5½ innings of Game 7, played October 4, he also had a 2-0 lead, both runs courtesy of Hodges.

A leadoff walk to Martin and Gil McDougald's bunt single placed Podres and the Dodgers in jeopardy in the Yankees' sixth. The dangerous Yogi Berra then sliced a pitch toward the left-field corner that appeared to be beyond anyone's reach. The baserunners never hesitated. Neither did Sandy Amoros, the little Cuban outfielder who had just entered the game for defensive purposes. Racing from left-center, he stuck out his glove and stabbed the ball just inside the foul line at Yankee Stadium.

How he got there in time, even he didn't know. "I run and run and run," was the only explanation he could offer, in part because he spoke very little English. He also had the presence of mind to throw quickly to Reese, whose relay to Hodges doubled off McDougald. Podres hung on for an eight-hit, 2-0 shutout. Fittingly, the final out was a ground ball to Reese.

The celebration in Brooklyn was indescribable. Amid the exhilaration, how was anyone to know that the borough's first World Series crown also would be its last?

The team seemed as strong as ever the following season. Snider hit 43 home runs, Hodges 32, Furillo 21 and Campanella 20. Erskine pitched his second no-hit game, against the hated Giants, and Big Newk had that phenomenal 27-7 season. But the Dodgers were aging and needed help. They found it in the unlikely form of Sal (The Barber) Maglie, whose knockdown pitches had been at the center of so many feuds when he toiled for the Giants.

GOODBYE DODGERS,
THANKS FOR A
WONDERFUL SEASON
WHICH MADE YOUR FANS
SO HAPPY.
NO REGRETS!

The fate of a Dodger fan: No Regrets.

Maglie had been acquired by the Cleveland Indians from the Giants for the waiver price in the midst of the 1955 season. Bavasi purchased his contract from the Indians in mid-May 1956. Although he was 39 years old, he proceded to win 13 of 18 decisions for the Dodgers, including a no-hit victory over the Phillies in the final week of the season. And when Brooklyn prevailed by one game over Milwaukee in the pennant race, Maglie was honored with the starting assignment in the first game of the Series.

He won, 6-3, and when the Dodgers overcame a 6-0 deficit to win Game 2, 13-8, the Yankees' hex appeared dead. Then New York evened the Series with 5-3 and 6-2 victories. Maglie started the fifth game for Brooklyn and pitched brilliantly, yielding but two runs on five hits in eight innings. On most days, it might have been enough. But not on October 8, 1956. That's when Larsen made his bid for eternity, setting down all 27 Dodgers. Pinch-hitter Dale Mitchell was caught looking at strike three to end the game.

Labine kept the Series alive the following day in Brooklyn, shutting out the Yankees and notching the victory when Robinson lined a ball over Enos Slaughter's head in the 10th inning. But then came Big Newk and the final humiliation. Berra hit two-run homers in the first and third innings off the Brooklyn ace, Yankee pitcher Kucks was at his best and the American Leaguers romped. The game and the Series ended with a Robinson strikeout.

But it wasn't the end of the old Dodgers. That came during the winter when the club in which he had invested his heart and soul dealt Robinson to the Giants for pitcher Dick Littlefield and cash. Unknown to the front office, however, Robinson had sold the rights to his retirement story to Look magazine. Robinson received $50,000 for the piece, more than he earned in any contract with the Dodgers.

Brooklyn fans, at least, were spared the shame of seeing Jackie in a Giants uniform as Robinson's retirement plans finally were divulged.

The Dodgers were a dispirited team in 1957, falling to third place. O'Malley, tired of the cramped conditions in Brooklyn and eyeing greener pastures, spent much of the season implementing plans to transfer the franchise to Los Angeles. On September 24, not quite two years after people danced in the streets over the result of a baseball game, the Dodgers made their final appearance at Ebbets Field. They beat Pittsburgh, 2-0, behind a lefthanded pitcher named Danny McDevitt. Organist Gladys Gooding ended the evening with a rendition of "Auld Lang Syne."

No longer was there reason to wait 'til next year. Fans of the Brooklyn Dodgers lost not only a team, but also the hope that team inspired.

NOTRE DAME
1941 to 1949

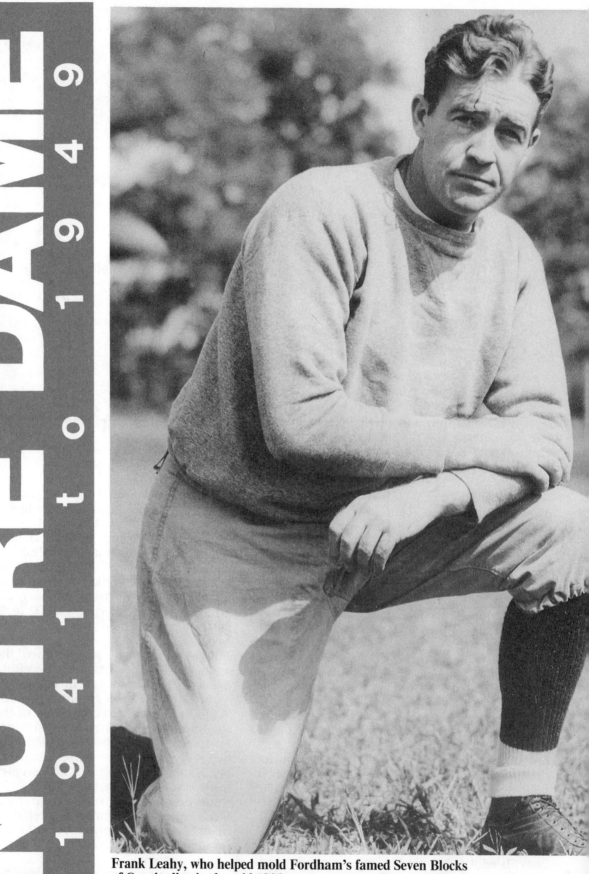

Frank Leahy, who helped mold Fordham's famed Seven Blocks of Granite line in the mid-1930s, was a stern taskmaster who pushed his teams as close to the brink—and perfection—as they could possibly get.

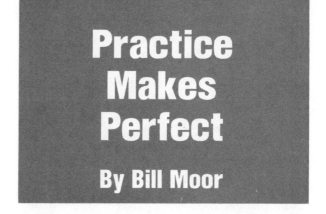

Practice Makes Perfect

By Bill Moor

To football fans and sportswriters, Frank Leahy was "The Master." To his Notre Dame players, he was "The Man." His assistants, sometimes fondly, sometimes not, called him "The Old Man."

By the end of his legendary coaching career at Notre Dame, Leahy had aged quickly, much like his own coach, Knute Rockne, had done more than a decade earlier. Leahy was only 33 when he took the Irish job in 1941 and 45 when he retired after the 1953 season.

During that period, he chose to travel a difficult road that was both intensely demanding and physically exhausting.

"After every practice, Leahy would run two laps around the goal posts as slow as one could imagine," said Joe Doyle, the longtime South Bend Tribune sports editor. "He looked like Father Time on his last legs."

But Leahy always made it through his runs. He always paid the price.

So did his great Notre Dame teams. Sure, they had tradition on their side, and talent, but it was the bone-weary work ethic demanded by the tutor-tyrant coach that molded the Irish teams of the 1940s into one of the greatest dynasties in sports history.

From 1941 through 1949, Leahy coached the team to four national titles and a 60-3-5 record in seven seasons. Like many of his players, he was away for the 1944 and '45 seasons while serving in World War II.

Over the last four years of the decade, the Irish never lost a game. Not one. The Class of '49, including Heisman Trophy winner Leon Hart, passed through Notre Dame without ever tasting defeat.

Not even Rockne had put together four years like that. Those were some of Notre Dame's finest football hours.

Yet some of the most impressive performances by those 1940s teams were never viewed by the public. Talented teammate met talented teammate in fierce, combative practice sessions. Assistant coaches would run four or five simultaneous scrimmages with the always-intense Leahy prowling like a hungry cat.

The practice field was where Notre Dame's dynasty was built. And that was where Frank Leahy truly was The Master.

"In 1946, I was just a 17-year-old freshman, but a lot of our players were veterans from the war who had played for Leahy in the early '40s," recalled Hart, a two-time consensus All-America at end who in 1949 became one of only two linemen to win the Heisman. "He figured that since many of them had been riding around in jeeps that their legs had turned rubbery. So when practice began that fall, we would go three times a day instead of two so they could get their legs back quicker."

Quarterback John Lujack, the 1947 Heisman winner, was one of those veterans. "By the time we got done with Coach Leahy's practices, we would get into games and think, 'Gee, this is pretty easy,'" he said.

The games were the only respite from Leahy's regimented program. He was so intense that one year, at the team's annual awards dinner in December, he announced that the first spring practice would be held the following day. Some of his players laughed, thinking he was making a joke. They weren't laughing when they got down to business in the fieldhouse the next afternoon.

This was the coach who once changed the travel plans of his team's return from a 40-0 victory at Pittsburgh (1948) because he wanted to get back earlier than planned. The reason: he wanted to practice his players as soon as Mass was over on Sunday. Despite the overwhelming victory, they had failed on one occasion to score from the 1-yard line, and that's where the two-hour practice began —and ended.

This was the man who once put lineman Bill Fischer back into the fray just a few plays after he had broken his nose. An assistant, thinking that Leahy did not know about the injury, ran up to tell him. "Well, there's nothing more that can happen to his nose now," Leahy replied.

A driven man himself, Leahy would push his squad as close to the brink, and perfection, as a team could get.

"The other assistant coaches and I were always talking players out of quitting," said former Notre Dame athletic director Ed (Moose) Krause, a topnotch Irish tackle in the early 1930s. "We kept telling them if Leahy was yelling at them, then that meant he thought they had the potential of being good football players."

Even Terry Brennan, a hard-nosed running back who later would succeed Leahy as the Notre Dame coach, found it almost unbearable at one point. He admits that his father had to talk him back on the team after a torturous "spring" season in 1946 that lasted from February into June.

"I once wrote an article about how one of Leahy's teams had put in seven times as much practice time as some of the later teams," Doyle recalled. "But my editor called me on it and said that couldn't possibly be. So I compromised and wrote they practiced three or four times as much.

"And then, wouldn't you know it, Neil Worden, a fullback for Leahy, called me and said that wasn't

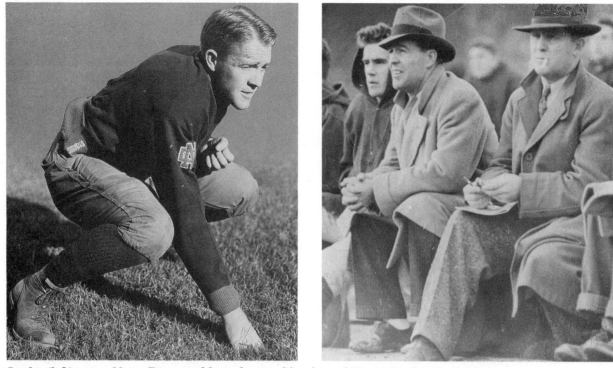

Leahy (left) was a Notre Dame tackle under coaching legend Knute Rockne in the late 1920s and the head coach (right, center) at Boston College in 1939 and '40.

The 1943 Notre Dame coaching staff: (left to right) Wally Ziemba, Leahy, Hugh Devore, Ed McKeever and Ed (Moose) Krause.

true. 'It was more than three or four times,' he said."

After those long practices, the players at least got to go back to their dorms. Leahy and his staff stayed on—and on and on. "There were many nights when we wouldn't get home until past midnight," Krause said.

The assistants did have one trick up their sleeves, though. "Some of us smoked cigars," Krause continued. "And occasionally, the smoke would get to him enough that he would end a meeting a little earlier than he planned."

Even then, Leahy wouldn't always head for his home in Long Beach (about 30 miles from South Bend). Two or three nights a week he would sleep on a cot in the old Notre Dame firehouse, where some of his players probably figured he was dancing in his own flames.

Leahy pushed himself to the limit with worry and work—and sometimes beyond.

"He took losing so personally," said Angelo Bertelli, Notre Dame's first Heisman winner in 1943. "It seemed like every time we lost, he would end up in the Mayo Clinic."

In the end, Leahy's trips to the hospital did almost catch up with his losses at Notre Dame, where his teams finished 87-11-9 in his 11 seasons.

His health problems were numerous, including spinal arthritis and pancreatitis. Most agreed that extreme nervous tension helped bring on many of his maladies.

Fittingly, it was in a hospital bed where Leahy officially got his first opportunity for a coaching job. It happened after the 1930 season when Rockne took Leahy, a tackle on that team, to the Mayo Clinic with him. Rockne was there for his phlebitis; Leahy needed a knee operation. They shared a room and long talks on football.

That's when Rockne showed his pupil several letters from other college football coaches asking him to send them an assistant. He let Leahy have his choice.

Ten years later, Leahy returned to Notre Dame after four successful stops, including six years as an assistant at Fordham where he helped mold the famed Seven Blocks of Granite line and two seasons at Boston College where he fashioned a 20-2 record as the head coach.

The news of his return was welcome on campus. The foundation for a dynasty had been poured. The Master was on his way home. Despite injuries that plagued his own career, Leahy had been a hard-nosed competitor for Rockne. Once, after Leahy dislocated an elbow, Rockne asked to see it. Leahy showed his coach the wrong one so he could play.

He expected the same sacrifices from his players. "We all need a little Christian Scientist in us," he used to say.

So it took some getting used to when Leahy replaced the mild-mannered Elmer Layden of Four Horsemen fame. Layden left to become the National Football League commissioner after a commend-

able 47-13-3 record.

Leahy wanted to do better. Deep down he wanted to match his old coach, Rockne, although he said publicly that "the days of undefeated Notre Dame are over."

He proved himself wrong in his very first season. With plenty of talent returning from Layden's 7-2 team of 1940, Leahy made some key position shifts and then directed his first Notre Dame team to an impressive 8-0-1 record.

Success wasn't without its price, however. Practices were brutal. Both blood and emotions sometimes poured out in the long, agonizing sessions on the practice field.

Nobody held back. "If we detect a man loafing," Leahy told his players, "we do not catch him a second time. Or if we do, we have to use binoculars."

"Some of the players thought he had four eyes," Krause said. "He could be on the other side of the practice field and bawl out a player he had seen make a mistake. He never used profanity but, boy, could he raise holy hell."

"At certain points of the season, many players would convince themselves they hated him. They usually changed their minds, even if it took time away from Notre Dame to realize how he had helped them. Yet they never forgot how tough and how demanding he was."

Or how persuasive.

Bernie Crimmins, who was expected to be the starting fullback on Leahy's 1941 team, received a surprise summer visit from his coach at his Louisville home. Leahy told Crimmins that, after studying films, he felt he would be better positioned at guard, where he could pull and lead the backs

Dynasty Data
Yearly Record
1941-1949

Year	W	L	T	Pct.	Avg. Score N.D.-Opp.	Coach
1941	8	0	1	.944	21-7	Frank Leahy
1942	7	2	2	.727	17-9	Frank Leahy
1943	9	1	0	.900	34-7	Frank Leahy
1944	8	2	0	.800	27-12	Ed McKeever
1945	7	2	1	.750	26-12	Hugh Devore
1946	8	0	1	.944	30-3	Frank Leahy
1947	9	0	0	1.000	32-6	Frank Leahy
1948	9	0	1	.950	32-9	Frank Leahy
1949	10	0	0	1.000	36-9	Frank Leahy
Total	75	7	6	.886	28-8	
Under Leahy	60	3	5	.919	29-7	

Additional Data

Best Years—1949 (10-0-0), 1947 (9-0-0), undefeated with one tie in three other seasons.

Worst Year—1942 (7-2-2).

Most Lopsided Victory—64-0 over Dartmouth, 1944.

Most Lopsided Defeat—59-0 to Army, 1944.

Most Consecutive Victories—21 games from Nov. 16, 1946 through Nov. 27, 1948.

Longest Undefeated Period—38 games from Sept. 28, 1946 through Dec. 3, 1949 (36 victories, 2 ties). Streak actually went to 39 games if Notre Dame's season-opening victory of Sept. 30, 1950 is included.

Most Consecutive Losses—2 games from Nov. 4 through Nov. 11, 1944.

Shutouts—The Irish held opponents scoreless in 32 games.

Times Shut Out—Notre Dame was shut out four times—all by Army. Two of the games ended in scoreless ties.

Strong-armed Angelo Bertelli, the key man in Notre Dame's 1942 switch to the T-formation, fires a pass over the middle (above) in the Irish's 1941 season-opening victory over Arizona.

downfield.

"Why, Bernard, you will be the most important player in our backfield," Leahy said. Crimmins agreed to the switch, admitting later that he fell for Leahy's snow job.

"He could make a player feel like he was two inches tall out on the practice field and then make him feel like he was the most important person in the world when he had him in the office," Doyle said.

He could be both convincing and conniving.

"Thank God for Frank Leahy," said Bertelli, who may have benefited most by The Master's arrival.

Leahy had tried to recruit Bertelli when he was coaching at Boston College. He liked what he saw then and quickly made Bertelli his passing tailback when he got to Notre Dame.

In the 1941 opener against Arizona, the sophomore connected on 11 of 14 passes and the Irish were on their way to a 38-7 victory.

Four lopsided victories later, on a rainy first day of November, the Irish failed for the first (and only) time to accomplish the ultimate goal, the only goal —a victory. Notre Dame was forced to settle for a

Two of the big weapons in Notre Dame's 1941 offensive arsenal were fullback Fred Evans and halfback Steve Juzwik. Evans (above) threads the Illinois defense after catching a pass from Bertelli, while Juzwik (below) looks for running room as the Illini defense moves in for the kill.

Irish fullback Jim Mello crashes over the Wisconsin goal line (far right) to score Notre Dame's only touchdown in a 1942 season-opening 7-7 tie. Patting Mello on the back is All-America end Bob Dove.

0-0 tie against Army that day—five years before a much more famous scoreless deadlock with the Cadets.

Nobody could have guessed that this 1941 contest would be a harbinger of the 1946 classic that pitted two college football powers in one of the great matchups of all time. But it did give some hint on how Leahy would react after any outcome other than a victory.

"It was as if someone had stabbed him in the heart," Krause said.

But the Irish then eked out close victories against traditional rivals Navy (20-13), Northwestern (7-6) and Southern Cal (20-18) en route to their 8-0-1 finish and final Associated Press No. 3 ranking.

Bertelli's passing prowess was evident throughout the undefeated campaign, but never more than against Navy. He completed 12 of 18 pass attempts that day for 232 yards and a touchdown.

Bertelli was not the only weapon in Notre Dame's impressive arsenal. Tackles Paul Lillis and Jim Brutz, center Wally Ziemba, consensus All-America end Bob Dove, quarterback Harry Wright, halfback Steve Juzwik, fullback Fred Evans and Crimmins all were key factors in the Irish's 1941 success.

Leahy, however, was far from satisfied. Before the 1942 season, he decided to break tradition while setting his own course away from the shadow of Rockne. He switched from his mentor's revered box backfield to the T-formation being used by the Na-

tional Football League's Chicago Bears with great success.

Moving Bertelli to quarterback was the key. Leahy called the youngster into his office one day in February 1942 and said, "Bert, you are the finest passer and the worst runner I've ever coached. We've got to do something about it."

The coach diagramed a play on his notepad.

"We were lucky last year, Bert," Leahy continued. "We didn't have any deception. Everybody knew when you were going to pass. You just took the ball from center, dropped back a few yards and threw. No deception. But they'll be laying for us next fall. Think you can play quarterback?"

"I guess so," Bertelli replied. "Why?"

Leahy sketched a new offensive diagram. "Because here's what we're going to try out in spring practice," he said. "It's the T-formation. . . . You'll play right behind center and handle the ball on every play."

"The 'T' was a natural for me," Bertelli recalled, "because I was not a very good runner."

Before that 1942 season, Leahy got Bertelli and some other teammates summer jobs painting the Notre Dame Stadium seats—seats they helped fill on fall Saturdays. His generosity was not without motive.

"Every free moment we had, we were spinning and spinning and spinning—working on the movement for the 'T'," said Bertelli. "I didn't think the season was ever going to get there."

Offensive starters for Notre Dame's 1943 national champions: (front row, left to right) John Yonakor, Zyggy Czarobski, John Perko, Herb Coleman, Pat Filley, Jim White and Paul Limont; (back row) Julie Rykovich, Mello, John Lujack and Creighton Miller.

And when it did, both Leahy and Bertelli were exposed to some serious second-guessing.

The Irish opened the campaign on a sour note, tying Elroy (Crazy Legs) Hirsch's Wisconsin team, 7-7. The worst was yet to come. The following week in Notre Dame's home opener, Georgia Tech handed Leahy his first loss at Notre Dame, 13-6.

It was enough to drive Notre Dame faithful into a frenzy, and Leahy's detractors quickly pointed fingers at his switch in offenses.

The adjustment to the new system was certainly part of the problem, but a rash of injuries also contributed to the slow start. Evans suffered a knee injury that forced him to sit out the season, ends Matt Bolger and Norm Barry went down for the count, fullback Gerry Cowhig was limited to two games and star halfback Creighton Miller played hurt through the team's first six games.

Other returning lettermen and newcomers, however, regrouped and eventually picked up the slack. Wright returned, Dove again captured consensus All-America honors and Ziemba anchored the line. Corwin Clatt and Jim Mello handled fullback duties while Bob Livingstone performed well at halfback.

But Leahy wasn't around to see Notre Dame's resurgence. He was resting in the Mayo Clinic. Leahy missed the next three games—all victories, including an exciting 21-14 win over Illinois—while receiving treatment for spinal arthritis, a condition traced to tension and overwork.

In Leahy's absence, assistant Ed McKeever ran the team while Wright, now a guard in the new system, called the offensive plays for Bertelli. Wright seemed to enjoy his new-found authority and became especially adventuresome on occasion.

Late in the Illinois game with the score tied, 14-14, he showed his moxie by calling a pass play out of punt formation. The gamble paid off and eventually led to the winning score. But Leahy, listening to the game on the radio from his hospital bed, almost had a heart attack.

After the game, Leahy called the winners' locker room and congratulated McKeever. Then he talked to Wright and asked the lineman if his play selection was any indication of how he felt about his coach's recovery.

Leahy returned for the next game—a 9-0 victory over Navy—and continued to lead his team to a 7-2-2 record that included a loss to Michigan and a season-ending tie with Great Lakes. The Notre Dame faithful, however, received a large dose of satisfaction from the Irish's 13-0 victory over Army.

The record was disappointing but the die had been cast. The T-formation was in and the Irish were on the threshold of becoming one of the greatest college football powers ever assembled.

But before Leahy could begin preparation for what he envisioned would be a banner 1943 campaign, he had to resolve a piece of urgent business involving Creighton Miller, the son of former Irish great Harry (Red) Miller (1906-09).

The Millers were wealthy enough that neither

Leahy (left) with triumphant members of his 1943 squad: (left to right) Czarobski, Creighton Miller, Lujack, Mello and tackle John (Tree) Adams.

Creighton nor his older brother, Tom, needed football scholarships to go to Notre Dame. As a result, Creighton apparently did not feel obligated to play spring football.

One afternoon, Leahy sought out his star running back for a spring practice. Creighton told his coach that he would rather play golf.

"Oooh, Creighton Miller," Leahy replied. "Football demands constant practice."

Miller stood his ground, answering that golf did, too.

So Leahy took a mulligan on that attempt and tried another approach. He went to Miller's father and convinced the old Notre Dame star that it was in his son's best interest to be on scholarship.

Creighton's reply to his father was: "You sold me down the river to that man."

But he went on to enjoy a fabulous 1943 season and Leahy was always quick to attribute much of that success to his ability to hit the holes in the T-formation more crisply because of his participation in the preceding spring drills.

Miller gained 911 yards on 151 carries in 1943 and also led the team in scoring, punt returns, kick-off returns and interceptions. He was one of five Notre Dame players to earn consensus All-America honors.

"I think Creighton was the greatest running back I ever saw," said Lujack, a sophomore in 1943 who would take over quarterback duties from the military-bound Bertelli midway through the season. "When we beat Michigan (35-12) that year, I've never seen a back have a better day."

Miller ran for 159 yards on just 10 carries as his proud father watched from the stands in Michigan Stadium. The last time the Irish had beaten the Wolverines was 1909, when the elder Miller was playing.

"Creighton suffered from high blood pressure and would have to sometimes lay down after a particularly long run," Lujack recalled. "I know because I used to sub for him during those times. He worried about his health and I think that's more of the reason that he didn't want to play spring ball.

Bertelli (second from left) was a member of a different team in late 1943 when he was awarded the Walter Camp Memorial Trophy honoring the year's top college player.

But I don't think Leahy fully understood that."

The coach apparently understood the secrets of success, though. With Bertelli in top form, his No. 1-ranked team rolled over its first six foes by an accumulative score of 261-31. That included the victory over No. 2 Michigan and a 33-6 triumph over No. 3 Navy in the sixth game.

But like all the other colleges, Notre Dame was losing many of its players to military service. After the Navy game, Bertelli's outstanding college career came to an end when he was drafted into the Marines.

"Gosh, it was as if I almost died when I had to leave that team," Bertelli recalled. "One day I was celebrating a great victory over Navy with a great group of guys and the next day, in a cold drizzle, I was heading off to Parris Island with 9,000 other recruits."

Lujack filled in admirably for his talented predecessor—literally. When Lujack complained that his cleats had become too tight, the trainer gave him Bertelli's old pair.

The transition was painless—at first. Lujack threw two touchdown passes and scored a touchdown himself as Notre Dame continued its relentless march with a 26-0 victory over third-ranked Army in Game 7. He then guided the Irish to victories over eighth-ranked Northwestern (25-6) and second-ranked Iowa Pre-Flight (14-13) before the roof caved in. Unranked Great Lakes scored a touchdown with 33 seconds remaining in the season finale to upset the Irish, 19-14.

Bertelli recalled listening to that game on a small radio in the Marine "rec" room. "I left the room crying," he admitted. "And when I walked outside, that's when I was handed the telegram that said I had won the Heisman."

Miller was fourth in the voting and Jim White, an outstanding Irish tackle, finished ninth. Both were consensus All-Americas along with Bertelli, end John Yonaker and guard Pat Filley. Center Herb Coleman was named to several All-America teams.

Despite all the honors, the loss to Great Lakes was a tough pill to swallow. Not only did it end Notre

Halfback Terry Brennan (left) and tackle George Connor (right) were key performers on the talent-laden 1946 and '47 Notre Dame teams.

Dame's quest for an undefeated season, it tarnished the Irish's first national championship. Notre Dame's final 9-1 record included five victories over ranked opponents, including four over teams that were ranked either No. 2 or 3 by the Associated Press at the time of the game. The Irish earned the No. 1 ranking after their second game and held it the rest of the way.

Ironically, one of the Great Lakes players who scored and later ended Notre Dame's last-ditch comeback effort with an interception was Emil Sitko, who had spent one semester at Notre Dame in 1942 and would return to play for the Irish after the war.

Leahy sought out Sitko after the game and the halfback asked how his old coach was doing.

"Not too well, Emil," Leahy replied. "My school lost today."

"So did mine, Coach," Sitko replied. "So did mine."

In 1946, Sitko joined Leahy, Lujack and many other Notre Dame "war veterans" as the nucleus of an Irish team that wouldn't lose again for four years.

But that kind of success would have to wait. The Irish ranks were depleted in 1944 and '45 because of World War II and Leahy himself left Notre Dame to serve as an officer in the Navy. Under McKeever in 1944 and Hugh Devore in '45, a makeshift Notre Dame team that included only five lettermen from 1943 compiled respectable 8-2 and 7-2-1 records but were embarrassed by some powerful service teams. Army demolished the Irish, 59-0 and 48-0, while Navy pounded out a 32-13 victory in 1944 and a 6-6 tie the next year. Great Lakes thumped the Irish, 39-7, in the 1945 season finale.

But those seasons, if not those two Army scores, were soon forgotten when The Master and his veterans came marching back to campus.

"I really think that Leahy joined the service so he would have the respect of his players who did go off to war," Doyle said. "At that point, he probably was of the age and had enough children so that he wouldn't have to serve. But it was important to him that his older players felt he had made the same sacrifices they had."

Leahy returned to his alma mater rejuvenated. He was not alone.

"It was just so great to be back in school and playing football for all of us veterans," recalled Lu-

The atmosphere was intense when 74,121 exuberant fans jammed Yankee Stadium (above) to watch the 1946 Army and Notre Dame teams play to a classic 0-0 tie.

jack, who had served two years in the Navy. "We had great spirit and we didn't have any jealousies among us. It was a great group of people to be around."

Players who had earned letters from as far back as 1942 returned from the service to join young talents like the 17-year-old Hart.

Hart, of course, would go on to become Notre Dame's third Heisman Trophy winner (1949), but in 1946 he was just another talented newcomer in a crowd of stellar performers.

"When I got to Notre Dame, I was one of 21 ends —13 of them lettermen," he said. "You had to learn rather quickly to survive."

Near the end of an early 1946 game, Leahy gave Hart his first playing time. The youngster was so excited that he dashed onto the field, looked back over his shoulder as an Irish assistant coach yelled instructions and accidentally ran over teammate Livingstone, who was coming off the field.

Poor Bob Livingstone! Once, when the talented running back missed a tackle, Lujack, standing next to his coach on the sideline, reportedly called his teammate an SOB. Leahy scolded Lujack for such a remark and said another outburst like that would cost him his scholarship.

But when Livingstone missed another tackle not too long after the first one, Leahy turned to his team and said, "Gentlemen, I fear that Jonathan Lujack is right about Robert Livingstone."

Leahy couldn't even crack a smile when he said it. "He had no sense of humor that I could see," Bertelli recalled.

"I think he had a sense of humor but it was a sly one," Doyle said. "The players probably sometimes missed it and even laughed at him behind his back because of some of the things he said. But he could be funny at times, whether he intended to be or not."

"I remember the time when Leahy took the team to the Notre Dame cemetery to visit Rockne's grave," Lujack said. "He apparently thought if Rock could use the Gipper to help win a game, then he ought to be able to use Rock in a similar way. We were to say a prayer over Rockne's grave. But I guess I prayed faster then most of the rest and so when I was done, I decided to see who else was buried there. A couple of us found the grave of George Keogan, the old basketball coach, and we were standing over it when Leahy spotted us.

" 'Oooh, lads, come back over here,' he said. 'Visit that man during the basketball season.'

"And he was serious."

Whether Leahy had a sense of humor was open to debate, but there was no questioning that he always meant business on the football field.

With Lujack at quarterback, Terry Brennan and Sitko at running back and such linemen as Zygmont (Ziggy) Czarobski, Fischer, Jim Martin, John Mastrangelo, George Strohmeyer and George Connor, the Irish were awesome in 1946.

"We allowed just four touchdowns and no extra points that season," Lujack said. "That may have been our best team."

But even with his considerable talent, Leahy didn't back off on his scrimmage regimen.

"Before some Saturday games, Leahy would scrimmage his players even on late Friday afternoon," Doyle said. "That would be unheard of today. He believed that the practice field—and scrimmages in particular—were where the great teams were made. He didn't believe in lifting weights. In fact, players could get in trouble if he found out they were using them."

"I remember that for a time he had me working with George Connor a half hour before the regular practices because he missed two blocks in one game," Krause said of the consensus All-America end (1946 and '47). "It didn't matter to him that Connor had 20 good ones in the same contest."

And practices were torturous. "It was a survival of the fittest," Brennan said.

If injuries occurred, no problem. The Irish had plenty of depth. In fact, Leahy always had two teams ready to go in a game—a big advantage in those days of single-platoon football. And the Irish's second team was almost as talented as the first. The Irish came at their opponents in waves. Thirteen different players rushed for more than 100 yards, led by Sitko's 346 and Brennan's 329. Notre Dame rolled up 3,061 yards on the ground, tops in the nation, as well as 911 yards via the air.

"We just wore down a lot of teams," Connor recalled.

Illinois fell first, 26-6, as Sitko started it off with an 83-yard run to set up a touchdown—maybe a gift to Leahy for Sitko's part in the 1943 Great Lakes upset victory.

That was a nailbiter compared to what followed. In order, the Irish ran over Pittsburgh (33-0), Purdue (49-6), Iowa (41-6) and Navy (28-0) to set up a showdown with powerful Army.

Coach Earl Blaik's Cadets were coming off consecutive undefeated seasons and boasted 25 straight victories in search of their third straight national championship. Leahy emphasized the embarrassment Notre Dame had suffered at the hands of Army in 1944 and '45 and posted a sign in the Irish locker room with a simple message: "59-0 and 48-0."

Army, with its great Mr. Inside-Mr. Outside running back tandem of Doc Blanchard and Glenn Davis, was ranked No. 1 by the Associated Press and the Irish were No. 2. The Cadets, like the Irish, had steamrolled unmercifully through their early schedule.

Lujack countered Army's dynamic duo with the game of his life despite spraining an ankle earlier in the week. But neither he on the one side nor Davis and Blanchard on the other could get the ball into the end zone.

There was offense that day in sold-out Yankee Stadium: Army gained 276 yards to Notre Dame's 271.

But 74,121 expectant fans watched in amazement as the defenses held on both sides. The Irish reached the Army 4-yard line in the second quarter for the game's best scoring opportunity but lost the ball on downs. Lujack killed Army's best scoring chance when he made an open-field, game-saving tackle of Blanchard when the back appeared headed for the end zone.

Ironically, Blanchard had captured the Heisman Trophy in 1945 while teammate Davis would win the award in 1946 and Lujack in '47.

"Since then, some people have written that I took great delight in that tackle of Blanchard," Lujack said. "There was no great delight. I just wanted to win that game. Later, I was told that may have been the first time that Blanchard had been pulled down in the open field by one man. Had I known that before the game, I might not have been able to make the tackle."

Krause recalled Leahy being devastated by the 0-0 tie in what some still label "the game of the century." But the players seemed to bounce back quickly. In fact, the following week, near the end of a late practice, Czarobski started his teammates chanting, "We wanna eat, we wanna eat."

By the time Leahy walked over to examine what was being said, the chant was changed to "We wanna eat the Wildcats"—the Northwestern Wildcats, Notre Dame's next opponent.

Czarobski was a great lineman, but he may have been an even better comedian. His quick sense of humor and loose tongue helped counteract the dourness of Leahy.

"From the moment we met Ziggy until the day he died, he captured our team," Lujack said. "And I think Leahy liked him too. Deep down, he knew

Notre Dame vs. Most Frequent Opponents

1941-1949
(5 or More Games)

Opponent	W	L	T	Pct.	Avg. Score N.D.-Opp.
Northwestern	8	0	0	1.000	22-8
Illinois	6	0	0	1.000	27-7
Pittsburgh	6	0	0	1.000	42-3
Iowa	5	0	0	1.000	35-5
Tulane	5	0	0	1.000	41-5
USC	5	0	1	.917	24-8
Navy	7	1	1	.833	24-7
Georgia Tech	4	1	0	.800	28-7
Army	3	2	2	.571	9-16

The Irish could throw a number of backfield combinations at undermanned opponents in 1946 and '47. One of Leahy's favorite units consisted of (left to right) Emil (Red) Sitko, Lujack, John Panelli and Bob Livingstone.

how important Ziggy's presence was to the team."

When Leahy once decided it was time to go back to the basics, he pulled out a ball and said, "Lads, this is a football."

Ziggy replied, "Coach, not so fast."

"Ziggy had such a quick sense of humor that he even could come up with things in the huddle that would have his teammates in stitches," Doyle recalled. "But a dominating team can afford to be funny."

After the Irish did eat the Wildcats, 27-0, they closed out the season with strong performances against Tulane (41-0) and Southern Cal (26-6). When Army barely squeaked out a victory over Navy, pollsters awarded the Irish the final No. 1 ranking and national championship.

That was just the beginning. With the nucleus of the 1946 team returning, including Brennan and Sitko in the backfield behind Lujack, Notre Dame rolled to a 9-0 season and its second straight national title. Several regulars, like Mello, Mastrangelo and end Jack Zilly were lost to graduation, but there were plenty of top-notch replacements, like Hart, fullback John Panelli and guard Marty Wendell. And talented Frank Tripucka moved into the backup quarterback position, preparing Leahy for a smooth 1948 transition.

That 1947 squad was so deep and talented that 29 of its players went on to play professional football.

The only close game that season was a 26-19 victory over Northwestern, the week after the Irish

had finally earned its long-awaited revenge over Army, 27-7. Notre Dame outscored its outmanned opposition that year, 291-52, with Lujack capturing the Heisman and Lujack, Connor and Fischer gaining consensus All-America honors.

"That victory (over Army) may have been Leahy's most pleasing," Krause said.

It also would be his last over the Cadets. The Army administrators decided that the series that had started in 1913 should be at least temporarily halted because of the bigger-than-life scope the game was being given. That and the fact that Leahy's Irish looked like they would dominate a non-wartime Army program.

A few years earlier, Michigan had ended a brief return of its series with Notre Dame and other teams were beginning to bail out as well.

Part of the reason was Leahy.

"There were jealousies among the coaching profession toward Leahy," Krause said. "They didn't like getting beat by him even though I honestly can say he didn't run up the score. But there was something about him that must have galled others. He wasn't Rockne on that point. Rockne could beat people and they could take it. It wasn't the same with Leahy."

Krause recalled the time he sat with Purdue Athletic Director Red Mackey at a state banquet after one of Notre Dame's national championship years. That's when Leahy said that he wasn't sure if his team would even be able to get a first down in the

Notre Dame co-captains in 1949: end Leon Hart (left) and tackle Jim Martin.

upcoming season.

"Mackey didn't know what to make of a statement like that," Krause said. "I think it upset him that a coach would make that kind of statement. I tried to explain that Leahy was always saying things like that and he knew they shouldn't be believed."

But people didn't easily forget and some refused to forgive as the Irish rolled on to victory after victory. And there was no letup in sight.

Lujack and many of the other service veterans were gone when the 1948 season rolled around, but Notre Dame's winning ways continued.

Tripucka stepped in smoothly for Lujack as Bob Williams would do the following year for Tripucka.

"Leahy always had a smooth transition with his quarterbacks," Doyle said. "When one would graduate, he would have another one ready."

The transition at other positions was equally painless. Ralph McGehee and Jack Fallon took over for Connor and Czarobski at the tackle spots while Brennan, Sitko and Panelli returned for another

season in the backfield. The beat continued.

Although the Irish had to survive a couple of Big Ten challenges that season—28-27 in the season opener against Purdue and 12-7 over Northwestern —they were 9-0 and ranked No. 2 as they headed to Los Angeles and a season-ending date with Southern Cal. Their winning streak stood at 21 and they had not been beaten in 27 games.

But the Trojans were up to the challenge on that early December day. The unranked hosts scored a touchdown with less than three minutes to play to forge a 14-7 lead while Tripucka sat dejectedly on the sideline with a broken bone in his hand.

But just before the ensuing USC kickoff, Notre Dame sophomore running back Bill Gay turned to a referee and asked how much time was left.

"Time enough, sir," Gay responded when he received his answer.

Gay returned the kickoff 86 yards to the Trojan 13. Sitko scored with 33 seconds remaining and Steve Oracko's extra-point kick salvaged the tie and kept the Irish unbeaten streak intact.

Notre Dame's 1949 quarterback was Bob Williams (left), who is pictured barking instructions to members of the Irish offense during a practice session.

Although Michigan was awarded the national title that season by virtue of its final No. 1 Associated Press ranking, the Irish were No. 2 and still unbeaten over three seasons.

There was to be a dramatic changing of the guard in 1949. Gone was 1948 All-America guard Fischer as well as Tripucka, Brennan, Panelli, Wendell, Fallon and center Bill Walsh. Only Sitko returned to a backfield that now featured Bob Williams at quarterback and Frank Spaniel and Larry Coutre at the halfback spots. Still the Irish rolled.

Outscoring their opposition, 333-66, the Irish were 9-0 and ranked No. 1 as they again entered what would prove to be a dramatic season-ending showdown. This time the opponent was unranked Southern Methodist and the game was to take place in Dallas.

The game appeared to be an easy conclusion to Notre Dame's third national championship in four seasons. The Mustangs would be playing without Doak Walker, their 1948 Heisman Trophy-winning running back, because of an injury and only Kyle Rote, another talented back, posed any kind of offensive threat to the Irish defense.

But somehow SMU muscled up and gave the Irish all they could handle. After Notre Dame had taken a 20-7 lead, Rote scored two touchdowns to tie the score.

Hart, who already had been named the 1949 Heisman winner, was moved to fullback to help the Irish offense get moving again and it finally did, with halfback Billy Barrett scoring the winning touchdown with about eight minutes to play.

Rote, however, was primed to lead another SMU comeback. The Mustangs moved to the Irish 5 before Hart's vicious tackle temporarily knocked the Mustang star out of the game. SMU failed to score and Notre Dame had another unbeaten season—its fourth in a row.

"That victory was nice, but I guess the streak didn't really mean as much to me then," Hart said. "But the older I get, the more I cherish those years."

Because Hart was scheduled to go to New York to accept his Heisman award, Rev. John Cavanaugh, Notre Dame's president, suggested that Hart take a plane.

The big end balked at the suggestion. "The team had taken the train down to Dallas," Hart recalled. "I think the way that Rockne died (in a plane crash in 1931) still weighed heavily on many people's minds at the university. Quite frankly, I wasn't all that excited about flying, either. And besides, I wanted to ride back with my teammates."

Father Cavanaugh immediately understood Hart's reluctance.

"Forget I even suggested it," he said apologetically.

So Hart rode back on the train with the rest of the Irish. "It was a wonderful trip," he recalled. "I had just played in my last game and we had won."

He and his teammates had never lost in an Irish uniform. But two games into the 1950 season, Notre Dame finally fell. Archrival Purdue pulled off the upset, 28-14. Three more losses followed that fall.

There would be other good seasons under Leahy, but the domination of the 1940s was over. The dynasty had ended.

The memories remain. "Those were great years," Lujack said.

And great teams.

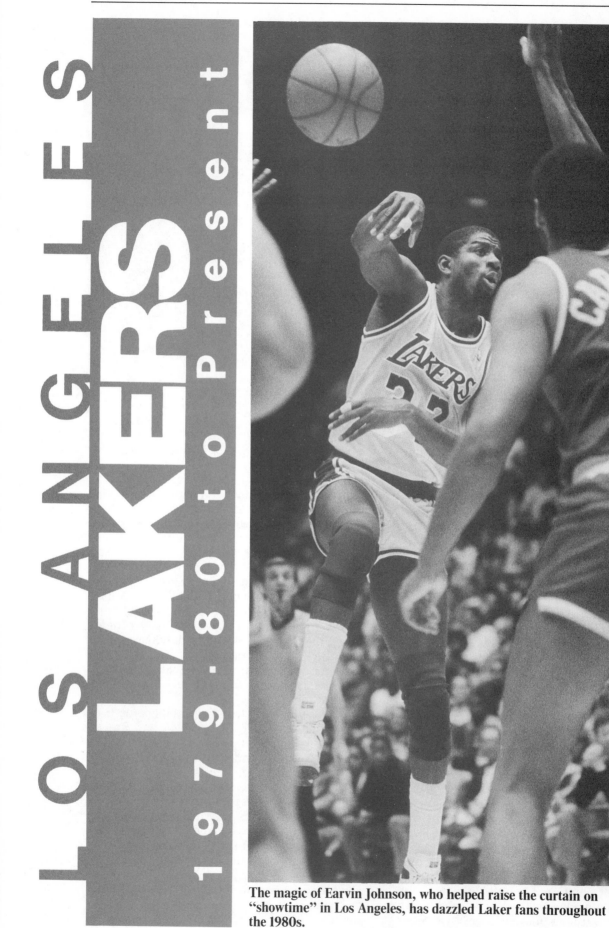

LOS ANGELES LAKERS

1979-80 to Present

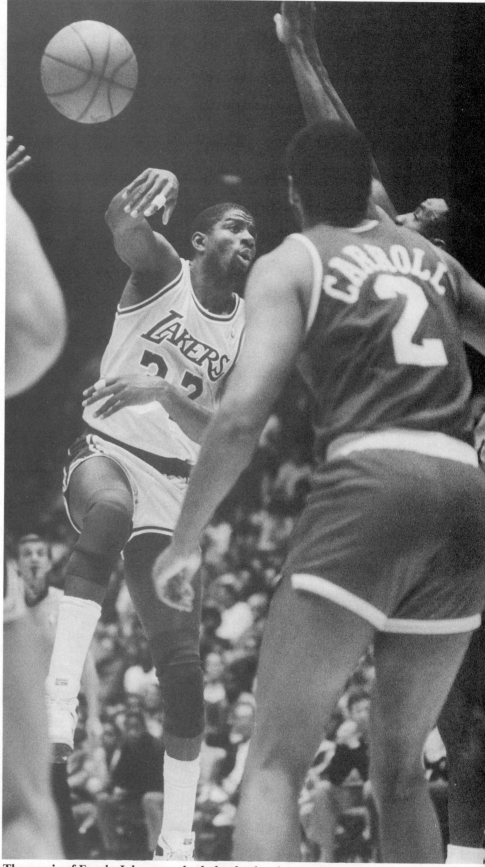

The magic of Earvin Johnson, who helped raise the curtain on "showtime" in Los Angeles, has dazzled Laker fans throughout the 1980s.

I n West Virginia, Fred Schaus, former coach of the Los Angeles Lakers, was too nervous to watch. Instead, he went out to his yard to pull weeds while his wife supplied him with bulletins.

In Los Angeles, a nervous Tommy Hawkins brushed cobwebs off his old Lakers uniform before slipping into the suit and then catching the final minutes on television.

Jerry West also watched apprehensively at home in Los Angeles. A former Laker superstar who had ascended to the club's general-manager position, he was too superstitious to go to the scene of the event. The locale was Boston Garden.

Frank Selvy, a Laker in both Minneapolis and Los Angeles, watched the nail-biter in Hilton Head, S.C. Jack Kent Cooke, former owner of the storied National Basketball Association franchise, viewed the game in Virginia.

And just what was making all these people so extraordinarily uptight? It was Game 6 of the 1985 NBA Finals, a contest in which the Lakers were attempting to exorcise evil spirits. These spirits dressed themselves up in green and white and were otherwise known as the Boston Celtics.

Just how evil—in Lakers' minds, anyway—were these spirits? We're talking top-of-the-line wicked. The Celtics and Lakers had met in six NBA Finals in the 1960s, and the Lakers, despite the presence of superstars West and Elgin Baylor for most of the competition, had lost all six times. In their last Finals clash, in 1984, Boston triumphed in seven games. And in their only other championship-series encounter, in 1959 (when the Lakers franchise was a year and a half away from deserting Minneapolis for Los Angeles), the Celtics also prevailed. Celtics 8, Lakers 0.

As the 1970s dawned, Boston's dominance had Los Angeles players and fans wondering if the Lakers ever would win an NBA crown in Southern California. The Minneapolis Lakers, after all, had captured five league titles. The L.A.-based Lakers finally made their breakthrough in the 1972 Finals, but the triumph came against the New York Knicks and not the Celtics. Los Angeles won again in 1980 and 1982, beating the Philadelphia 76ers in the Finals each time. These were special moments, to be sure, but, oh, to win the big one against the Boston Celtics. The revenge. The vindication. The satisfaction.

It was now June 9, 1985, and Los Angeles led Boston three games to two in the battle for the NBA championship. Not only were Schaus, Hawkins, West, Selvy and Cooke keenly interested in what would unfold on the parquet floor in Boston, so was the entire sporting nation. In a smashing performance, Los Angeles stormed to a 111-100 conquest as center Kareem Abdul-Jabbar and forward James Worthy combined for 57 points.

It was just the midway point for the Lakers' dynasty of the '80s, but for a club that had been foiled so many times by the Celtics, it was the zenith.

"When the Lakers walked out of Boston Garden

Do You Believe In Magic?

By Steve Springer

with a victory," Hawkins said, "we were free at last, free at last. It felt like two tons of weight had been lifted off my chest." Hawkins had played on three of the 1960s Laker teams that lost to the Celtics in the Finals, West had been a standout on all six of those Los Angeles clubs, Schaus had coached four of them and Selvy had been a member of two of the squads.

Like Hawkins, Los Angeles Coach Pat Riley was ecstatic.

"This is the start of Laker mystique," Riley said. "There goes Boston—the mystique, the con and the deception. When we get our championship rings, we're going to have a diamond set on a parquet floor. . . ."

For the Lakers of the 1980s, the winning tradition actually goes back four decades to the frozen north, where the looming presence of center George Mikan, the NBA's first superstar, cast a long shadow over the rest of the league. With the 6-foot-10, 245-pound Mikan muscling his way to such scoring averages as 28.3, 27.4 and 28.4, Minneapolis captured its five NBA championships in a six-season stretch ending in 1953-54.

The roots go back three decades to 1959, the year in which budding entrepreneur Jerry Buss, who bought the Lakers franchise in 1979, purchased his first apartment building and, in Lansing, Mich., a baby named Earvin Johnson was born.

The first major step toward a new dynasty was taken in 1975 when the Lakers pulled off one of the biggest trades in league history, obtaining Abdul-Jabbar, the dominant center of his generation, from the Milwaukee Bucks as part of a six-man deal.

And the ultimate step was taken in 1979 when the team drafted Johnson, already known by that time in name and deed as Magic.

Finally, the cast was complete, the stage was set and the curtain was about to rise on "showtime," a dynasty for the '80s.

Before this decade even entered its late stages, the Lakers had captured the imagination of a nation, pumped life into a potentially moribund sport and changed the very nature of big-time athletics by proving that sports and entertainment could provide a healthy mix.

Sure, Laker basketball is a whistling, no-look, bullet pass from Magic, a towering Kareem sky hook and a swooping James Worthy dunk. But it's

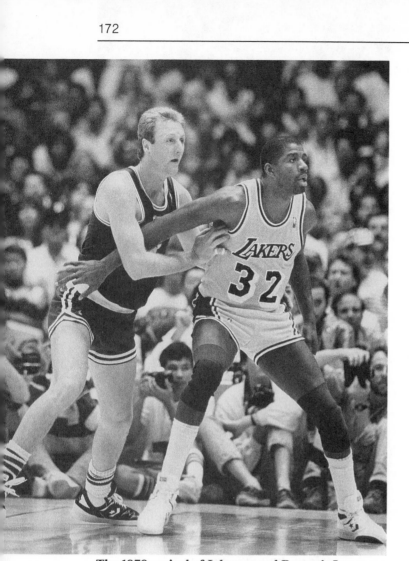

The 1979 arrival of Johnson and Boston's Larry Bird set the stage for a decade-long rivalry between the players and the NBA's premier franchises.

also the Laker girls, Dancing Barry and Jack Nicholson, Dyan Cannon and friends in $250 courtside seats.

It's not just a game. It's a happening. An event.

"Jerry Buss recognized that this is the entertainment capital of the world," said NBA Commissioner David Stern. "The team matches the community. He made the Forum the place to be."

It wasn't always this way. In fact, before Magic and Larry Bird entered the league after the 1978-79 collegiate season, the NBA was in the doldrums. It definitely ranked third in the pro-sports world, behind football and baseball, and some observers even considered the league a bush operation.

New blood and new excitement were needed, and Johnson and Bird helped to supply same. It didn't happen overnight, but it happened.

Remember the Lakers' title-clinching victory over the 76ers in the 1980 NBA Finals when Magic played center in place of the injured Kareem?

For many fans, the memory of that contest is pretty dim. They either failed to see the game on television or didn't view it via a live telecast. The game was shown on a tape-delay basis to most of the country late at night.

That's a measure of where the NBA stood on an esteem scale in those days. Can you imagine the Super Bowl or the World Series being tape-delayed?

Things were darkest in the 1980-81 season, with 16 of the 23 teams losing money. Four franchises were up for sale with no buyers in sight. There was talk of merging several money-losers.

That, however, is ancient history now. The NBA has become a bona fide third major sports entity. League attendance has risen more than 25 percent since that 1980-81 season. The NBA alone, among the major sports leagues, continues to show a steady rise in television ratings. A team losing money is nearly unheard of.

What caused such a drastic turnaround? An influx of incredibly skilled athletes into the NBA, starting with Johnson and Bird and continuing with Isiah Thomas, Dominique Wilkins, James Worthy, Michael Jordan, Akeem Olajuwon, Charles Barkley, Patrick Ewing and Karl Malone; better management throughout the league; improved marketing; tough drug-control laws, and a salary cap that both contains costs and spreads the talent pool.

But don't discount the appeal, now nationwide, of "showtime." It's no coincidence that the rise of the league has paralleled the ascent of the Lakers.

That ascent has taken the Lakers into hallowed territory, their championship banners giving the Forum the look of a historic shrine, an appearance that once was the sole province of Boston Garden.

It's almost difficult now to remember the frustration and failure that once dogged this Laker franchise. It's hard to recall that before those banners filled a wall in the rafters of the Forum, there were balloons up there, serving as the perfect symbol of all the frustration.

Never was there more gnashing of teeth than after Game 7 of the 1969 Finals. Before that Celtics-Lakers contest, the ever-confident Cooke had his staff place balloons—lots and lots of balloons—up in the rafters, set for release when the Lakers finally emerged triumphant. And these Lakers, owning the home-court advantage and featuring not only West and Baylor but also Wilt Chamberlain, seemed fully capable of putting an end to all the anguish they had suffered at the Celtics' hands. Los Angeles had won its division championship handily and breezed into the Finals with eight victories in 11 playoff games; Boston, conversely, had finished only fourth in its division but rolled into the Finals with a hot hand in its first two playoff series.

Red Auerbach, the Celtics' general manager and former coach of the Boston club, was furious when he walked into the building and saw those balloons.

"Those things," Auerbach barked, "are going to stay up there a hell of a long time."

And they did.

Down by 17 points with just under 10 minutes to play, the Lakers cut that deficit to seven points five minutes later when Chamberlain, Los Angeles' gifted 7-foot-1 center, limped off the court with a knee injury.

Chamberlain was soon ready to return. His coach, however, had other ideas. Bill van Breda Kolff, climaxing a long-running feud with Chamberlain, told his center, "We're doing well enough without you." The Lakers had cut the deficit to one point in Wilt's absence.

So Chamberlain remained where he was. And the balloons remained where they were. The Lakers fell once again to their arch-rivals, 108-106.

"I think the Lakers were a dynasty in the '60s," Riley said. "They just couldn't beat the other dynasty (the Celtics). The Lakers were right there, playing for the championship so many times. They were as great a team as ever. But there happened to be probably the greatest dynasty of all time right there with them."

The drought finally ended in the 1971-72 season when the Lakers set league records with 33 consecutive regular-season victories and 69 triumphs overall en route to beating the New York Knicks in five games in the Finals for their first title in Los Angeles.

That team had the look of a dynasty—guards West and Gail Goodrich both averaged more than 25 points per game, Chamberlain was still a force in the middle and Jim McMillian and Happy Hairston were solid at the forward spots—but the club lacked the feel of same. It just didn't have the magic touch to sustain its success.

Until nearly a decade later, that is, when the young man from Michigan came along.

Earvin Johnson had been nicknamed "Magic" for his sleight-of-hand feats in leading Lansing's Everett High School to a Michigan state championship in 1977. He then lived up to the billing at Michigan State where, as a sophomore, he was the key figure in the Spartans' run to the NCAA championship in 1979.

But when he was drafted into the NBA as a 19-year-old undergraduate in '79, Johnson, selected No. 1 overall, found many non-believers. This ain't college, kid. Don't be bringing that razzle-dazzle, rah-rah stuff up here.

There even had been some doubters in the Lakers' front office.

"There was some thought among my counselors that Sidney Moncrief (Arkansas) might have been the better choice," said Cooke, who still was the Lakers' owner when the draft decision was made but soon sold the franchise to Buss. "Never any question in *my* mind. I said to my counselors, 'I don't give a damn what you say, it's going to be Magic Johnson.'"

Magic displayed his trademark spirit—punctuated by a wide-eyed grin and high-five salutations—right from the start as a professional. But in the beginning, it was regarded as rookie naivete.

In Magic's first regular-season game, the Lakers defeated the San Diego Clippers on a Kareem sky hook at the buzzer. Magic, wild with exuberance,

When Johnson joined the Lakers, he became fast friends with fellow guard Norm Nixon (above), who was running the team's high-powered offense.

ran over and threw his arms around his big center, giving him a huge hug.

Abdul-Jabbar, the quintessential cool professional, wasn't quite ready for that. "Hey," he told the rookie, "we've got 81 more of these."

The kid had reason to be excited, having shown in his first official game as a pro exactly what he could do at that level. He had scored 26 points against the Clippers, pulled down eight rebounds, handed out four assists and made one steal. Magic Johnson probably would have been just as thrilled if he had struggled personally in that game; it's simply the nature of the man to revel in team-wide success.

Ten years and five NBA crowns later, Johnson hadn't lost any of his enthusiasm.

"I'm still that guy. I still get excited. We do it maybe in a different way where I won't tire Kareem out so much," Johnson said with a laugh. "But I'm still excited. Once I lose that, then it's time to go."

But it wasn't all laughs and high fives in that first season. Fourteen games into the 1979-80 campaign, the team lost its coach, Jack McKinney.

A longtime head coach at the collegiate level and an assistant with the NBA's Portland Trail Blazers,

Jack McKinney, architect of the Lakers' run-and-gun style, was sent to the sidelines by a bicycle accident during the 1979-80 season.

McKinney had been hired by Buss to replace West, who had bowed out from a job he found difficult to deal with. West had a hard time coaching players who couldn't approximate the standards he had set.

Which included nearly everybody.

Enter McKinney, who immediately installed the fast-break offense that was to carry the Lakers to 10 years of glory.

McKinney's own brief moment of glory came to a tragic end on a seemingly innocent bicycle ride through his Palos Verdes neighborhood to meet his assistant and best friend, Paul Westhead, for a game of tennis. McKinney never made it, his bike tumbling down a hill, leaving the helmet-less coach in critical condition with severe head injuries.

McKinney eventually got his health back, but never his job. Memory lapses left him incapable of running the team.

At one point, Buss was tempted to put McKinney back in charge. But a chilling incident convinced Buss that was not practical. McKinney, attending a game, walked past Buss and was greeted by the Lakers' owner. The coach ignored the gesture and kept walking—he had not recognized his boss.

So the torch was passed on an "interim" basis to Westhead, who had coached collegiately at La Salle, and he led the Lakers into the playoffs. Under McKinney, Los Angeles had won 10 of 14 games; with Westhead guiding the club, the Lakers won 50 of their last 68 regular-season contests.

It was in the 1980 playoffs that Johnson first defined his favorite phrase, "winning time." His play in the regular season had not silenced all of his critics. Not even an 18-point scoring average and a 7.7 rebound mark could quiet everyone.

After Magic was made a starter in the All-Star Game by vote of the fans, Boston Coach Bill Fitch said, "It's a travesty. Magic is a good enough kid, but some of those people must have thought they were voting for Dennis Johnson (Seattle) when they voted for Earvin Johnson."

On a similar front, NBA players, voting in a New York Times poll, compiled a list of the Western Conference's best guards in 1979-80. Magic didn't make the top *six*. Bird, the Celtics' sensational newcomer out of Indiana State, was voted Rookie of the Year.

"Winning time," though, demonstrated clearly that Magic Johnson, even at the tender age of 20, was a cut above. In the playoffs, Magic started pulling rabbits out of his hat in a manner that would become so familiar over the next decade.

The tone was set early, on a seemingly routine play in a Western Conference semifinal game against the Phoenix Suns. The Lakers, ahead two games to none in the best-of-seven series, were leading by three points with a little more than two minutes to play in Game 3 at Phoenix. Magic, dribbling up the court, had the ball slapped away. Walter Davis picked it up and threw a long, lazy pass downcourt to a waiting Paul Westphal. No hurry. No sweat. All alone, Westphal could lay it in for the

Paul Westhead, who replaced McKinney in 1979-80, is congratulated by Jamaal Wilkes after the Lakers had dispatched Philadelphia to win their first title of the decade.

two points that would leave the game a tossup.

But Westphal soon had company.

Somehow, someway, Magic sprinted all the way to the other end of the court, sneaked in while Westphal waited for the one-bounce lob to settle in his arms and stole the ball right out from under the Suns' guard. Johnson then bolted back up the court and fired a bullet to Abdul-Jabbar, who finished off matters with a slam dunk.

Phoenix never recovered—either in the game or the playoff round. The Lakers eliminated the Suns in five games.

Asked about the third-game play later, Magic said, "It's magic, baby."

But like any great performer, Johnson saved his best act for the grand finale, Game 6 of the NBA Finals against Julius Erving and the Philadelphia 76ers. It already had been a tumultuous championship series.

After Game 2, veteran forward Spencer Haywood, a Laker reserve and former American Basketball Association and NBA standout, was suspended "for activities disruptive toward the team." Then, before Game 5, Buss, his hand forced by a news story emanating out of the East, announced that McKinney's days as Los Angeles coach were officially over.

Game 5 itself was drama-packed. Abdul-Jabbar suffered an ankle sprain in the third quarter and went to the sidelines, but he returned and netted 14 of his game-high 40 points in the final period. Guard Norm Nixon incurred a finger fracture, reducing his effectiveness. Despite the injuries, Los Angeles persevered and came away with a 108-103 triumph. The Lakers now led the series, three games to two, with Game 6 scheduled for the Spectrum in Philadelphia.

It was a forlorn group of Lakers, though, who

A smiling Johnson lends a hand to champagne-soaked Lakers Owner Jerry Buss during the team's 1980 championship celebration.

gathered at the airport for the trip to Philadelphia. The players had learned only moments earlier that Abdul-Jabbar, hobbled by the ankle injury, would not be joining them.

But one Laker, the youngest on the squad, was anything but down in the dumps. He got aboard the jetliner and strode directly to the window seat in the first aisle on the left side.

Kareem's seat on every flight.

"Never fear," he told his teammates, that grin as wide as ever. "E.J. is here."

That old naivete back again?

Not quite.

Johnson not only took Abdul-Jabbar's seat, but his position as well. When the two teams marched out on the court for the tipoff, Magic was in the center spot.

"This was gonna be the greatest moment in my life," he said. "I knew that." And so many years and so many accomplishments later, that statement probably still holds up.

While Magic indeed played in the middle that night, he also saw duty at forward and his usual guard spot. He put on a performance that dazzled the Spectrum and the late-night television audience, scoring 42 points and collecting 15 rebounds and leading the Lakers to their first NBA title of the '80s. Johnson sank 14 of 23 field-goal attempts in Los Angeles' 123-107 triumph, made all 14 of his free-throw tries, had seven assists and recorded

three steals.

There were plenty of other heroes. Jamaal Wilkes scored a career-high 37 points, including 16 in the third quarter. Michael Cooper, knocked cold by Darryl Dawkins, got up and converted two important free throws. Reserve Brad Holland hit several clutch baskets, and the injured Nixon came up with a key steal.

Despite the contributions by all, the night was Magic's.

"I don't think any of us will live to see a better performance than that," said broadcaster Chick Hearn, who has seen it all since assuming his Laker duties in 1961.

"Without Kareem, I'm a little more free to do my thing," Johnson said in measured, modest tones. When the rookie sensation was told he had been named Most Valuable Player of the 1980 NBA playoffs (despite Abdul-Jabbar's 31.9 scoring average over 15 games), Magic said: "If it wasn't for the big fella, we wouldn't even be here. When we get back to Los Angeles, we're going to hug and kiss him all night."

The effervescence that Earvin Johnson had displayed after the opening game of the season had changed not one whit by season's end.

The NBA crown meant Johnson had now been a member of championship teams in high school, college and pro ball in three of the last four seasons. "This is the biggest thrill," he said, "because it's the highest level of basketball there is. Everybody thought we were going to come in here and fold without Kareem. But we didn't."

While the seeds of a dynasty had been planted, Magic II wasn't anything like the original.

Johnson injured his knee early in the 1980-81 season and missed 45 games. He returned to action at less than 100 percent, with both his knee and his feelings hurt. In his absence, Nixon, his close friend and the Lakers' point guard before Magic's arrival, had been given the controls once more.

Nixon couldn't deny that he liked the feeling of running the ball club and said so in a Los Angeles Times story that included a few shots at his buddy.

"I thought Magic would come in and have to adjust to our game," Nixon was quoted as saying, "but we had to adjust to him."

Magic contained his anger for a while, but he exploded at the worst possible time, in the midst of the playoffs. After the Lakers lost the first game of a best-of-three mini-series to the Houston Rockets, Magic wondered aloud about what he perceived as jealousy.

"If Norm Nixon feels that strongly about having the ball," Magic said, "we'll get him a ball, put his name on it and he can keep it under his arm during the game. It'll be his ball."

Strong stuff. Stunning repercussions.

Distracted by all the controversy, the Lakers were knocked out of postseason play by upstart Houston, which had finished the regular season with a losing record. Magic, still at the center of the storm, fired up an air ball in the closing seconds of the final game with the outcome still in doubt.

But as storms go, that was pretty mild stuff compared to the twister that lay dead ahead.

Buss took Johnson and Nixon to Las Vegas after the season ended to talk over their differences. The two returned home a close-knit pair once again, both on and off the court.

Peace at last?

Only for a short time. Beyond the quiet summer of 1981, clouds were gathering for an even bigger storm, one that threatened to tear apart this budding dynasty. This time, the rift placed Westhead on one side and several of his players on the other.

When the Lakers reported to camp in the fall of 1981, they found changes in the offense. It was minor stuff, said Westhead, aimed at refining Los Angeles' half-court game. It was major stuff, though, in view of some of the players, who believed the innovations would cripple the team's major weapon, its devastating fast break.

"He (Westhead) left the ways that we were successful," Abdul-Jabbar said, "and that made it hard for us to get things done. It was like wearing somebody else's suit. You're not going to look that great."

Johnson tried to intercede and was told firmly by Westhead, "This is what we run!"

Period.

The tension grew. An early-season meeting was held at the Forum involving Buss, special consultant West and General Manager Bill Sharman to determine whether the situation was irretrievable, whether Westhead ought to be let go.

Buss felt as if he were sitting on a time bomb. Three days later, it exploded.

Following a game in Salt Lake City, Westhead called Magic aside and bawled him out because the coach thought Johnson had not been paying attention to his instructions during a timeout.

Dynasty Data
Yearly Record
1979-80 to 1987-88

Season	W	L	Pct.	Avg. Score L.A.-Opp.	Place	GA(+)/GB	Coach
1979-80—(Pacific Division)	60	22	.732	115-109	1	+ 4	Jack McKinney, Paul Westhead
1980-81—(Pacific Division)	54	28	.659	111-107	2	3	Paul Westhead
1981-82—(Pacific Division)	57	25	.695	115-110	1	+ 5	Paul Westhead, Pat Riley
1982-83—(Pacific Division)	58	24	.707	115-110	1	+ 5	Pat Riley
1983-84—(Pacific Division)	54	28	.659	116-112	1	+ 6	Pat Riley
1984-85—(Pacific Division)	62	20	.756	118-111	1	+20	Pat Riley
1985-86—(Pacific Division)	62	20	.756	117-110	1	+22	Pat Riley
1986-87—(Pacific Division)	65	17	.793	118-109	1	+16	Pat Riley
1987-88—(Pacific Division)	62	20	.756	113-107	1	+ 9	Pat Riley
1988-89—(Pacific Division)	57	25	.695	115-108	1	+ 2	Pat Riley

Playoffs

Season	First Round	Western Conference Semifinals	Finals	NBA Championship	Total Playoff Record
1979-80	Earned bye	4-1 vs. Phoenix	4-1 vs. Seattle	4-2 vs. Philadelphia	12-4
1980-81	1-2 vs. Houston				1-2
1981-82	Earned bye	4-0 vs. Phoenix	4-0 vs. San Antonio	4-2 vs. Philadelphia	12-2
1982-83	Earned bye	4-1 vs. Portland	4-2 vs. San Antonio	0-4 vs. Philadelphia	8-7
1983-84	3-0 vs. Kansas City	4-1 vs. Dallas	4-2 vs. Phoenix	3-4 vs. Boston	14-7
1984-85	3-0 vs. Phoenix	4-1 vs. Portland	4-1 vs. Denver	4-2 vs. Boston	15-4
1985-86	3-0 vs. San Antonio	4-2 vs. Dallas	1-4 vs. Houston		8-6
1986-87	3-0 vs. Denver	4-1 vs. Golden State	4-0 vs. Seattle	4-2 vs. Boston	15-3
1987-88	3-0 vs. San Antonio	4-3 vs. Utah	4-3 vs. Dallas	4-3 vs. Detroit	15-9
1988-89	3-0 vs. Portland	4-0 vs. Seattle	4-0 vs. Phoenix	0-4 vs. Detroit	11-4
					111-48

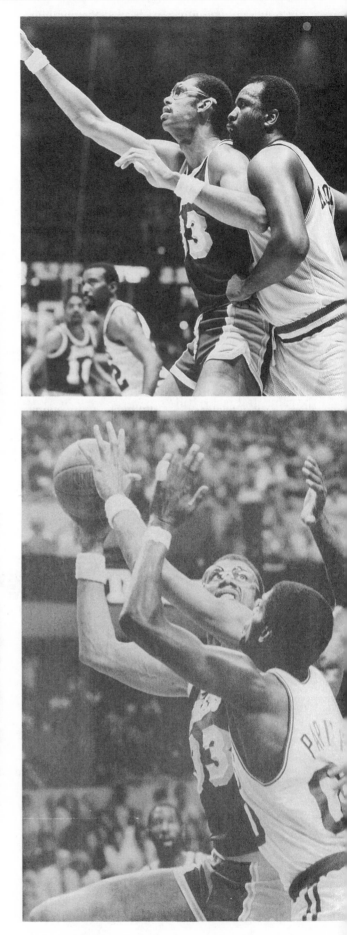

Big man Kareem Abdul-Jabbar was understandably giddy (above) when the Lakers defeated the 76ers again in 1982. But there were more battles to be fought. Abdul-Jabbar (above right) battles Philadelphia's Moses Malone in the 1983 NBA Finals and Boston's Robert Parish (below right) in the 1984 title series.

The Lakers of the 1980s were not all Magic Johnson and Abdul-Jabbar. The silky-smooth Wilkes (left) was a big factor in the early part of the decade, while talented James Worthy (right) joined the team in 1982-83.

"You might as well sit me down," Magic said, "because I ain't being used anyway. Just sit me down."

Thinking it over, Magic decided to sit himself down. Permanently. When the media confronted him in the Lakers' locker room moments later, Johnson went public.

"I can't play here anymore," he said, speaking softly but with the kind of determination he'd always shown on the court. "I want to leave . . . I want to be traded . . . I'm not happy now."

Somebody was going to leave all right, but it wasn't Magic.

Buss informed Westhead the next day that he was gone, then told the media that afternoon in a hastily called press conference that West would become the "offensive coach" and that Pat Riley, a Westhead aide, would "stay as coach." The terminology seemed a mite confusing, but Riley proved to be the man in charge.

Buss had moved quickly, having fired Westhead 11 games into the season and given the job to a man with no previous experience as a head coach. Riley, in fact, had been a member of the Lakers' broadcast team as recently as November 1979.

A gamble? Jerry Buss was used to same. He had been rolling the dice all his life.

A child of the Depression, Buss moved from bread lines in southwestern Wyoming as a boy to an engineering job in Southern California's aero-space industry as an adult.

That was quite a jump, but Buss had an even more distant goal—financial independence. So he and a fellow worker, Frank Mariani, put $83.33 aside from each paycheck until they had enough to invest $1,000 apiece toward the purchase of a West Los Angeles apartment building.

It was to be just the first link in a chain that would spread across the Sun Belt and the financial spectrum.

One building led to two, then four, and on and on until, by 1979, Mariani-Buss consisted of a $350 million real-estate empire that included 45 limited partnerships and 400 employees overseeing some 200 pieces of land and 1,000 houses.

Jerry Buss was 46 years old and living a dream life. Yet he was bored to death.

So he turned to sports, a life-long passion, first as owner of the Los Angeles Strings of World Team Tennis. However, he wanted a bigger court on which to play, and he got it in mid-1979 when he paid Jack Kent Cooke $67.5 million for the Lakers, the Kings and the Forum.

Buss didn't delude himself by thinking he suddenly knew more about basketball than the average fan, which is what he still was, deed of ownership or not. So he figured he'd lean on two guys who certainly did know more, West and Sharman, both former players and coaches and longtime fixtures at the Forum.

Michael Cooper (left) has captured the hearts of Laker fans with a decade of defensive excellence and quality sixth-man play, while Byron Scott (right) has won over skeptics with his strong shooting and intensity.

A victory over longtime nemesis Boston in the 1985 NBA Finals was critical for the Lakers. Los Angeles forward Kurt Rambis battles Bird for a loose ball (right) and the Lakers whoop it up (left) as the curtain falls on the Celtic jinx.

That was fine until Buss found out that West, who had coached the team for three years through the 1978-79 season, didn't want to continue in that capacity. Sharman, on the other hand, was content in his role as general manager. So, Buss named West a consultant, kept Sharman as GM and named McKinney, an assistant under Jack Ramsay at Portland, as his coach.

When that didn't work out because of McKinney's misfortune, he got Westhead—a turnabout that proved troublesome for the new coach. With common basketball roots in Philadelphia, McKinney and Westhead had been longtime close friends. McKinney, in fact, had gotten Westhead several jobs. The wives and children were close.

And, suddenly, Westhead was offered the position McKinney had lost, the job of a lifetime, the opportunity to sit at the controls of a basketball machine that had the potential to steamroll its way through the years, leaving a permanent mark on the game.

"Jack (McKinney) will not be the coach of this team," Buss told Westhead when he offered to remove the "interim" from Westhead's title. "Do you want the job or do we get somebody else?"

Westhead wanted it, guilt and all. And he took it.

"They can't share our joys," said Cassie West-head, Paul's wife, of the McKinneys, "and we can't share their sorrows."

But there was plenty of sorrow—disappointment, anyway—for Westhead and his family as well. While guiding the team to the NBA crown in the 1979-80 season as "acting coach" after replacing the injured McKinney in early November, Westhead, as *the* coach, directed the Lakers to a 54-28 record in 1980-81 but suffered that playoff upset at the hands of the Houston Rockets. He then had Los Angeles on a five-game winning streak when he was dismissed with a 7-4 record early in the 1981-82 campaign.

Now, it was Riley's turn. Being handed the reins of a powerhouse team out of control was quite a challenge—and opportunity—for the former Kentucky standout and NBA reserve, who had been a member of the Lakers' 1972 championship team.

So what did he change?

"Nothing. I had no time to change anything," Riley said. "The offense was never the problem. They (the players) used that as a crutch for whatever reason."

With Westhead gone, the Lakers threw away the crutches. And started running. And running. And running. All the way to another title.

Like a wild horse freed from a corral, the Lakers

Coach Pat Riley shows off the title trophy that proclaimed the Lakers as the 1984-85 NBA champions.

burst back into high gear, fast-breaking past one opponent after another until they eventually beat the 76ers in six games in the NBA Finals.

Magic had faced a lot of criticism for his role in the Westhead firing, but even that faded in the euphoria of another title. Johnson, the playoff MVP just as he had been two years earlier, helped fuel the Lakers to sweeps against Phoenix and San Antonio in the Western Conference semifinals and title series and was his usual magnificent self against Philadelphia in the Finals.

The Lakers' cast was much the same as in 1980, with Johnson and Nixon holding forth in the backcourt (and Michael Cooper at the ready), Abdul-Jabbar at center and Wilkes at one of the forward slots. Rookie Kurt Rambis proved a strong rebounder and tough defensive player at the other corner, manned previously by Jim Chones. Forward Mitch Kupchak, a Laker after spending five seasons with the Washington Bullets, played in

only 26 games before going down with a severe knee injury.

The next two seasons had plenty of excitement as well, but both ended with a bitter taste. In 1982-83, the Lakers, beset with injuries (Kupchak remained on the sidelines and flashy rookie James Worthy missed the playoffs because of a bad leg), won 58 games but were dispatched in the Finals in four games by a Philadelphia club that had been bolstered by the acquisition of Moses Malone.

In the 1984 Finals, Los Angeles met its old nemesis, Boston, after a 15-year cessation to their title-round hostilities. This series finished just like all the previous Lakers-Celtics struggles, with a lot of "what-might-have-beens" bandied about for Riley's team.

Worthy threw away a pass that proved costly in Game 2, a contest in which Magic dribbled away nearly all of the time remaining in regulation (the score was tied and Boston went on to win in over-

The Lakers' second triumph over Boston in the NBA Finals (1987) was punctuated by the cheerleading antics of Johnson on the steps of City Hall during the victory celebration.

By 1988, forward A.C. Green, pictured defending against Detroit's Vinnie Johnson in the title series, had become an integral part of the Laker machine.

time). Johnson then made a bad pass and missed some crucial free throws in another overtime loss in Game 4, and he proceeded to have the ball stolen away twice at the end of Game 7, which Boston won by a 111-102 score after holding only a 105-102 edge in the late going. The Celtics had now beaten the Lakers in all eight of their Finals matchups, with four of the series going the seven-game limit.

"We choked," Riley said.

The Lakers would get a chance to make amends the next spring. In this clash of juggernauts—the Celtics compiled a 63-19 regular-season mark and the Lakers went 62-20—there was little to indicate things would be different in the 1985 Finals, with the Celts blowing past the Lakers, 148-114, in Game 1 at Boston Garden. The game forever would be known as the Memorial Day Massacre.

Emotionally, would the Lakers even show up for Game 2? Would the curse ever end?

Riley, always a motivator, stole a page from the playbook of the master of the art of motivating, Knute Rockne. In the locker room at the Garden prior to Game 2, Riley called upon his own "Gipper," relating to the Lakers the words of his father shortly before Lee Riley's death in 1970. "Just remember," said the senior Riley, who had a cup of coffee in major league baseball and served as a minor league manager, "somewhere, someplace, sometime, you're going to have to plant your feet, make a stand and kick some ass."

This was the place, the time and the stand. Los Angeles rebounded for a seven-point triumph.

"Game 2, to me, is still the most important game this team has ever played," Riley said. "I think the team just finally gathered the strength and realized who they were and broke through."

The Lakers went on to win three of the next four games, with the clincher—the monkey-off-their-back game—coming at Boston Garden as franchise members past and present heaved a collective sigh of relief. Front-line standouts Abdul-Jabbar and Worthy scored 29 and 28 points, respectively, while the backcourt twosome of Johnson and second-year pro Byron Scott combined for 28.

The Lakers fell to Houston in the 1986 Western Conference title round, but stormed back for league championships in 1987 and 1988 by defeating Boston (again) and Detroit, respectively, in the Finals. The back-to-back crowns were the first in the NBA since the Celtics ruled in 1968 and again in 1969.

The march to the '88 championship was particularly grueling for Los Angeles, which was extended to seven games in successive playoff series against the Utah Jazz, the Dallas Mavericks and the Pistons. Only a team of the highest skill and character could have survived such rigors.

In the 1989 playoffs, the Lakers took dead aim at a third consecutive NBA crown. They swept Western Conference series against Portland, Seattle and Phoenix and entered the Finals against Detroit with an 11-0 postseason record. Most astonishing in that amazing run was Los Angeles' comeback from a 29-point deficit in the series-clinching victory against the SuperSonics.

While opponents failed to slow the Lakers, an injury bug did. Scott was sidelined for the Finals because of a hamstring injury incurred in practice, and Magic went down with a similar injury in Game 2 of the championship round. The talented Pistons, clearly capable of beating a full-strength Lakers team, took advantage of the situation and dispatched Los Angeles in four games.

No one, though, was questioning what Riley and his players had accomplished over the years.

Indeed, numerous men of skill and character contributed to the Lakers' dynasty, which in the 1980s produced five NBA champions, three runners-up, a cumulative regular-season record of 591-229 (.721) and four consecutive seasons of 62 or more victories.

There was Kareem Abdul-Jabbar, the NBA's all-time leading scorer, who played in the league for 20 seasons, to age 42, contributing those killer sky hooks and his intimidating presence in the middle. When people reflect on the Lakers of the '80s, the union of Kareem and Magic may be considered the sports world's greatest 1-2 punch since Babe Ruth and Lou Gehrig.

But Abdul-Jabbar, who retired after the '89 Finals, and Johnson had a lot of help. There was Michael Cooper, contributing a decade of great defense and inspired sixth-man play. There was Wilkes and, later, Worthy, at small forward, front

**Magic Johnson shoots over Detroit's Dennis Rodman during action in the Lakers'
seven-game NBA Finals victory in 1988.**

The road through the 1988 playoffs was filled with potholes, but the Lakers survived and Riley was vindicated for guaranteeing a title repeat.

With Laker banners hanging in the background and the final posted on the scoreboard, happy fans storm the court to celebrate their team's title-winning triumph over Detroit in '88.

men for those magical passes on the break. There was Kurt Rambis and, later, A.C. Green, at power forward, pulling down rebounds and providing muscle and hustle. There was Scott, confronted by hostility from his new teammates when his draft rights were acquired from the San Diego Clippers in a 1983 trade for the popular Nixon, but who went on to earn respect with his deadly shooting and overall play. And there was the bench strength provided by people like Bob McAdoo and, later, Mychal Thompson.

Plus, there was Cooke, who had his sights set on Magic; Buss, who created the winning environment; and West and Sharman, who flourished in those surroundings, wheeling and dealing and helping to build and maintain this dynasty by drafting Worthy, obtaining Scott and coming up with McAdoo and Thompson just when they were needed most.

There was McKinney, who designed the fast break; Westhead, who won a title with it; and Riley, who won the other four championships of the 1980-1989 time frame.

Riley always came prepared, with the right strategy and the right words, like his pre-Game 2 speech in the 1985 Finals and his guarantee of a second straight NBA title before the champagne had dried up after the '87 celebration.

But most of all, there was Magic. That first hug of Kareem in Johnson's first game proved just the beginning of a decade-long celebration.

"Magic Johnson made a believer out of Kareem," broadcaster Hearn said. "I think that hug gave Kareem a sense of being wanted, needed, loved and respected. And I think the rest of the guys took off from there.

"It's a feeling that Magic brings, even today (the late 1980s). When he's out of the game, it's a different game. Not just because of his talents. He is a leader. He is the glue that holds them together. He might be the best player that ever lived. He might be."

In the late 1970s, Riley believed his future was in broadcasting. But even if he had envisioned coaching as his livelihood, he never could have imagined the success he has enjoyed.

"There's an old saying," Riley recalled. " 'When your reality exceeds your dreams, don't tell anybody.' Make it seem like it just happened because you were good.

"It's been a great opportunity for me, one that I will never, ever forget. I'll be here for 10 or 12 years with this team and, then, that's going to be it for me. Because there will never be another team like this."

CLEVELAND
BROWNS
1946 to 1955

**Cleveland Coach Paul Brown (right), The Great Innovator, with
assistant Bill Edwards in the late 1940s.**

David Becomes Goliath

By Dave Newhouse

It was a nightmare with cleat marks. Every coach, every player who played those postwar Cleveland Browns teams experienced the same restless, sleepless nights.

Lying in the dark, they'd see Marion Motley, the giant fullback, charging at them like the lead elephant in a stampede. Or Otto Graham, the T-formation quarterback, cutting them apart with feathery passes and nifty runs. They'd picture Lou Groza knocking their defensive linemen out of the trenches, then dropping back to kick 50-yard field goals. Or Horace Gillom, whose punts seemed to be suspended in midair, inventing something called "hang time." Or they'd stare at the ceiling and watch Dante Lavelli and Mac Speedie, running their intricate patterns—and running free. Then something would flash before the eyes, and it would be Bill Willis, too fast to be blocked.

And, mostly, they'd see Paul Brown. They'd wonder, perhaps even shout out in the evening's still, "What is he up to now? How will he beat us this time?" How could they sleep before facing The Great Innovator, knowing they'd face the same inevitable fate on Sundays.

When coaching was a six-months-on, six-months-off profession, Brown began working year-round with a year-round staff. When other coaches were playing golf in the spring, Brown and his assistants were the first to study films, grading every move of every player. While other coaches diagramed plays on chalkboards as their sole means of teaching, Brown tested his players, not only on every play in the playbook (which he also introduced), but on their "ability to learn" through psychological testing.

Brown was the man responsible for the four-man defensive line and the breaking down of the color barrier in pro football's postwar era. He recognized that the kicking game was overlooked as an offensive weapon. While other teams relied on the traditional "safe" passing zones, Brown allowed his quarterback to throw anywhere on the field.

How could anyone beat those Browns teams, with talent that was the best of its time and a coach who was far ahead of his time? Well, you didn't beat them, not very often anyway.

In their first 10 years of existence, from 1946 through 1955, the Browns played in 10 league championship games, winning seven times. They were a perfect 4-0 in the All-America Football Conference, winning the league title in each season of the league's history (1946-49), before claiming National Football League championships in 1950, 1954 and 1955. Never has pro football witnessed such consistent domination—and with 28 teams competing today compared with 12 at the end of the Browns' reign, it probably never will again.

The Browns of Paul Brown simply overwhelmed the competition. To accurately describe them, pick a word between "dominant" and "awesome." One word comes to mind: "dynasty."

"I don't think the Green Bay Packers or Miami Dolphins could stand up to us," said Lavelli, recalling two other teams associated with the 'D' word. "The Packers never had a passing attack like we did. And we were there for 10 years, while the Dolphins were there for two or three."

"You have to categorize teams by their times," Groza said, "and we were the best of the heap."

By far. The Browns' regular-season record over their first 10 seasons was 105-17-4. They outscored opponents by a 2-1 margin (3,545 points to 1,734).

"You could see that there were no weaknesses," said college coaching great Ara Parseghian, a Browns halfback in 1948 and 1949, when an injury cut short his career. "The kicking game, offense, defense, leadership—they were all strong. This was one tough football team."

No weaknesses, indeed. For along with his innovative, inventive qualities, Brown knew talent and where to find it. He was the first coach to make scouting his passion and, consequently, a science.

Brown, you see, had begun the scouting work that would make the Browns a winner even *before* the franchise was formed. He had compiled his own mental file of football talent as he moved up the coaching ladder—from Severn Prep in Maryland, where he began his career with a 16-1-1 record in 1930-31; to his high school alma mater, Massillon (Ohio), where his first dynasty took shape with an 80-8-2 mark over nine seasons; to Ohio State, where he coached from 1941 through 1943, producing a national championship in 1942; to the U.S. Naval Training Station in Great Lakes, Ill., where he took a bunch of servicemen and upset fifth-ranked Notre Dame, 39-7, in the Irish's final game of the 1945 season.

Brown formed the nucleus of that first Browns team with players he had coached, coached against or scouted in high school, college and the service, including Graham, Motley, Groza, Lavelli, Willis and center Frank Gatski, all of whom would be inducted into the football Hall of Fame, as well as Speedie, halfback Edgar (Special Delivery) Jones and most of the rest of that first gathering.

It was one of the finest conglomerations of talent ever assembled—which pro football would learn only too soon. Perhaps with that in mind, AAFC Commissioner Jim Crowley (one of Notre Dame's legendary Four Horsemen) boasted before the start of the league's 1946 inaugural season, "We'll have

The 1952 Cleveland coaching staff included such impressive names as (left to right) Howard Brinker, Blanton Collier, Brown, Weeb Ewbank and Fritz Heisler.

better games and better teams than the NFL because our players are better."

Ironically, it was another former Horseman, NFL Commissioner Elmer Layden, who had fired a salvo that would ensure the rival leagues would experience anything but harmony. Asked whether the NFL would welcome interleague games with the AAFC, Layden snapped, "Tell them to get a football first, then play a game."

On June 4, 1944, Chicago Tribune sports editor Arch Ward had laid out plans for his newest brainchild in a meeting with prospective club owners at a St. Louis hotel. Ward, organizer of baseball's All-Star Game and the football College All-Star Game (the now defunct showcase held in Chicago that pitted the top graduating college seniors against the defending NFL champion), worked to place AAFC franchises for that first season in New York (Yankees), Brooklyn (Dodgers), Chicago (Rockets), Los Angeles (Dons) and four cities without NFL representation: San Francisco (49ers), Buffalo (Bisons), Miami (Seahawks) and Cleveland, which actually had an NFL franchise, the Rams, when the AAFC was nothing but a paper league. But after winning the NFL title in 1945, the Rams moved to Los Angeles, cast adrift in a sea of red ink.

Acting on the advice of Ward and another news-

paperman, John Dietrich of the Cleveland Plain Dealer, Cleveland multimillionaire Arthur (Mickey) McBride sought out Paul Brown as coach of his new AAFC franchise. It was a recommendation that would prove prophetic.

Brown already had a strong following in northern Ohio due to his success at Massillon but, more important, had begun to experiment with techniques that would revolutionize professional football. It was wartime now, and Brown was serving a two-year hitch as a coach at Great Lakes.

"There were no real pressures," Brown said years later, "so I did a lot of experimenting. I experimented with everything I was ever curious about in football. We did a lot of things that were different.

"I studied the T-formation in its looser aspects, getting away from the tight-T that was generally in use. We even did things with different kinds of stances. One year, our backs stood straight up; the next season, because of a flaw we found in studying movies, we switched to the three-point.

"Much of the stuff that we put in as new on the Browns in the All-America Conference, we'd worked on first with the Great Lakes team."

Brown, offered complete control of the Cleveland team as coach and general manager, was persuaded to sign, though he admitted, "I wasn't sure that I would like coaching the pros because I did not know if they would have the same kind of spirit."

"I am an amateur at heart," he told McBride, "and we'll probably be the most amateurish professional football team in the country."

That was the operative key for Brown, who wanted players with a love for the game, not of money.

The new league would open for business after World War II, when former college and NFL stars returned home from battlefields in Europe and the Pacific, or from "soft duty" on the football fields of America, playing for a number of powerful service teams that became a supply line for the AAFC. This fledgling league was willing to pay big money, enough to lure more than 100 former NFL players and many of the elite College All-Stars into the fold.

That Brown had the best team in the AAFC was partly due to his aggressive recruiting. Fully committed to building his postwar football power, he directed the foundation work from his post at Great Lakes, drawing from his mental catalog a list of prospects, many of them in the service and some of those with college eligibility remaining. Ohio State denounced Brown's tactics when he set his sights on a number of Buckeyes, including Lavelli and Groza, who received his first pro contract "while I was in Okinawa. I liked it. I was getting paid (extra) to be in combat."

"We're not trying to snatch athletes who want to return to college," Brown stated. "However, we're going to run our business aggressively—that means to win."

Brown's boldest stroke was his signing of Willis

The Browns' offensive triggerman through their dynasty years was quarterback Otto Graham (60), shown here breaking a long gain in an AAFC game against the New York Yankees.

Brown celebrates his first AAFC title in 1946 with Lou Rymkus (left), Edgar (Special Delivery) Jones (90) and other happy Cleveland players.

and Motley, the first blacks to compete in professional football since 1933 and the only two blacks to play in the AAFC that first season. "I didn't care what color they were . . . I wanted men of character who could play ball," Brown recalled. "I knew I was rocking the boat with that decision to invite Motley and Willis to our first camp."

To play for Brown, players had to accept strict discipline. There had to be obedience and loyalty. This was his code, and if anyone broke it, no matter how talented, he was gone. Future Hall of Fame defensive lineman Doug Atkins, the club's No. 1 draft pick in 1953, got into Brown's doghouse and was traded to the Chicago Bears after only two seasons.

Most of the Browns who had been mustered out of the service found themselves in something like another branch of the military. Each player at training camp carried a mimeographed schedule which detailed where he would be at a particular time. Every hour, every minute was accounted for: when, where and what a player would eat, when he would sleep, when he would get up, when he reported for taping, for practice, for meetings. Almost every facet of daily life was accounted for, except breathing. And the regimented Cleveland players may have wondered if Brown would regulate that,

too.

"Paul was very intense up until 10, 15 years ago," Lavelli said in a February 1989 interview. "He had complete, total dedication. He had horse blinders on—he knew nothing but football. Everybody knew about those beady eyes. He was always a detailed man. Little things became big things. If you were supposed to meet at 3 p.m., he wanted you there at 2:55.

"But I don't remember Paul swearing at a guy in 25 years. He'd give a look or make a biting remark, but he never swore. In those days, a coach had more control over a player's discipline. And Paul had 33 of *his guys*. Look at his success. Eleven of the first 23 Super Bowls were won by guys who played for Paul or who coached under him: Chuck Noll has won four, Bill Walsh three, Don Shula two, Weeb Ewbank one, Don McCafferty one."

"Paul was ahead of his time in teaching and organization," said Parseghian, who guided Notre Dame to national championships in 1966 and 1973. "It was classroom, then performance. It's a mistake for any coach to emulate anyone. There's only one Paul Brown, only one Red Blaik. But the singleness of purpose is what Paul brought to coaching—that football wasn't just a job, but something you gave your life to.

**Marion Motley (right), the Browns' bruising
fullback, follows Edgar Jones' block (above) in an
AAFC game against the Yankees.**

"Another thing that Paul taught me was not to
leave your game on the practice field. We had light
practices with the Browns on Thursdays and Fri-
days. While other coaches were beating their teams
to death during the week, Paul wanted his teams to
be at their absolute peak on Sunday."

Brown was most interested in the mental aspects
of football. He wanted to know how much the
mind could take, how much it could retain, how it
would react under pressure. "I'm not interested in
players who do not think," he said.

He tested his players constantly, on the practice
field and in the classroom. The Browns, who took
notes on everything, had to know their assignments
or there would be punishment; too many blown
assignments and there would be banishment.

"There was a time," Brown said in 1953, "when
all you had to know about a football player was
whether he was big, tough and fast. Now you have
to know whether he's *smart*, big, tough and fast."

Brown used the results of his intelligence tests to
separate every group of rookies into three classifica-
tions.

"The top third we want," he said. "The middle
third we want if they're good enough physically.
The lower third we don't want no matter what
their physical qualifications. They'd only hurt us.

One of Graham's talented targets was the aptly named Mac Speedie, a breakaway end who could also maneuver in heavy traffic.

Somewhere along the line, the dumb guy will get your football team into trouble—probably on the field, maybe off. We found we can't afford to fool around with him. He makes mistakes that beat you."

All things being equal, Brown focused on defense when it came to intelligence. That's where he wanted his smartest players.

"About the most an offensive mistake can cost you is a small loss of yardage or a failure to gain," he explained. "A defensive mistake can cost you a touchdown, and a touchdown can cost you a game."

Welcome to Pro Football 1A, Paul Brown professor. Attendance mandatory, tests frequent and failure imminent for those who will not—or cannot—do the required work.

And the final grades? In the four-year run of the AAFC, the Browns led in scoring defense every season and in passing defense three times, no small task in a league that had gifted passers in Y.A. Tittle, Frankie Albert, Glenn Dobbs and George Ratterman.

Brown made another thing crystal clear when the Browns first banded together at Bowling Green

University in the summer of 1946. "Our accent's on speed here," he said. "You can't lick speed, and we hope to present one of the fastest-moving elevens in pro football history."

The lords of the NFL snickered over that projection, those who even listened. Who does Paul Brown think he is, they told themselves, working in an inferior league with overinflated egos? But Brown wasn't blowing smoke. He knew what he had . . . and what he had was the perfect concept on how to build a winning football team.

"Everyone was pretty fast at his position," Lavelli remembered. "Paul picked players for positions by their builds. He built a team on speed and physique. We weren't bigger than other teams, but we were quicker, and that was the deciding factor in the second half of our games."

Given this club's hand-picked talent, however, most games were decided in quick fashion. The 1946 Browns came roaring out of the chute, drawing 60,135 fans (more than any NFL team ever had) to Cleveland Municipal Stadium to witness their 44-0 annihilation of Miami on September 6 in the first AAFC regular-season game. When the Browns capped a seven-game winning streak by beating Los

The other half of Cleveland's great receiving duo: sure-handed Dante Lavelli.

This young halfback went on to greater glory as coach at Notre Dame: Ara Parseghian.

Angeles, 31-14, in front of 71,134 hometown fans, NFL eyes popped.

Among those seven victories were two against the Yankees, who would wind up Eastern Division champions with a final 10-3-1 mark. After being thrashed, 24-7, in Cleveland in the first meeting, Yankee Coach Ray Flaherty, coach of the NFL's Washington Redskins from 1936 through 1942, berated his players for losing to "a Podunk team with a high school coach." That contemptuous remark found its way back to the Browns, who, after wrapping up the Western Division title with a 12-2 record, delighted in beating New York for the AAFC championship, 14-9.

The Browns' offense was virtually unstoppable that first season, scoring 423 points to set a pro mark (the 1941 Chicago Bears had set the NFL standard with 396 points in an 11-game season).

"Even more striking," the conference mused in its record book recapping the season, "was their avoidance of interception. Only seven out of 237 tosses were stolen. . . . This is particularly unusual in view of the fact that Otto Graham, ace Browns flinger, and his cohorts were usually shooting for big yardage when they passed—and long forwards are sup-

posed to be easy to intercept."

Otto Everett Graham Jr. was the first player Brown signed, which would prove portentous as Graham became the heart of the Cleveland dynasty. When he retired for good after the 1955 season, Cleveland's era as pro football's dominant team and Brown's era as a perennial championship coach were all but over.

"The test of a quarterback is where his team finishes," Brown said. "By that standard, Otto was the best of them all."

In a 10-season pro career, Graham quarterbacked the Browns to 10 championship game appearances and seven league titles. Nine times he was an all-league selection and five times the league leader in passing yardage.

He had been a single-wing tailback at Northwestern from 1941 through 1943 and had twice defeated Brown's Ohio State teams. Graham was a dangerous ballcarrier, blessed with the ability to throw while running right or left. He was extremely aggressive, but not overwrought with emotion. He was, in essence, the perfect candidate to deal the ball in Brown's T-formation offense.

"Otto is first of all a great passer," said Brown,

Special Delivery Jones was a double-threat halfback who could run over or around would-be tacklers . . .

who followed Graham's progress in the Navy's football program. "But, more than that, he has a good channel of thought, he has the peripheral vision, and he's the type of fellow personally who will create team spirit on a ball club."

"I could throw the ball as accurately as anyone who ever played," Graham allowed in a March 1989 interview, "(and) I was a good leader. I didn't chew guys out like Norm Van Brocklin or Bobby Layne. My leadership came from example, basically. I didn't drink or smoke. Never have. We won a lot, so guys looked up to me."

Some critics may have challenged Graham's achievements, contending that Brown called the offensive plays through his "messenger guards" that rotated on every play (another of the coach's inno-

vations). That was blown out of proportion, which Graham pointed out during his final season.

"In the first four years in the old league, I doubt if he ever called more than six, seven or eight plays a game," Graham said. "When we started off in the National League, he increased his calls, but not by much. The year before last (1953) I would say he called 50 percent of the plays, and last year 95 percent. It's his belief that the quarterback has enough responsibility out there without worrying about the selection of plays. I respect his opinion, but I disagree with him 100 percent and he knows it. . . .

"I believe these fellows playing pro ball are actually playing coaches. They're pros. They know a lot better than anyone else what they can do at a given moment. Lou Groza, for instance, might

. . . as well as catch Graham's passes as an extra receiver coming out of the backfield.

come back in a huddle and tell me that the opposition tackle is charging too hard and can be trapped. I want to call a play right then and there to take advantage of that situation.

"There were times when I ignored Paul's calls," he admitted. "When my plays worked, he didn't say much. When they didn't, he'd let me know about it."

Graham, a two-way player early in his career, was the consummate athlete by any standard. He was a consensus All-America in basketball (though not in football) at Northwestern and played one season for the Rochester Royals when they won the National Basketball League championship in 1945-46. Skeptics scoff at the notion that football players of yesteryear could hold up against today's bigger,

faster generation. The skeptics obviously never saw Graham play.

"I view Otto Graham as the absolute complete player," Parseghian said. "I'd match him with any quarterback today for touch and timing on the ball. They say that Joe Montana doesn't have the strongest arm, but he gets the ball into the end zone. Graham was the same way.

"If you couldn't catch Otto Graham's passes, you couldn't catch anyone's. He threw a beautiful ball. He had the ability to lead you perfectly, or to drop the ball just over the defenders into your hands. I don't think many of the players . . . could touch today's players, but Graham could touch them."

Make no mistake, Graham's talent was timeless, for true greatness knows no calendar. Graham was watching Super Bowl XXIII between San Francisco and Cincinnati when he heard his name mentioned. "The announcer said I had gained more yards (8.63) per pass attempt than any quarterback who ever played," he said. "I was amazed."

He shouldn't have been. But he rejects the thinking that he was the heart of the Browns, and that his retirement slowed down the team's pulse.

"It's like anything else—any team doesn't stay on top forever," he said. "They didn't just have me. I was one factor, but there were a lot of factors. We were a team all the way, and no team in history will do as well as we did. It's impossible in today's game."

By Graham's second season, however, there was no disputing that he was the guiding force of the Browns' offense. Voted the league's Most Valuable Player, he passed for a career-high 25 touchdowns (a figure he would match in 1948) and completed 60.6 percent of his attempts, helping Cleveland break the Sammy Baugh-led Redskins' all-time team record for passing accuracy. The Browns, who bettered another pro mark by amassing 5,547 yards in total offense (an average of 7.1 yards per play), finished the regular season with a 12-1-1 record, then stuck it to Flaherty and the Yankees once more, 14-3, in the league championship game in New York.

The Cleveland offense showed more imaginative flair that year, most particularly in a Novemeber 2 game against Buffalo. With the Browns backed up to their 1-yard line, Graham stunned his teammates by calling for a screen pass, floating a butterfly to Speedie over the end as the defense came blowing in. Speedie caught the ball on the goal line and raced down the sideline for a touchdown.

"Our plans permitted the quarterback to pass from any part of the field, including the times when we were deep in our own territory," Brown said years later. But, he added with a laugh, "I wouldn't expect that one to work very often. It was a terrible gamble, even for those days."

Speedie wound up leading the league in receiving, finishing just ahead of Lavelli, who had tied for the lead in the AAFC's first year. Both were named to the all-conference team after the season, an honor

Championship celebrations were an annual rite during Cleveland's AAFC days and Brown always enjoyed center stage. No. 20 is team captain Lou Saban.

many Browns had a lock on during the history of the All-America. After Graham, a selection each season, Cleveland had all-league performers in Motley (1946-47-48), Willis (1946-47-48), Speedie (1947-48-49), Lavelli (1946-47), tackle Lou Rymkus (1947-48) and linebacker Lou Saban (1949).

There was no way to hide it: The Browns were too talented, too good, too much. When they needed a big play, any number of men came through, right up until the final seconds when Groza would finish off an opponent if his teammates hadn't already done so.

Groza, pro football's first successful long-distance placekicker, wasn't a "specialist" by any stretch—he also happened to be an All-Pro offensive tackle six times in the Browns' first eight NFL seasons. "I kicked because I had the competitiveness," he reflected in retirement, "but my intent was to play tackle."

Limited to only three games of freshman football at Ohio State before entering the Army, Groza was principally a kicker in the Browns' first two seasons, learning the line play techniques of Brown's precision offense in practice and limited duty in games. He worked his way into the regular job at left tackle by his third season, contributing as much to the offense with his protection for Graham and blocking for Motley as he did with "The Toe," for which he will forever be linked.

Groza, an original Brown who outlasted Paul Brown in the organization, established his kicking supremacy in the AAFC's maiden season, booting 13 field goals and 45 extra points, pro records in both categories. When he wrapped up his 21-season career after the 1967 campaign, Groza was the NFL's all-time scoring leader and owner of a host of other records, including most games played, extra points made, field goals made and consecutive games scoring (107).

"I reasoned that there are just so many turnovers in football, just so many times when your offense has a chance to score," Brown said. "I wanted to take advantage of every possible opportunity.... That's where a long-range field-goal kicker like Groza helped us put a lot of games out of reach of the opposition which didn't have a kicker like him."

Groza boomed 51- and 50-yard field goals in just his first season, 53- and 51-yarders in 1948 (when he hit the crossbar on a 57-yard effort) and five more from at least 50 yards out in the NFL. That long-strike ability left even some of his teammates spellbound.

"I remember when the goal posts were on the goal line," Parseghian recalled. "One day, Groza lined up to kick a 53-yard field goal. I said, 'What's happening here? Do they have a trick play?' He made the kick, absolutely made it. I was seeing *a new game.*

"I always admired Groza, grinding away at tackle. Then if the drive stalled, he'd move back into a kicking position. Remember, this was a long time before the soccer-style kicker. You'd have shoes that weren't as clean, from playing in the mud and snow. Before Groza would kick, he'd take a towel and wipe off his shoes. He wasn't all clean and rehearsed like the kickers of today.

"And the kicking game not only had Groza, but Horace Gillom," Parseghian went on. "With most punters, the ball goes up and it comes down. But with Gillom, he'd just put the ball into orbit, it would level off and go for a while, and then it would come down. I'd match him with today's punters, all right."

Gillom, who lined up as much as 14 yards deep, kicked the ball for distance besides hanging it high. His longest NFL punt was 80 yards against the New York Giants in 1954. With his deep drop, the ball probably traveled 94 yards, nearly the length of a football field. He still holds the club record for career punting average (43.8 yards, not including AAFC totals) and backed up Speedie and Lavelli at end throughout his career.

A high school opponent of Brown's Massillon teams, Gillom joined Cleveland in 1947 along with linebacker Tony Adamle, another former Buckeye who made a profound impression on Parseghian.

"Saban and Adamle played linebacker and made most of the tackles," he recalled. "Adamle was a tough son of a gun, mentally and physically. He dressed once with an ankle as big as a balloon. I thought there was no way he'd play, but he did. There's *nobody* in the game today who's tougher than Tony Adamle."

Brown recognized that tenacity and appointed Adamle team captain after Saban retired following the 1949 season.

If Adamle would make it as a linebacker today, then pity anyone who took on Willis, who was lightning disguised as a lineman for the Browns from 1946 through 1953. "Bill Willis was about the first guy who convinced me that I couldn't handle any guy in the world," said Clyde (Bulldog) Turner, the Chicago Bears' Hall of Fame center.

At 6-foot-2 and 215 pounds, Willis was listed as a middle guard but became the pioneer of what is now the middle linebacker's position. At times the center of a five-man front, he often took advantage of his speed and agility by dropping back from the line and exploding toward the play.

"He was so quick, they just couldn't block him," Parseghian said. "He was gone. I mean, *gone.*"

A member of Brown's national championship team at Ohio State, Willis was brought out to Cleveland's first camp in 1946, when the racial conditions in pro football mirrored baseball's segregated look. Brown saw nothing in the AAFC constitution that barred blacks, however, and he had Willis suited up minutes after he arrived in camp. What Willis did next, to Browns center Mike Scarry, would be re-enacted against every center he ever faced.

"I watched the ball intently, and as soon as Scarry tightened his grip, I charged," Willis said. "For four, five minutes, I charged over, under and through Mike Scarry. The offense couldn't get a play off. One time, I landed on Otto Graham. Paul said, 'That's enough.' That night, he signed me to a contract."

Brown was colorblind. He signed Motley during that same camp and Gillom the following year. And although the Los Angeles Rams opened the door to blacks Woody Strode and Kenny Washington in 1946 to break the NFL's string of 12 seasons of all-white participation, the AAFC officially beat its rival to the punch, beginning league play three weeks earlier than the NFL.

As it turned out, the AAFC tried to beat Willis *with* the punch. Though the league office was becoming enlightened, the message hadn't reached some of the white players.

"They'd throw fists to the jaw, they'd step on you, throw elbows instead of trying to block you, clip you when you weren't looking," Willis said, the

Dynasty Data

Regular Season
Yearly Record
1946-1955

Season	W	L	T	Pct.	Avg. Score Clev.-Opp.	Place	Coach
1946	12	2	0	.857	30-10	1	Paul Brown
1947	12	1	1	.893	29-13	1	Paul Brown
1948	14	0	0	1.000	28-14	1	Paul Brown
1949	9	1	2	.833	28-14	1	Paul Brown
1950	10	2	0	.833	26-12	1†	Paul Brown
1951	11	1	0	.917	28-13	1	Paul Brown
1952	8	4	0	.667	26-18	1	Paul Brown
1953	11	1	0	.917	29-14	1	Paul Brown
1954	9	3	0	.750	28-14	1	Paul Brown
1955	9	2	1	.792	29-18	1	Paul Brown
Total	105	17	4	.849	28-14		

†Tied for position.

Playoffs

Season	Playoff	—(NFL (AAFC 1946-49)— Championship	Total Playoff Record
1946		14-9 N.Y. Yankees	1-0
1947		14-3 N.Y. Yankees	1-0
1948		49-7 Buffalo	1-0
1949	31-21 Buffalo	21-7 San Francisco	2-0
1950	8-3 N.Y.Giants	30-28 Los Angeles	2-0
1951		17-24 Los Angeles	0-1
1952		7-17 Detroit	0-1
1953		16-17 Detroit	0-1
1954		56-10 Detroit	1-0
1955		38-14 Los Angeles	1-0
Total			9-3

Additional Data

Best Record—1948 (14-0-0).
Worst Record—1952 (8-4-0).
Most Lopsided Victory—62-3 over Washington, 1954.
Most Lopsided Defeat—56-28 to San Francisco, 1949; 55-27 to Pittsburgh, 1954.
Most Consecutive Regular-Season Victories—16 games from Nov. 27, 1947 through Dec. 5, 1948.
Longest Regular-Season Undefeated Streak—27 games from Oct. 19, 1947 through Oct. 2, 1949 (25 wins, 2 defeats).
Most Consecutive Regular-Season Defeats—2 games from Oct. 27 through Nov. 3, 1946; Dec. 13, 1953 through Sept. 26, 1954; Dec. 19, 1954 through Sept. 25, 1955.
Shutouts—The Browns shut out their opponents 17 times.
Times Shut Out—The Browns were shut out only once—by the New York Giants in 1950.

All eyes watch Lou Groza's field goal sail through the uprights with 28 seconds remaining as the NFL newcomers post a 30-28 victory over the Los Angeles Rams in the 1950 title game.

taunts still with him more than 35 years after retiring. "Lou Rymkus told me that if anyone fouled me, 'Don't get into a fight. We'll take care of it.' But I never went to Lou. I had a rather devastating forearm. When I proved to guys that I could take it, things got much better."

Racial problems didn't exist on the Browns, Willis said. "I had played against most of these guys in the Big Ten, so it was like old home week when I joined the Browns. I've always said that the thread follows the needle. As Paul Brown reacted to myself, Motley and Gillom, the rest of the players had to follow. I was made to feel as important as Lou Groza and Otto Graham."

Willis lined up in a sprinter's stance, down on all fours, instead of the conventional three-point stance of the time.

"I was very strong for my size and, like I said, I had a pretty good forearm," he said. "I'd charge sometimes by using my left hand, but first I'd unleash a forearm and straighten the center up. Then I was by him. But I had a variety of charges. I'd go under the center—right through him—until he got lower and lower in his stance. When that happened, I'd spring like a cat and go right over the top. And in many instances, I wouldn't even be touched."

The Browns themselves were untouchable in 1948, so powerful that they survived the loss of Lavelli (to a broken leg) for nearly half the season and went undefeated in 14 games—three of which were scheduled within an eight-day span. The Browns beat the Yankees in New York on Sunday, No-

vember 21, flew to Los Angeles and beat the Dons on Thursday, Thanksgiving Day, then traveled to San Francisco and defeated the 49ers on Sunday, November 28. A week before the trip, 82,769 fans—the most ever to watch a pro football game—turned out at Municipal Stadium to watch the Browns and undefeated 49ers play for the Western Division lead.

Before the season, Brown dealt the draft rights to Michigan All-America back Bob Chappuis to Brooklyn for Dub Jones, a lanky 6-foot-4 halfback who would develop into a trusty running-receiving back for Cleveland through 1955. "Our best all-around receiver," Graham once said. "He could do everything. He had a good pair of hands, he was a very good faker ... he knew what he was doing all the time."

Hammering his way to 964 yards, Motley wrested the league's rushing title from two-time champion Spec Sanders of New York, Graham led in passing yardage and was named co-MVP (with the 49ers' Frankie Albert) and Speedie topped the AAFC in receptions. Buffalo claimed the Eastern Division title with a 7-7 record but was no match for the Browns in the title game, losing 49-7. Not until 1972, when the Miami Dolphins were 17-0 overall, was an NFL team able to sweep through a season undefeated and untied, including postseason play.

For the second consecutive year, the Browns' backfield excelled in the title matchup, with Motley rushing for 133 yards and three touchdowns and "Special Delivery" Jones running for one score and catching a pass for another. In the 1947 championship against New York, Motley had carried for 109 yards, but Jones delivered the death knell with a third-quarter touchdown run, the final points in Cleveland's 14-3 victory.

"Jones wasn't particularly fast," Graham would remember, "but he was a great money player, always good for short yardage. He could really cut and he was a rough one to bring down."

The AAFC had completed its third season and three things had become obvious: The league had no stability, the Browns were too overpowering and, consequently, killing off interest in the league.

The Miami Seahawks had folded at the end of the first season and been replaced by the Baltimore Colts, who would undergo a change of ownership before their second season. The Chicago Rockets, a new coach (or committee of coaches) at the helm every year, became the Hornets in 1949, when ownership changed hands—for the third time. Branch Rickey stepped in to run the struggling Dodgers in 1948. The AAFC had a merry-go-round look, but wasn't getting any closer to grabbing the brass ring.

Before the start of the 1949 season, O.O. (Scrappy) Kessing became the league's third commissioner, taking over with these memorable words: "Our league is not dead, not dying and not going to die." After Kessing cleared his throat, the AAFC dropped its two-division format when only seven teams could suit up for 1949, the Dodgers and Yankees having merged their listing ships.

Scrappy's words notwithstanding, the AAFC was dying—and almost dead—save for two viable franchises: Cleveland and San Francisco. Paced by a high-octane attack, the 49ers had set pro records for total points and offense in 1948, and their four-year AAFC regular-season record of 38-14-2 ranks second only to the Browns' 47-4-3 mark. The 49ers' dealt the Browns two of their four losses, including one in 1949 that brought out the wrath of Paul Brown.

On October 9 in San Francisco, the 49ers crushed Brown's forces, 56-28, snapping Cleveland's 29-game unbeaten streak that stretched back into the 1947 season (including two championship-game victories). Appearing calm after the game, Brown told reporters, "The pressure of that streak is off. We ought to be all right now." But on the flight out of San Francisco, he went on a tirade. He threatened firings, releases, trades. He accused the Browns of becoming bigheaded and vowed to make them pay in practice—those players he decided to keep around.

Brown's invective in the suddenly unfriendly skies was reported nationally and brought him considerable criticism. Here was a coach whose team was running roughshod over a crumbling league, and one rare defeat had turned him against his players. What more could one tyrant want?

As always, Brown knew precisely what he was doing. The following Sunday, the Browns ripped into the Los Angeles Dons, who served as innocent,

though convenient, scapegoats for Brown's fury. Fists and elbows flew. Faces were bloodied. Cleveland was assessed a league-record 16 penalties but set a team scoring record in bludgeoning the Dons, 61-14. A week later, Cleveland exacted revenge on the 49ers, but barely, 30-28, before 72,189 at Municipal Stadium.

Aside from that one 49ers game, however, the Browns averaged just over 23,000 fans for five other home games; in 1946, the average draw had been more than 57,000.

"We were too good, if that sounds possible," Brown said. "Even in Cleveland, the fans stopped coming because they just assumed we'd go out and dominate the opposition so strongly, there would be no contest."

The Browns finished 9-1-2 in their final AAFC season, with Graham again leading the league in passing yardage and Speedie in receptions. Both finished as the AAFC career leaders in their respective statistical categories, with Motley first in rushing. Only 22,550 fans turned out at Municipal Stadium on December 11 to watch the Browns methodically wear down the visiting 49ers, 21-7, in the final AAFC championship game.

Thus, the AAFC died with Scrappy's words as its epitaph.

Three teams would be brought in out of the cold by the NFL: Baltimore, San Francisco and, naturally, Cleveland, "The one prize the National League wants," wrote Gordon Cobbledick of the Cleveland Plain Dealer. And the league wasted little time in testing this much touted franchise, scheduling the Browns against the Philadelphia Eagles, the NFL champions the previous two seasons, in the very first game of the 1950 NFL season. It was put-up or shut-up time.

"This was the highest emotional game I ever coached," Brown said. "We had four years of constant ridicule to get us ready."

The game would be played in Philadelphia, without a trace of brotherly love. Reputations had to be defended, or proved. The Browns were from a "Humpty Dumpty league," while the Eagles were represented by future Hall of Famers in Steve Van

Cleveland vs. Most Frequent Opponents

(5 or More Regular-Season Games)
(1946-1955)

Opponent	League	W	L	T	Pct.	Avg. Score Cle.-Opp.
Chicago Cardinals	NFL	12	0	0	1.000	29-14
Chi. Rockets/Hornets	AAFC	8	0	0	1.000	30-12
Baltimore Colts	AAFC-NFL	7	0	0	1.000	27-5
Brooklyn Dodgers	AAFC	6	0	0	1.000	37-13
New York Yankees	AAFC	7	0	1	.938	25-10
Pittsburgh Steelers	NFL	11	1	0	.917	30-16
Washington Redskins	NFL	10	1	0	.909	34-14
Buffalo Bisons/Bills	AAFC	6	0	2	.875	30-13
Los Angeles Dons	AAFC	7	1	0	.875	30-14
San Francisco 49ers	AAFC-NFL	9	3	0	.750	24-20
Philadelphia Eagles	NFL	8	4	0	.667	23-18
New York Giants	NFL	7	4	1	.625	21-15

One of the toughest and most tenacious of Cleveland's defenders was linebacker Tony Adamle, the team captain in 1950.

Buren (who would miss the game to injury), Pete Pihos, Alex Wojciechowicz, Chuck Bednarik and their coach, Earle (Greasy) Neale.

The Eagles had shut down the Los Angeles Rams, 14-0, for the 1949 NFL championship and were convinced they'd teach Cleveland the same kind of humility. But the Browns were ready not only for the Eagle defense, but the "Eagle Defense": a 5-4 alignment that had outside linebackers "chucking" the ends. The defense became popular with virtually every other coach, pro and college, of the era. Except Brown, that is. Its problem against both the run and pass, he said, was the lack of a middle linebacker.

"We began spreading our offensive line a few inches on each play," he revealed years later. "Of course, their defensive linemen took post on the shoulder of an offensive man, so they began to spread, too. Before long that big middle guard was isolated over the center with no one in position to help him."

The Browns had the perfect play to attack the Eagles' vulnerable middle—the draw—and the perfect man to execute it—the bruising, overpowering Motley, who would lead the NFL in rushing in his first try with 810 yards, and set a standing NFL single-game record when he averaged 17.09 yards a carry against Pittsburgh (11 carries, 188 yards).

The Browns' draw play happened by accident one day in the AAFC. "Otto got such a hard rush that he handed the ball to Motley in desperation," Brown recalled. "The defense had overrun Motley in their desire to get to the quarterback, and Marion swept right through them for a big gain. We looked at the play again and decided it couldn't help but work. In a short time, it became Marion's most dangerous weapon."

Weighing nearly 240 pounds, the 6-1 Motley was bigger than some linemen and most linebackers (where he also played) of the age. Seeing him blast through the line and into the secondary with a full head of steam gave smaller defensive backs pause.

"Motley had quick feet and great running sense," Parseghian remembered. "A great back is one who comes into the line and still makes yardage even if the hole is one hole away. The lousy back is the one who runs up your back. Motley could bowl you over, but he could also find the hole. That's why he'd be a great back today."

A member of Brown's Great Lakes team, Motley was the Browns' leading rusher in six of his eight seasons in Cleveland and averaged 5.7 yards per carry in his pro career; Jim Brown, who would arrive as a Browns rookie in 1957, holds the NFL career mark with 5.2 yards per attempt.

Cleveland's offense was, essentially, Motley and Graham working in tandem: Motley was a devastating pass-blocker for Graham; Graham used the pass fake to turn loose Motley on the draw. Brown loved to misdirect defenders and trap them. Thus, his reputation grew as a "pass-and-trap coach."

"All right, so I'm a pass-and-trap coach," he said

during those dynasty years. "But any coach having Graham and Motley would do what we do. With that kind of passer, and with that big Motley to protect Graham or go up the middle, a guy would be daffy not to pass and trap. Why it got so in the last couple of years that our opponents were packing the middle with three men to stop Motley on our draw plays. That was good, because then we could run our halfbacks outside."

Or flip a flare pass to one angling out of the backfield. The Browns' halfbacks carried the ball randomly, but they were used often in the team's passing scheme.

"Paul always said, 'Let them choose their weapons,'" Graham said, reflecting back to those glory days. "If they decided to drop back to stop the pass, then we ran up the middle. And if they decided to stay up close and stop the draw or trap, then we threw over them."

With everything in place—the talent and the perfect game plan—the Browns met the Eagles in a showdown of the two best teams from two different leagues. "It was really like a war," Lavelli remembered. "Like jump-off time on D-day." Only this clash was as one-sided and short-lived as the Six-Day War. The Browns pummeled the Eagles, 35-10, before a stunned crowd of 71,237.

After Philadelphia took a 3-0 lead in the first quarter, Graham connected with Dub Jones on a 59-yard scoring pass. And before the Eagles managed their lone touchdown in the fourth quarter, Graham had thrown scoring strikes of 26 yards to Lavelli and 13 yards to Speedie—pro football's first pair of great ends.

Lavelli had great hands, deceptive moves and, although other receivers had bigger numbers, was the best third-down receiver of his era. Speedie had abounding talent as well, although his forte was—what else—speed.

"It's hard to separate Speedie and Lavelli, but of the two, I would say Mac had more natural ability than Dante," Graham said near the end of his career. "He was a better faker and made everything look easy. On the other hand, although Dante had to work harder, he would catch a ball a lot better than Mac. Let's say I threw a looper. Dante would go up in the air flailing his arms and legs, but he would be more apt to come down with the ball . . . he had a stronger pair of hands."

"There was," said Lavelli, "a saying back then: 'When in doubt, down and out to Lavelli.'"

Graham, Motley, Speedie, Lavelli, Dub Jones. . . . Cleveland simply had too many weapons for even the talented Eagles. The Browns passed and trapped for 487 yards against Neale's Eagle defense, using Motley selectively (11 carries for 48 yards) to set up the pass. Graham completed 21 of 38 attempts for 346 yards, showing the Eagles a passing technique they'd never encountered—a quarterback throwing to a spot, instead of a man.

"We would be on top of receivers," said Philadelphia defensive back Russ Craft, "but they caught

Dub Jones, a trusty, do-everything halfback for the Browns and father of Bert Jones, an NFL quarterback for 10 seasons.

the ball anyway because the pass was so well-timed."

A lot of faces from the AAFC wore "I-told-you-so" smiles that day.

The Browns and Eagles would cross paths again in 1950 . . . and again the Browns had something to prove. Brown, stung when some Eagles knocked him as the coach of "a basketball team," refused to let Graham throw a pass in the rematch, and Cleveland knocked off the Eagles using only a ground game, 13-7. Point proven.

The Browns had bolstered their already formidable ranks for the NFL wars, having claimed hard-rushing defensive end Len Ford, another future Hall of Famer, from the Los Angeles Dons and, from Buffalo, guard Abe Gibron, a Pro Bowl selection in four of his seven seasons in Cleveland.

Brown's troops breezed through their schedule with a 10-2 record, suffering both defeats at the hands of the New York Giants: a 6-0 loss in the third week (the first time Cleveland had ever been shut out) and a 17-13 beating three weeks later. The two teams wound up tied for first in the league's American Conference, but Groza booted the Giants out of the championship picture with two field goals in a postseason playoff. His 28-yard field goal snapped a 3-3 tie with 58 seconds remaining, and the Browns added a safety moments later to set up, in Paul Brown's words, "the greatest game I've ever seen."

That would be the 1950 NFL championship game, Browns vs. Rams, Cleveland's thriving monarchs vs. Cleveland's former paupers. It would be the Rams' first return visit to their roots, a wild-west homecoming played out in Browns weather (numbing cold) on Browns turf (the frozen playing field of Municipal Stadium).

These Rams, however, knew what to do with a football, whatever the conditions. They had Hall of Fame-bound quarterbacks in veteran Bob Waterfield and Norm Van Brocklin and future Hall of Fame receivers in Elroy (Crazylegs) Hirsch and Tom Fears. The game was only 27 seconds old when Waterfield teamed up with Army's former "Mr. Outside," Glenn Davis, on an 82-yard touchdown pass. Graham responded in kind, however, with a scoring strike to Dub Jones on Cleveland's first possession.

Thus, a back-and-forth offensive mode was established. Los Angeles' Dick Hoerner scored on a plunge, Graham twice passed to Lavelli for touchdowns and Hoerner scored again on a plunge midway through the third quarter. On Cleveland's first play from scrimmage following the ensuing kickoff, however, Motley fumbled, and Los Angeles' Larry Brink picked up the ball and lumbered into the end zone. Waterfield's conversion put the Rams ahead by more than a touchdown, 28-20.

To the Browns' dismay, a bad snap on the conversion attempt following Lavelli's first touchdown now loomed larger than ever. But Graham would not be denied, and Cleveland cut the Los Angeles

Guard Abe Gibron (above) and end Len Ford (below): two tough men in the trenches during the Browns' NFL glory years.

Lou Groza (right) with Philadelphia's Chuck Bednarik and Pro Bowl director Paul Schissler receiving the 1955 Most Valuable Player award presented by The Sporting News.

lead to one point when Otto flung his fourth touchdown pass, this time to Rex Bumgardner, and Groza added the extra point midway through the final period.

Late in the quarter, Graham drove the Browns toward pay dirt again, only to fumble as he scrambled for a first down across the Rams' 21. "All of a sudden I was blind-sided," he said. "I wanted to dig a hole right in the middle of that stadium, crawl into it and bury myself forever."

But the Browns' defense held at this point, getting the ball back into Graham's hands with 1:48 to play. Starting from his own 32-yard line, Graham scrambled for 14 yards, then completed three consecutive passes to move the ball to the Los Angeles 11. On a quarterback sneak, he gained another yard but, more important, moved the ball to the center of the field.

Time out. Twenty-eight seconds remained. As Groza dropped back for a decisive field-goal attempt, the celebration started.

"Guys were jumping up and down on the sideline even before I kicked," Groza said. "I didn't see it because I was concentrating on kicking. The field was frozen."

But the Browns knew their man. Rain, mud, ice, snow—Groza always delivered. He thumped it through and Cleveland had won its fifth straight championship, 30-28. Brown's Browns: champions in any league, by any measure.

"It was really a glorious occasion," Groza recalled warmly. "My biggest thrill? Oh, yes, because it had so much writing on the cake."

Writing, frosting ... what did it matter. The Browns, once doubted, were now truly redoubtable. Of all his great Cleveland teams, Brown remembers his 1950 squad most fondly. "The game has changed, and players are bigger, faster and stronger," he said years later. "But there will never be a better group for love of the game and desire to win."

The Browns rolled to the American Conference title again in 1951, winning their final 11 games after losing the season opener to their old foes, the 49ers. On November 25, Dub Jones took the Chicago Bears apart almost single-handedly, scoring six touchdowns to tie Ernie Nevers' single-game NFL record. "He fools you because of the way he's con-

Lavelli hauls in a 50-yard touchdown pass from Graham in the Browns' 1955 NFL title-game victory over the Rams.

structed," Brown said after the game. "He doesn't look strong enough to stand the punishment the backs absorb in this league. But Dub has the speed, the guts and the know-how of a great player."

The Browns met the Rams once again for the title, this time in Los Angeles, but the Rams pulled out a 24-17 victory on Van Brocklin's 73-yard touchdown pass to Fears with 7:25 to play.

That defeat would have a carry-over effect. The Browns returned to the championship game in 1952 and 1953, but were beaten each time by Bobby Layne and the Detroit Lions, 17-7 and 17-16, respectively. In the 1953 matchup, Graham completed only two of 15 passes for 20 yards. "This is the worst I've felt in my life," he said afterward.

It wasn't a good time for the team in general. Though they were a combined 19-5 over those two seasons, the Browns were going through changes. After the 1951 season, three of Cleveland's biggest contributors had retired—Adamle (who would come back for 1954), Rymkus and Cliff Lewis, who had been Graham's backup but also a defensive whiz who intercepted more passes (24) in the AAFC than any other player. Brown would pick up insurance at quarterback by acquiring George Ratterman, the Notre Dame product who had starred with Buffalo in the All-America.

Speedie had jumped to Canada after the 1952 season. So had dependable tackle John Kissell, who would rejoin the Browns in 1954. Motley and Willis played their last games for Cleveland in 1953, as did two other original Browns, guard Lin Houston and defensive end George Young. Future Hall of Famer Mike McCormack would offset the loss of Willis, but the remaining Cleveland players nevertheless were reading that the team was too old, that the dynasty was on the brink of collapse.

But Paul Brown had told something to his team many times. "Paul said to hold ourselves up as the (baseball) Yankees of football," Groza remembered. "And that's what we did."

The thing about dynasties, outside of their dominance, is that they don't disintegrate immediately upon speculation. They have a staying power, an ability to rejuvenate, that isn't easily detected by the common eye.

After a 1-2 start in 1954, the Browns won eight in a row and rolled to another conference title, meeting Detroit in the NFL championship game for the third consecutive year. The Lions, fresh off a last-minute, 14-10 victory over the Browns in the final game of the season, executed a mastery over Cleveland that had long ago passed the frustration stage for the Brown players. Cleveland had never beaten Detroit in regular or postseason play, its lone victory against the Lions coming in a 1950 preseason contest.

The Lions saw a different Cleveland team this time, and a true-to-form Graham. Otto the Great, playing in what he said would be his last game, threw for three touchdowns and ran for another three himself, and the Browns made Detroit pay

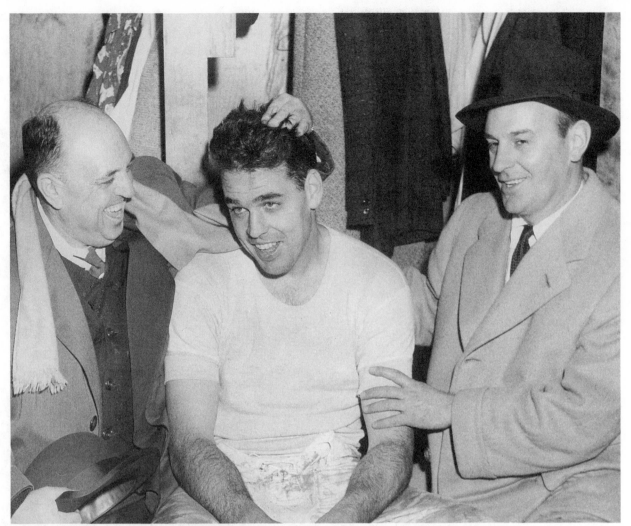

Graham (center) with Otto Graham Sr. (left) and Brown after Cleveland's 1955 title-game victory, the quarterback's last professional game.

badly for the past, 56-10.

Although Graham had announced that the 1954 season would be his last, Brown coaxed him back into uniform when Cleveland got off to a rocky start during the 1955 exhibition season. Without the benefit of training camp, the amazing Graham not only led the league in passing (based on average gain, 8.33 yards per attempt), but directed the Browns to the league's best record, 9-2-1. Playing the Rams for the championship in Los Angeles, Graham closed out his career by passing for two touchdowns—including a 50-yarder to Lavelli—and running for two more in a 38-14 pasting of the Rams.

Ten years, 10 trips to the throne room, seven crowns. Then the castle changed its locks. The Browns would make it back to the NFL championship game (excluding conference championship games in the Super Bowl-era seasons of 1968 and 1969) only three times over the next 33 years, the last in 1965. Well, there's only one Otto Graham.

Paul Brown was forced out as coach of the Browns following the 1962 season after a falling out with new Owner Art Modell. Five years later,

Brown was inducted into the Hall of Fame. He was, however, by no means retired, and one year later, in 1968, was coaching the American Football League's Cincinnati Bengals—the second franchise he helped found. In the Bengals' first year in the NFL, 1970, Brown guided Cincinnati to the AFC Central Division title.

Brown coached the Bengals for eight seasons, stepping down after Cincinnati posted an 11-3 mark as division champions in 1975. He moved into the Bengals' front office as vice president and general manager, overseeing an organization that reached the Super Bowl twice in the 1980s. Each time, the Bengals were turned back at the summit by Brown's old AAFC rival, the 49ers, 26-21 in January 1982, and 20-16 in January 1989, when Brown was 80.

In an interview with the Cincinnati Post prior to Super Bowl XXIII, Brown agreed that he'd like to add a Super Bowl title to his long list of achievements. "It doesn't have to be for Paul Brown . . . I'd like it for the players and coaches."

It was vintage Paul Brown. A man who never forgot a player.

NEW YORK
ISLANDERS
1979·80 to 1982·83

Two players who figured prominently in the Islanders' four-year
Stanley Cup reign were left wing/center John Tonelli (left) and
nonpareil defenseman Denis Potvin.

I t was the changing of the guard, the end of one era and the dawn of another.

New York Islanders defenseman Denis Potvin had just exchanged the traditional handshake that ends the hockey season. In each of the previous four years, he had passed through the line receiving congratulations for helping the Islanders win the Stanley Cup. But on this sultry spring night of May 19, 1984, as Northlands Coliseum in Edmonton throbbed in celebration, Potvin had marked the end of the Islanders' dynasty by extending his hand and congratulations to Wayne Gretzky and the Edmonton Oilers.

"I feel I've been part of something special," Potvin said. "To turn the Cup over to the Oilers is no shame at all. When I went through the line shaking hands at the end of the game, their players said how much they had idolized us. Wayne Gretzky said that. It made me proud. One great hockey team passed the torch to a team that deserved to win."

It wasn't just the torch and a symbolic silver trophy that was passed on, but a legacy perhaps no other team could uphold as the Islanders had.

Granted, the Oilers would usher in a new game in the National Hockey League, winning three more Stanley Cups over the next four seasons with a sleek offensive attack that was artistry in motion. They were the forefathers of the generation of speed skaters who would revolutionize the sport, weaving and circling and tying everything together with precision passing.

But the Islanders were throwbacks to another era, a blend of styles like the old Montreal Canadiens. And there is no denying the bottom line: Since the NHL was organized for the 1917-18 season, only the Islanders and Canadiens have won as many as four consecutive Stanley Cups.

In more ways than one, New York may have been the last of the great, old teams. The Islanders played defense the way it had been played in the frontier days before helmets and goalie masks. They threw bone-crunching body checks in their own end of the ice, and their defensemen, with few exceptions, remained tethered to the front of the net.

Sure, the Islanders could score, seemingly at will and especially on the power play. But they were more deadly than flashy, with a patent on teamwork and confidence. "A lot of teams kept wondering why we went on winning for so long, saying we weren't that good," recalled forward Bob Bourne, an Islander for 12 seasons. "But we *were* that good, and the reason we won all those years is that we believed it when no one else did."

Under Coach Al Arbour, they frustrated and ultimately defeated opponents with a brand of hockey built on close checking and positional play, a competitive appetite honed by hard work, and the unity created by General Manager Bill Torrey, who built the club from the infancy of expansion in 1972.

By the time they arrived, winning their first Stanley Cup in 1980, four original Islanders remained

Bring Fourth The Cup

By Pat Calabria

from the team's first season, and most of the rest were veterans of what was a painstaking struggle first to win respectability, and then a championship.

"One ingredient that people forget to mention about those great teams is that many, many of the players were involved in the franchise from the first or second or third years," Torrey recalled. "They went through the bad times, the team got better, and when we started to win, a lot of those players were bonded by the process. It was sort of like being in the Army together, going through boot camp and doing battle, getting wounded. Then you come home and you say to the buddies in your platoon, 'Gosh, look what we went through.'"

Torrey, who was born across the street from the Montreal Forum, was the first employee hired by Islanders Owner Roy Boe in February 1972. "Right from the start I committed myself to a definite youth program," he said. "I told Roy to expect nothing from the expansion draft. I even told him we'd have to get rid of most of the players we picked up in that draft just as fast as we could."

Formerly the vice president of the Oakland Seals, Torrey set realistic goals. "Nobody expects us to be a Cup contender next year," he said, "but in three to five years, we should be doing respectably."

Torrey's mission was to build a reliable defense, find a young goalie who might blossom into stardom, and only then turn his attention to goal scorers. With patience as his virtue, he would develop that talent through the amateur draft, stockpiling his picks and consenting to trades only when he was certain to get the best of the deal.

Torrey got off to a tremendous start. He landed Billy Smith, a 21-year-old goaltender with the Los Angeles Kings, in the 1972 expansion draft, and center Lorne Henning, right wing Bob Nystrom and left wing Garry Howatt (all members of the first Cup team) in the amateur draft.

He laid the foundation for his defense with one stroke in 1973, selecting Potvin—already heralded as the next coming of Bobby Orr—with the No. 1 pick in the draft. A year later, he turned his attention to offense, picking bruising left wing Clark Gillies in the first round, then Bryan Trottier, an unsung 17-year-old center who was passed over 21 times before Torrey stole him in the second round. With pick No. 214, he added slick-passing defenseman Stefan Persson, a former member of the Swedish national team who would become a fixture on the power play.

His offensive coup came in 1977, however, when sharpshooter Mike Bossy was had with the 15th pick in the draft. Bossy would score 53 goals in his first season (a standing NHL rookie record) and become the third of Torrey's draft picks (along with Potvin and Trottier) to win the Calder Trophy as the league's top rookie.

The Islanders' first Stanley Cup championship team included 17 players developed through the draft and only five—most notably center Butch Goring—who arrived by trade. Torrey, in search of that commodity that inexperienced draft picks rarely offer ("character," he called it) tearfully parted with right winger Billy Harris, his first pick in the Islanders' first amateur draft, and defenseman Dave Lewis to obtain Goring from Los Angeles as the Islanders sputtered down the stretch in 1980. Goring made his presence felt without wasting time. "Logically and realistically," he told reporters after his first game as an Islander, "I think we can win the Cup this year."

The Isles were a team without an exploitable weakness—a balanced combination of talent, toughness and character.

In Bossy, the Islanders had the league's highest-scoring right wing, a sniper with a quick wrist shot who would score more than 50 goals in each of his first nine seasons (an NHL record) and net 573 in his career, sixth on the NHL's all-time scroll. "I hardly ever look when I take a shot," he once said. "I don't look for a goalie's weakness. If I shoot it quickly enough, it doesn't matter where he's strong or weak, it will end up in the net."

In Trottier, they boasted the league's best two-way center, a deft puck-handler who made twisting, eye-opening turns that left goaltenders confused—and ultimately victimized. A gifted playmaker, he also would score 30 or more goals 11 times and become the team's all-time scoring leader.

In Gillies, the club had a frightening and physical left wing who battled for goals in the trenches or, when challenged, knocked out opponents. In Goring, a pesky checker, clutch face-off man and expert penalty killer. In "Battlin' Billy" Smith, the best goaltender in playoff history, a feisty netminder who would win 88 postseason games (an NHL record) and wield his stick like a sword to protect his crease.

And in Potvin, the Islanders had the league's most adept defenseman, the cornerstone of the franchise for 15 seasons. Forever compared to Orr, Potvin was judged a better passer, a more physical checker and more defensive-minded than the Bruins' spectacular No. 4, who was regarded as more innovative, a better skater and more dangerous offensively. Yet Potvin became the only defenseman to tally 1,000 points in a career, eclipsing Orr's record for career goals by a defender (310 to 270) along the way. Throughout his career, Potvin was a superb navigator for a ruthless power play.

More than anything, it was the ferocity of the power play that set the Islanders apart from the rest of the league. In the 1980 Stanley Cup finals, they would score 15 power-play goals in six games, the standing NHL record for one playoff series, then 31 power-play goals altogether in the 1981 playoffs, another standing mark.

"When the Islanders are on the power play," Vancouver Canucks goalie John Garrett once remarked, "it's like sharks at a feeding frenzy." And for mealtime music, the organ at Nassau Coliseum pounded out the ominous theme from the movie "Jaws"—Da-dum . . . Da-dum . . . Da-dum—whenever the Islanders gained a man advantage.

What's more, the Islanders had an effective and exciting penalty-killing unit, one that would set records in both the 1980 and 1981 playoffs for short-handed goals (seven and nine, respectively) with the likes of Goring, Bourne, Trottier and unsung players such as Anders Kallur and Billy Carroll.

There were fourth-line reserves who delivered

Dynasty Data
Yearly Record
1979-80 to 1982-83

Season	W	L	T	Points	GF	GA	—Finish— Div.	Overall	Coach
1979-80	39	28	13	91	281	247	2	5	Al Arbour
1980-81	48	18	14	110	355	260	1	1	Al Arbour
1981-82	54	16	10	118	385	250	1	1	Al Arbour
1982-83	42	26	12	96	302	226	2	6	Al Arbour

Playoffs

Season	Preliminary Round	Quarterfinals	Semifinals	Stanley Cup Finals	Total Playoff Record
1979-80	3-1 vs. Los Angeles	4-1 vs. Boston	4-2 vs. Buffalo	4-2 vs. Philadelphia	15-6
1980-81	3-0 vs. Toronto	4-2 vs. Edmonton	4-0 vs. N.Y. Rangers	4-1 vs. Minnesota	15-3
1981-82	3-2 vs. Pittsburgh	4-2 vs. N.Y. Rangers	4-0 vs. Quebec	4-0 vs. Vancouver	15-4
1982-83	3-1 vs. Washington	4-2 vs. N.Y. Rangers	4-2 vs. Boston	4-0 vs. Edmonton	15-5
					60-18

Additional Data

Best Season—1981-82 (54-16-10).
Worst Season—1979-80 (39-28-13).
Best Records vs. Opponents—15-2-1 vs. Colorado-New Jersey (8-2-1 vs. Col., 7-0-0 vs. N.J.); 11-3-0 vs. Toronto; 10-2-2 vs. Chicago.
Worst Records vs. Opponents—4-9-1 vs. Boston; 5-8-1 vs. Buffalo; 4-4-6 vs. Minnesota.

General Manager Bill Torrey (left) built the Islander machine that captured four straight Stanley Cups. Coach Al Arbour (right) was the technician who made it run smoothly.

when called upon, and an anonymous collection of defenders who were shaped into a tough, fearless unit. With the notable exception of Potvin, the Islanders' defense in their first championship year consisted of such uncelebrated players as Bob Lorimer, Dave Langevin, Ken Morrow and Gord Lane.

"If I had to put my finger on something that strikes me about those teams, it would not be the great players we had," Bossy said. "What made us stand apart is the great role players we had—guys who really understood they had a role to play and understood that role was really important, even if it wasn't the most glamorous job. Most teams don't have players like that, or can't get them."

It was, then, entirely appropriate that Henning—an original Islander but by 1980 a spare center—began the play that resulted in an overtime goal by Nystrom—another original and a plugger who never scored more than 30 goals in a season—to seal the club's first Stanley Cup.

The Islanders—individually or collectively—never did suffer from identity crises, not even during their dreadful first season. They were bad, and they knew it.

"We used to face 50, 60 shots some games, but I had no complaints," Smith said. "I was fighting and enjoying it. The fans liked it; they knew they were

getting their money's worth. There was no pressure. How can you put pressure on a team that's completely awful?

"We were the biggest joke going, and even the players knew it. You'd go into a game knowing it was going to be a bombing. The idea was lose, but lose honorably."

And the Islanders had no peers when it came to losing. Fifty games into their first season, Coach Phil Goyette was fired after winning only six times. The Isles finished 12-60-6, the worst record in NHL history at the time. The NHL's other expansion entry, the Atlanta Flames, posted a 25-38-15 mark.

"I don't think I went into a city where I didn't see the headline, 'Hapless Islanders,'" Torrey said. "I thought they were talking about some town in Long Island I hadn't heard about."

The Islanders knew their place in the New York hockey hierarchy—as subordinates to the rival Rangers, who played a slap shot away in the world-renowned palace of Madison Square Garden, in front of a faithful following and a roster of celebrities. The Rangers had a deep, if checkered, history as one of the NHL's earliest franchises. The Ranger sweater had been worn by Hall of Famers Lynn Patrick, Bryan Hextall and Andy Bathgate, just to name a few.

Four of the Islanders' top guns: (left to right) center Bryan Trottier, Potvin, left wing/center Bob Bourne and right wing Mike Bossy.

In contrast, the Islanders' home ice, Nassau Coliseum, was a quiet, antiseptic arena, located not in a bustling city but on a stretch of Long Island plain, not far from where a young pilot named Charles Lindbergh took off for Paris in the "Spirit of St. Louis" in 1927. Even after the Islanders in their very first playoff series upset a veteran Ranger team in 1975, the club didn't easily cultivate its own legion of fans. Many of the Coliseum seats were, in fact, occupied by longtime Ranger fans who couldn't get tickets to the Garden.

"For a long time, we were the new kids on the block, that team from the suburbs," Bourne said. "We were stuck with that tag."

Torrey didn't deny the image, running a franchise that was short on capital and sparse in glamour. Where other teams beat drums and turned on spotlights for special occasions and pregame introductions, the Islanders never followed suit. Torrey invested much of his time on scouting trips, resisting temptations to deal youth or draft picks for jaded veterans. "The people in New York thought

we were brand X compared to the Rangers," he said. "So we could afford to be brand X for a while."

Boe, who had paid $6 million for the franchise and a few million more as indemnity to the Rangers for invasion of their New York territory, never questioned Torrey's plan. "I knew I had to be patient," he said. "It was like raising children. Bill's philosophy was to go with the youngsters, and I agreed that was where our future would be."

The club made a giant leap forward before the start of its second season, recruiting Arbour as coach and securing Potvin with the No. 1 pick in the draft. Arbour was a defensive fundamentalist, a former defenseman on three Stanley Cup winners who had also coached the St. Louis Blues for parts of three seasons.

"That was a very, very important move," Torrey said. "That first training camp with Al was like boot camp. I can remember Ralph Stewart literally crawling off the ice one day, and guys like (Ed) Westfall were bitching something awful. That was

One of Torrey's key picks in the 1972 expansion draft was Billy Smith, who would become the winningest goaltender in playoff history.

the sign we were getting somewhere."

Under Arbour, New York again wound up in last place in the eight-team East Division, finishing 19-41-18. But after surrendering an all-time NHL high of 347 goals in their first season, the Islanders sliced their goals allowed total to 247. "Teams beat us," Torrey said, "but they had to work to do it."

By the third year, the goals were down to 221 (only two teams allowed fewer) and the Islanders marched all the way to the Stanley Cup semifinals. Coming off their first winning season (33-25-22), they upset the Rangers in the preliminary playoff round, rebounded to beat Pittsburgh after losing the opening three games of the quarterfinals, then battled the Philadelphia Flyers—the eventual Cup champions—to seven games before bowing out.

In a poll of his managerial peers after the season, Torrey was chosen The Sporting News' 1975 NHL Executive of the Year. The young talent was ripening and Torrey continued to build through the draft.

Trottier, who had remained in junior hockey an

extra season after being drafted as an underage selection in 1974, set an NHL rookie scoring record with 95 points (32 goals, 63 assists) in the 1975-76 season, complementing a defense that set a standing club mark for fewest goals allowed (190). The Isles made it as far as the Stanley Cup semifinals but were eliminated in five games by the Canadiens, who went on to claim their first of four straight Cup championships. Montreal prevailed over the Islanders again in the semifinal round of the 1977 playoffs.

Before the Islanders could claim that first Stanley Cup for their young franchise, one obstacle had to be overcome.

In building his team, Torrey hadn't neglected to add muscle, but the Islanders sometimes neglected to use it. To be sure, Potvin was one of the most intimidating defensemen in the league, employing his stick like a pitchfork when he didn't use the brute strength that earned him the nickname "Bear." Howatt, only 5-foot-9, was known as the "Toy Tiger" for his role as enforcer and catalyst on

Butch Goring was known around hockey circles as a pesky checker, a clutch face-off man and an expert penalty killer.

the ice. And few henchmen dared provoke Gillies.

Yet in the 1978 playoffs, New York was upset and undone by the back-alley behavior of the Toronto Maple Leafs in a brutally physical quarterfinal series.

Toronto Coach Roger Neilson, after his barbaric troops were likened to "veritable meat grinders" while losing the first two games of the series, vowed a comeback. "We will hit them harder and harder and harder," he assured reporters.

In a savage fourth game, Nystrom was sucker-punched by Toronto hit man Dan Maloney and pummeled onto the ice. Tranquil Jude Drouin took a high stick across the back of the head. Bossy, the 53-goal scorer voted Rookie of the Year, was checked headfirst into the boards in the fifth game.

"To call it brutal would be the understatement of the half-century," Stan Fischler wrote in The Sporting News. Nonetheless, the Leafs ousted New York from the playoffs in seven games.

Once again the next year, the Islanders were bullied out of the playoffs—this time by the hated Rangers in the semifinals—after exceeding the highest of expectations during the regular season. On the brink of folding the previous summer (the club was an estimated $20 million in debt), the Isles had reorganized their finances under new ownership and blitzed through the schedule, amassing a league-high 116 points with a 51-15-14 record.

Where defense had been the cornerstone of the team's early successes, the Islanders now were an offensive machine as well. Paced by the "Trio Grande" of Trottier, Gillies and Bossy, the league's most potent line, New York led all teams in goals scored.

Trottier topped the circuit in individual scoring with 134 points (47 goals, 87 assists) and was voted the NHL Most Valuable Player. Gillies tied for ninth with a career-high 91 points, and Bossy (fourth with 126 points) boosted his goal count to a league-high 69 in just his second season. Only Phil Esposito, who netted 76 goals for the Boston Bruins in 1970-71, had ever scored more.

"(Bossy) has enough sense to keep from getting clogged up in the middle," Isles goalie Glenn Resch observed. "He'll hang back on the perimeter of the slot and dart in and out. Gee, he gets on a loose puck fast. He'll slap at them blindly, but a lot of those go in. His success is based on the theory that the man without the puck is the most dangerous man in the play."

Supplying more firepower from the back line, Potvin became the second defenseman, next to Orr, to tally 30 goals and 100 points in one season, finishing with 31 goals and 70 assists for 101 points.

Around the league, Torrey was being compared with Sam Pollock, the architect of the Canadiens' dynasty the Islanders were trying to overthrow. "In my mind, there's only one person in the league who can do what Sam Pollock did," NHL President John Ziegler said. "That person is Bill Torrey."

That huge disappointment against the Rangers, however, carried into the 1979-80 season. The intensity prevalent over the course of the previous regular season was missing. So, too, was Potvin, who was lost for more than half the year with a thumb injury. While the team struggled to reach the .500 level, Torrey was criticized for not making a trade to shake up the ranks.

Torrey finally made his move as March unfolded. First, he added Ken Morrow, a silent, bearded defenseman who was a member of the U.S. Olympic team that had won the gold medal at Lake Placid, N.Y., weeks before. And at the stroke of the trading deadline, he acquired Goring, the scrappy, first-rate center he needed to support Trottier and ease the burden of a one-line offense.

"I reached the conclusion the team couldn't win

about two months ago," Torrey said after completing the deal. "All along, right from the start, I said that the centermen in our organization had to improve or we'd have to look elsewhere.

"Well, it became apparent we had to look elsewhere. Yeah, I could have gotten a stopgap to fill in, but in my judgment that's not what this team needed. And I was prepared to go further, but the proper deal never presented itself."

From the time Goring came aboard, the Islanders went 8-0-4 to finish the regular schedule. Goring netted six goals and five assists in those final 12 games, though he deflected much of the credit for the turnaround. "I just think this team was ready to take off," he said. "If it took someone like me to get it going, well, great."

The Islanders finished second behind Philadelphia in the Patrick Division with a 39-28-13 record but clearly were hitting their stride. They dismissed Goring's old Los Angeles teammates in the opening round of the playoffs, then headed to Boston for the playoff series that, many believe, made the franchise.

It was against the Bruins that the Islanders once and for all took on the personality of their serious and devoted coach. Arbour had served in 14 NHL seasons as an unspectacular defenseman who survived on instincts for good positioning and toughness. "As a player," said Scotty Bowman, his coach with the Blues, "he had the ability to dig deeper when he had to, to make himself go harder when he was hurting or when the team needed it. That's toughness."

Total commitment was what Arbour demanded of himself as a player; he expected the same from his players as a coach.

"Al was really a tough driver," Potvin recalled. "He'd drive you and drive you. He'd do things that were repetitive, over and over, repetitive to the point that it was a bore, and then he'd watch you make a mistake in practice and he'd stop the play and yell at you. But it became so automatic, the things he taught, that I'd turn around and make a pass and it would land on somebody's stick. It made me look great, but really, here's my teammate knowing exactly what I'm going to do by repetition."

Charming off the ice, Arbour was a stern tactician behind the bench, often fashioning a frosty stare from behind his steel-rimmed eyeglasses. From the moment the quarterfinal series began in cramped, old Boston Garden, it was evident that the Islanders never had been so serious, either.

"We were a different team than we ever were before that," Arbour remembered. "We seemed to know how important that series was, how much rested on it. We were ready. Looking back, that series was really the perfect preparation for us to win a Stanley Cup."

As if they needed additional incentive, the Islanders got it while sitting in their hotel rooms before the opener. A TV sportscaster predicted not

Center Lorne Henning was an original Islander who played a key role in the overtime goal that sealed New York's first title in 1980.

only that Boston would easily win the series, but that the big, bad Bruins would walk all over the lamb-like Islanders.

On the bus ride to the rink, the Islanders were uncommonly quiet. Not a word was spoken as they filed out of the bus and into the locker room. The silence there was broken only by the rustle of equipment being strapped into place and tape being wound around sticks.

"When I saw the look on their faces," Arbour said, "I knew right away what it meant. They were a little nervous, sure, but they were angry. I liked that."

Boston was a rough, surly club led by Terry O'Reilly, a gallant and aggressive right winger. The Bruins included brawlers John Wensink, Al Secord and Stan Jonathan, as well as dangerous scorers in Rick Middleton and Ray Bourque. But the critical difference between the teams was to be found between the pipes.

Tending the Bruins' net was 39-year-old Gerry Cheevers, playing in the final season of an illustrious career. The Islanders, after alternating between Smith and Resch for years, had decided to give the playoff reins to Smith. It was a decision they would not regret.

Smith was about to begin carving out a legend as one of the best pressure performers in Stanley Cup history. Playing the Bruins was right up his alley. He goaded the Boston players and their fans, cheered his teammates when they exchanged punches with the Bruins and turned away shot after shot.

"It was a big series for me," said Smith (who posted a 15-4 record overall playing in 20 of 21 postseason games). "But I've always said that us winning came down to one thing: We stood up for ourselves. We had Clark Gillies to thank for that."

From the opening minutes of the first game, the Bruins physically challenged the Islanders. This time, it was a challenge the Islanders would meet, exorcising all those ghosts of past failures. Four times in the series Gillies fought and bloodied O'Reilly, although between periods, the Islander left wing sat on a stool in the locker room, losing his lunch. The Bruins had never seen these Islanders, nor had the rest of the league, for that matter.

"It wasn't hockey," Gillies laments today. "It was a circus. It was obvious they wanted to try and intimidate us, like other teams had. We knew we couldn't back down, and we didn't."

Gillies, in fact, struck the biggest blow of the first game, but did it with his stick. His goal 62 seconds into overtime lifted the Islanders to a 2-1 victory. The next night, Bourne scored at 1:24 of overtime.

The Islanders had beaten the Bruins twice, on their own ice, in overtime. More important, they had made it clear they would have to be beaten on the scoreboard, because they were standing their ground.

"People said our team could be pushed around," Gillies said after the series. "Maybe that was true once. It's not anymore."

After splitting two games at Nassau Coliseum, the Islanders headed back to Boston, where they rallied in the fifth game for what would be a crucial victory in terms of their development as champions. The goal siren had wailed twice for the Bruins in the opening minutes, but the Islanders, calm and poised, slowly pecked away at the lead. With Smith blanking the Bruins for the final 56 minutes, Arbour's troops emerged with a hard-fought 4-2 victory and a berth in the semifinals, their fifth trip there in six seasons.

"What did that series do for us?" Bourne mused. "It convinced us we could really go all the way, and it convinced the other teams we could, too. After

that, no one treated us the same way anymore. We had respect."

The carousel did not stop. Smith continued his remarkable play, holding the Buffalo Sabres scoreless for a 106-minute stretch in the first two games of their semifinal series. The Isles won both contests, giving them seven straight playoff victories on the road. They dispatched the Sabres in six games, setting up their first-ever Stanley Cup final against division rival Philadelphia.

Again, the lessons learned against the Bruins served the Islanders well. They won the opener in Philadelphia on Potvin's goal during a rare power-play advantage in overtime. After the Flyers earned a split at home by winning Game 2, the Islanders swept the next two games on Long Island, taking a commanding lead against a team that had strung together a record 35-game unbeaten streak during the regular season.

The Flyers tried to outmuscle the Islanders, but failed. They tried to intimidate the Islanders, but couldn't. Faced with elimination, they resorted not to punching, but to offensive punch, routing Smith 6-3 in Game 5 to force a sixth game at Nassau Coliseum. To accommodate CBS, which would provide the first network telecast of an NHL game since 1975, the starting time was moved from evening to afternoon, making for a steamy milieu inside an arena hot with Cup fever.

The rink was pounding in wild celebration—albeit a premature one—by the end of the second period, when Nystrom scored in the final seconds to put New York ahead 4-2. The Flyers were down—but not out. They struck back for two goals in the third period, sending the game into sudden death. "Did I panic?" Smith said. "I was scared skinny."

The Islanders already had played six overtime games in these playoffs—and won five—but on the threshold of a Stanley Cup championship, they were untypically shaken.

"We all knew we just about had to win, that the Flyers would be very tough in a seventh game back in Philly," Henning said. "And we knew that if we lost the series after leading three games to one, we'd never be able to forgive ourselves—and probably no one else would forgive us, either."

Henning, a balding, bookish center, had endured eight years with the Isles because of his intelligent passing and ability to kill penalties. During the regular season, he had played in fewer than half of the games, and now was skating in the playoffs only because of an injury to Kallur. Nonetheless, he had scored three shorthanded goals so far to tie a playoff record, and just over six minutes into overtime, Arbour summoned him from the bench.

From his own end, Henning spotted John Tonelli racing up the right flank and shot a perfect pass up ice. Tonelli, another Torrey draftee and refugee from the World Hockey Association, was a plodding skater, a grinder noted for his work in the corners. But now, he flashed across the Philadelphia blue line, eluded a Flyers defenseman and re-

Left winger Clark Gillies (left) was a frightening physical specimen who worked hard in the trenches and eventually became the Islander enforcer. Ken Morrow (right) was a steady defenseman who helped keep opposing snipers away from Smith.

layed the puck to Nystrom, who was darting toward the net. "All I had to do was shovel it in," said Nystrom, who flipped a pretty backhander past Pete Peeters for the biggest goal in club history. The Islanders were never the same again.

"It was the greatest thrill in the world, so I still find it hard putting into words after all this time," Nystrom said, looking back. "It was a fairy tale."

The Islanders' championship was, indeed, remarkable. In only eight seasons, they had risen from a laughingstock expansion team to the Stanley Cup. And only two years earlier, new Owner John O. Pickett had rescued the club from the brink of bankruptcy.

The Isles had brought the New York metropolitan area its first Cup since 1940, but Smith drew an even thicker boundary between Islander and Ranger fans. "It's not New York City's cup," he protested. "It belongs to Long Island."

And it belonged to Trottier, too, who was voted MVP of the playoffs for recording a record-breaking 29 points. "(The Cup) means that much more because there were those who said I couldn't perform in the playoffs," he said.

Some opponents were convinced that the Islanders themselves were one-season wonders, a theory the Isles dismissed in 1980-81. "Last year, 'choke' was the word that followed us around," Potvin said. "After we won the Cup, it was 'fluke.' We're going to prove to those people who doubted

Center Anders Kallur, a member of the Islanders' crack penalty-killing unit, brought his services from the Swedish national team.

Bob Nystrom leaps for joy after scoring the 1980 overtime goal that defeated Philadelphia and gave the Islanders their first Stanley Cup. Also celebrating is Henning, who set up the winning goal with a breakaway pass.

The scoreboard tells the story as defenseman Gord Lane (left) and Tonelli celebrate a five-game victory over Minnesota in the 1981 Cup finals.

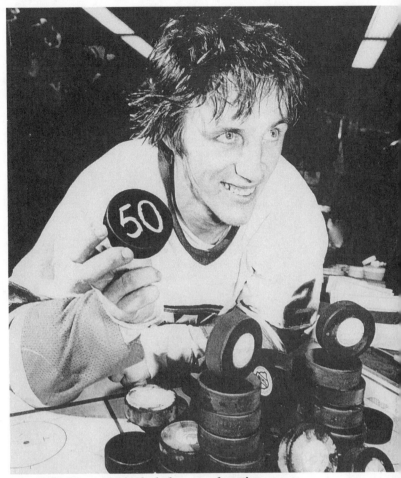

The 1980-81 season included a record-setting performance by Bossy, who tied Maurice Richard's mark by scoring his first 50 goals in 50 games.

us all along that we're a damn good team. We're going to force people to give us that respect."

A hero months before, Henning became an assistant coach, passing on his penalty-killing chores to Carroll, a good-checking center called up from the minors. Defenseman Tomas Jonsson joined the team, as well, and for the second straight year, Torrey swung a deal at the trading deadline, sending Resch to the Colorado Rockies for puck-rushing defenseman Mike McEwen.

"I didn't feel we needed to make big moves—we were the champs," Torrey said. "We did a little fine-tuning along the way, and it turned out just right."

The Islanders finished on a roll, losing only two of their final 17 games to post a league-best 48-18-14 record. They won the Cup for the second time by turning aside, in order, the 16th-place Toronto Maple Leafs, the 14th-place Edmonton Oilers, the 13th-place Rangers and the ninth-place Minnesota North Stars.

In many ways, a four-game sweep of the Rangers made the finals against Minnesota almost anticlimactic. The Islanders won the first three games from the North Stars, then wrapped up the Cup in Game 5, back on the Nassau Coliseum ice. "I think we could have won in four games," Bourne said,

years later, "but a lot of us wanted to go back home to clinch the Cup. I don't think we played as hard as we probably should have, you know?"

Yet sitting in the locker room after Game 5, Bourne was awed by the effort put forth by his teammates, particularly Trottier, who played the last five periods with a separated shoulder. "How can you come out and not work as hard as you can when you see him doing it," Bourne said, shaking his head in amazement.

Sitting a few feet away, blood drying where 40 stitches would soon be needed to close a gash from his lip to his chin, was Goring. "A little sonofagun," Bourne said. "Always was."

Goring had scored three goals in Game 3. He had forechecked recklessly and tenaciously. He had sparked the Isles' dangerous penalty-killing unit, which set a playoff record with nine shorthanded goals. He had scored two goals in the clinching game. And though Bossy (a 68-goal scorer during the season) had set a new playoff mark by tallying 35 points, one name had to be engraved on the Conn Smythe Trophy as the playoff MVP: Robert (Butch) Goring.

Once "chokers," then "flukes," the Islanders now were garnering some overdue respect. "If people

The highlight of the Islanders' 1981-82 season was a record 15-game winning streak that prompted this triumphant leap by Trottier.

want to give it to us now, fine," Trottier said. "We don't care about being compared with the Montreal Canadiens. At least I don't. We're just happy being the Islanders of the '80s."

The dynasty was firmly stamped in 1981-82, empowered by a third straight championship, a club-record 118 points (54-16-10) and a 15-game winning streak that erased the 1929-30 Bruins' NHL mark of 14 consecutive wins. Among the many records the Islanders left in their wake, this was one they savored.

"Every year, somebody's name is inscribed on the Stanley Cup," Torrey said. "But it's been 52 long years since anybody's done this."

Two smaller jewels were set around the crown—a Vezina Trophy for Smith, judged the top NHL goalie for his 32 victories and 2.97 goals-against average,

and Bossy's 147-point season (64 goals, 83 assists), a standing NHL mark for right wingers. (Smith's backup, Roland Melanson, was no slouch, either, posting a 3.23 goals-against average.)

The Islanders roared into the playoffs, whipping lowly Pittsburgh, 8-1 and 7-2, in the first two games of the opening round. Then, suddenly, the dynasty was imperiled.

Facing elimination, the Penguins somehow rallied, winning the third game in overtime and the fourth convincingly, 5-2. Back in Long Island for a decisive fifth game, they forged a 3-1 lead, an advantage they still held over the stunned Islanders with less than six minutes to play.

"It was just the kind of game which made us great," said Tonelli, who had totaled 35 goals and 93 points in a season that established him as one of the league's best left wings. "We were worried, sure. But not one person on the bench ever gave up or thought it was over. We were the 'Never-Say-Die' Islanders."

Taking matters into his own hands after McEwen cut the Pittsburgh lead to 3-2, Tonelli tied the game with just over two minutes remaining, then batted home a rebound at 6:19 of overtime to earn the club a dramatic victory.

"You have to credit the Islanders," Pittsburgh goaltender Michel Dion said. "They have the hearts of lions." And a sense of history, too, which Bourne touched upon after the series. "That's why we win," he said. "Because we never forget what it was like to lose."

That hurdle cleared, the Islanders had few problems in becoming the first U.S.-based franchise to win three consecutive Cups (and only the third club overall, next to Montreal, 1956-60 and 1976-79, and Toronto, 1947-49 and 1962-64). They eliminated the Rangers in six games and the Quebec Nordiques in four straight to advance to the finals against Vancouver. The Canucks, a clutch-and-grab team that had finished 30-33-17 in the regular season, couldn't impede the Islanders' relentless attack and lost the series in four games.

Not only did they confirm their dynasty, but the Islanders had done it with ease. Their victory was a victory of style. They had whipped Vancouver, a team of limited talent but lots of determination, with teamwork, imagination, speed, defense—and Bossy, who scored seven goals in the finals (tying Jean Beliveau's record) and 17 goals overall for the second straight postseason to sew up playoff MVP honors.

"It wasn't bad enough that you had to put up with Smith," one club official once remarked. "Sure, he'd get your goat with his tactics. But worse, you play all year to get to the playoffs, only to go up against the best money goalie going. And then Bossy. Well, he's circling your zone, waiting to pounce on the puck. You just *know* he's gonna turn it on."

The goal lamp, that is. Through the 1988 postseason, Bossy was the all-time NHL leader with 85 ca-

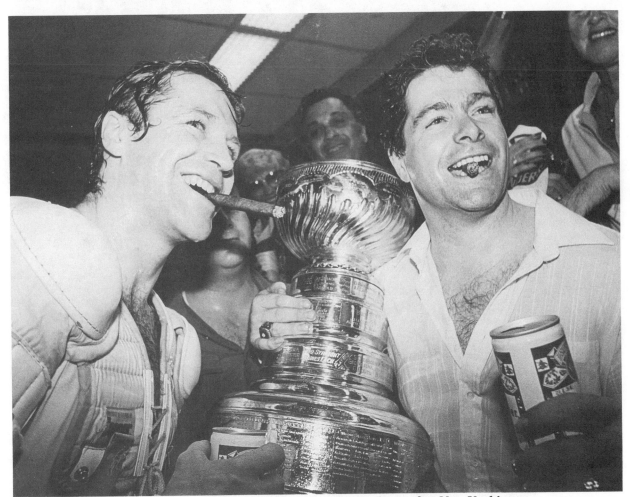

Potvin (left) and brother Jean, a former Islander, enjoy victory cigars after New York's 1982 Stanley Cup victory over the Vancouver Canucks.

reer playoff goals.

Even after that third title, however, a few enduring bolts of criticism found their way to Long Island. "There were many people in the league who didn't think we were that good and that was surprising," Torrey said. "The first year we beat the team that was the best in the league. The second year we beat some teams that hadn't had real good seasons, but had come on in the playoffs and were very tough."

And then came the unlikely final series against the Canucks. "A lot of people didn't give us much credit because they thought Vancouver being there was a joke," Potvin said.

A slow start in the 1982-83 season may have given credence to the criticism, bizarre though it was. The team slumped early due to a lethargic offense. There were subtle changes made because of injuries and an influx of youth. Arbour was a noticeably different coach by now. He was more mellow, but he also had restyled the Islanders' system, principally their methods of attack but also how they defended against free-wheeling offenses.

"The personality of the club has changed and I've changed," Arbour allowed. "I'm not as tough on them as I used to be. I've molded this team in a

certain way, so the guys know what's expected of them."

Said Torrey: "There's more speed in the game now and the players are bigger. It's to Al's credit that he was able to change with the times. He not only adjusted to changes, he created some of them."

The Islanders finished second in the Patrick Division, behind Philadelphia, and sixth overall in the NHL with a 42-26-12 record. They eliminated the Washington Capitals in the first playoff round, subdued the Rangers and Bruins in six-game series and headed into their fourth straight Stanley Cup final in a most unusual position—as underdogs to the Edmonton Oilers.

The Oilers, riding Wayne Gretzky's back, had emerged as the most explosive team in NHL history, and perhaps its most cocky. On one occasion, several Oilers had booed an opponent's power play from the Edmonton bench. The Oilers appeared to believe the press clippings that predicted a mighty Edmonton victory over the aging Islanders.

"It was the craziest thing," Bourne said. "Here we'd won three Cups. And people were talking about how we had to prove ourselves against the Oilers. We figured they had to prove themselves to us."

Smith leads the cheers and the celebration begins after the Islanders' 1983 Stanley Cup victory—a four-game sweep of the future-champion Edmonton Oilers.

In the end—and a quick ending it was—the Isles were the team roaring in self-satisfaction. "Put it this way," Nystrom said after the Isles completed a stunning four-game sweep. "I hope I don't see anything bad written about the New York Islanders for a couple of months."

Paced by Smith, the playoff MVP, they limited the turbocharged Oiler offense to six goals in four games. They held Gretzky, who had scored a league-leading 71 goals and 196 points during the regular season, to no goals and four assists. Why, Morrow, who had scored only eight goals in his career, totaled five points on three goals and two assists, more points than any Oiler.

The Islanders had fooled the skeptics again, embarrassed the Oilers and become only the second franchise to win four straight Stanley Cups—and they did it in only their 11th year in the league. During their four-year reign, they won a record 16 straight playoff series, fashioning a 60-18 record, including an eye-popping 16-3 record in the finals. They would advance to one more final series, losing to an improved and more mature Oiler team in the 1984 rematch. But to the Islanders, the disappointment of just falling shy of a record-tying fifth straight Cup didn't tarnish the dynasty at all.

"Right now," Torrey had said amid the celebration of the fourth championship, "we'd love to play those Montreal teams for a lot of money."

"We were the best damn team ever," Potvin maintains today. "Nobody can tell me any different. And I'll believe that until the day I die."

Bourne hoists the 1983 Stanley Cup, signaling the end of the Islanders' four-year stranglehold on the NHL.

After a 2-2-1 start as Oklahoma coach, Bud Wilkinson finished at 145-29-4.

Preparation isn't everything. It's the only thing.

That twist to a statement that a noted pro football coach supposedly uttered time and again sums up to a T—a split-T, even—the philosophy of one Charles Burnham (Bud) Wilkinson.

Describing what he perceived as the primary responsibility of a collegiate football coach, Wilkinson once said: "Part of his job, if it's competitive, is to try to win, of course. But, essentially, it's to prepare his people to play as well as he can teach them to play. And if he can do that, I think he feels, in spite of what other people might say, that he has accomplished his purpose."

Bud Wilkinson, it can be said without fear of contradiction, accomplished his purpose as coach of the Oklahoma Sooners. No team on any level of any athletic endeavor seemed more prepared for the task at hand than a Wilkinson-coached Oklahoma football team. It wasn't merely incidental, of course, that the Sooners compiled an .826 winning percentage in Wilkinson's 17 seasons at the helm and captured 12 straight league championships outright. After all, while winning wasn't the only thing for Wilkinson, it was undeniably the end result—the expected payoff—for all that preparation.

Wilkinson's strong views on the importance of preparedness—as opposed to the necessity of winning—came, strikingly enough, in 1958, just after he had guided the Sooners through one of the most successful 10-year periods that any team in any sport has ever experienced. From the 1948 season through the 1957 campaign, Oklahoma ran up a 97-7-2 record and won three national championships.

"During football season, a coach hardly has time to brush his teeth," Wilkinson said. "Four hours of preparation are needed for one hour of practice. If we're going to use our practice to maximum value, we have to know what we're going to do every minute. How much football we as coaches know will have no bearing on a single game. It's the skill and knowledge we're able to impart to our players that counts. The game is won or lost by the players, not by the coaches. . . ."

Wilkinson surely was correct—to some extent, anyway—about the ultimate responsibility for the winning and losing of football games. But there can be no question that a man possessing his unique leadership and organizational qualities had a special impact on Oklahoma football and the collegiate game overall. Oh, the Sooners had been reasonably successful before his arrival on the Norman, Okla., campus, but reasonably successful and astonishingly successful are two different things.

A standout player under Bernie Bierman at Minnesota in the mid-1930s and a former assistant coach at Syracuse, Minnesota and the Iowa Preflight School, Wilkinson made his Norman coaching debut in 1946 as an aide on Coach Jim Tatum's staff. The Sooners won eight of 11 games that season, but then lost their coach. After serving only one year as Oklahoma's man-in-charge, Tatum left to take over the top job at Maryland. He was replaced by a 31-year-old assistant: Wilkinson.

Wilkinson, a challenge-oriented individual who had tried to undertake a business career but found that field lacked the competitive fires he wanted, was eager to begin his new assignment. He set out immediately to employ what he had gleaned from the master, Bierman, a little more than a decade earlier.

" 'Don't become sold on the type of football that defeats teams you could defeat anyway,' " Wilkinson remembered Bierman as saying. " 'Base your play on standards most likely to defeat the champions. You can't fool a good team. The good ones don't take the fake. You've got to block 'em.' "

The Sooners, whose '46 season under Tatum included a Gator Bowl triumph over North Carolina State, found themselves owning only a 2-2-1 record halfway through Wilkinson's first season as coach. "I was not in the driver's seat in any capacity whatsoever. Oklahoma people realized how young I was," Wilkinson said of his standing with Oklahoma supporters after the so-so start. But the Sooners swept through the remainder of their schedule, beating Iowa State, Kansas State, Missouri, Nebraska and Oklahoma A&M, and the Wilkinson era was off and running. A 7-2-1 mark was impressive, all right, but, amazingly, it would wind up as one of the lesser seasons in Bud's regime in Norman.

Wilkinson entered the 1948 season feeling considerably more at ease than he did a year earlier. The victory over a good Missouri team in the eighth week of the 1947 season—a 21-12 triumph at Columbia, Mo.—had provided a major boost. "It was a key game in my career," the coach remarked more than 40 years later. "It solidified confidence in me by fans and backers."

Oklahoma's 1948 season began on a sour note, though, with the Sooners losing a 20-17 decision to Santa Clara, an outcome that Wilkinson acknowledged caused a "little disturbance" throughout Oklahoma. But Wilkinson's athletes pounded Texas A&M the next week and then spilled Texas and Kansas State, the latter game featuring a 96-yard punt return by the Sooners' Darrell Royal. It was a stirring touchdown gallop by Royal, but one that probably should not have even been attempted.

"You're not supposed to field the ball inside the

Dynasty Data
Yearly Record
1948-1957

Year	W	L	T	Pct.	Avg. Score Okla.-Opp.	Coach
1948	10	1	0	.909	32-11	Bud Wilkinson
1949	11	0	0	1.000	36-8	Bud Wilkinson
1950	10	1	0	.909	32-13	Bud Wilkinson
1951	8	2	0	.800	32-10	Bud Wilkinson
1952	8	1	1	.850	41-14	Bud Wilkinson
1953	9	1	1	.864	27-8	Bud Wilkinson
1954	10	0	0	1.000	30-6	Bud Wilkinson
1955	11	0	0	1.000	35-5	Bud Wilkinson
1956	10	0	0	1.000	47-5	Bud Wilkinson
1957	10	1	0	.909	30-8	Bud Wilkinson
Total	97	7	2	.925	34-9	

Additional Data

Best Record—1949, 1955 (11-0-0); 1954, 1956 (10-0-0).

Worst Record—1951 (8-2-0).

Most Lopsided Victory—66-0 over Kansas State, 1956.

Most Lopsided Defeat—14-7 to Texas A&M, 1951; 28-21 to Notre Dame, 1953; 7-0 to Notre Dame, 1957.

Most Consecutive Victories—47 games from Oct. 10, 1953 through Nov. 9, 1957.

Longest Undefeated Period—48 games from Oct. 3, 1953 through Nov. 9, 1957 (47 victories, 1 tie).

Most Consecutive Losses—2 games from Oct. 6 through Oct. 13, 1951.

Shutouts—The Sooners held opponents scoreless in 33 games.

Times Shut Out—Oklahoma was shut out only once—7-0 by Notre Dame on Nov. 16, 1957.

Darrell Royal was a gifted quarterback, punter and punt returner for Wilkinson's early Sooner teams.

10-yard line," Royal said, "and I think Coach Wilkinson was a bit upset. We had run a crisscross (Jack Mitchell had fielded the ball and slipped it to Royal), and that saved me. There was a perfect wall."

As the play unfolded, Wilkinson "wasn't particularly satisfied we had made the right decision." But, Wilkinson admitted with a bit of a twinkle in his eye, "by the time Darrell was sprinting past our bench, I was yelling, 'Go, Darrell, by God, go!' "

Texas Christian, Iowa State, Missouri and Nebraska also came out on the short end in '48 against Oklahoma, which then braced for a meeting with Kansas, with whom it had shared the league title in 1946 and 1947. In a Big Seven Conference game played on the Jayhawks' home field, the Sooners rocked Kansas, 60-7, as Royal and Mitchell reeled off punt-return touchdowns of 73 and 67 yards, respectively. Oklahoma was rolling; steamrolling, even. In fact, the Sooners, after dropping that '48 season opener, would not lose again until New Year's Day, 1951.

The '48 team wound up the regular season by edging past Oklahoma A&M, then toppled North Carolina in the Sugar Bowl. While All-America guard Paul (Buddy) Burris and standout quarterback Mitchell would not be around the following season, the Sooners would be returning a stable of fleet and strong backs. Royal, a top-flight defensive back and a talented punter, would take over at quarterback. His No. 1 operative in the backfield would be George Thomas, who had rushed for 835 yards and scored 10 touchdowns in '48, backed by Lindell Pearson and Leon Heath.

Wilkinson's 1949 Sooners ran the split-T offense to perfection, and that attack proved the ideal vehicle for the Oklahoma coach to emphasize what he considered the key elements to success. "Speed, deception and hustle are the essentials of any winning football team," Wilkinson said.

Explaining his preference for the split-T, which he learned while serving as an aide under Don Faurot at Iowa Pre-Flight, Wilkinson once said the Sooners operated out of that formation "because we think we can teach it more effectively than any other offense in the short period of practice time allowed us, and the fluid pattern of the play enables our individual linemen to move at will laterally." Guard Stan West and tackle Wade Walker were among Oklahoma's best movers and shakers along the forward wall in '49.

Wilkinson, who weaved the power of the single wing into his variation of the split-T by using pulling guards, an end-around for blocking purposes and spinners and half-spinners by the quarterback, never claimed to be an innovator.

"Most of us coaches are adapters and copycats," Wilkinson said. "There really are very few original ideas. Missouri Coach Don Faurot's idea of splitting the linemen—that's the split-T—was an original contribution."

The Sooners were pressed only twice in '49, winning by six points against Texas in their third game of the season and prevailing by seven against Santa Clara (the last team to beat Oklahoma) in the ninth contest. In the regular-season finale, the Sooners thumped Oklahoma A&M, 41-0, in a game highlighted by a 90-yard run by Thomas, who finished the season with 859 yards rushing and wound up as the nation's leading scorer with 117 points on 19 touchdowns and three extra-point conversions.

Oklahoma then battered Louisiana State, 35-0, in

White-clad Santa Clara players watch in vain as the Sooners' "Mule Train," Leon Heath (40), breaks into the clear for a long scoring run in a 1949 game.

the January 2, 1950, Sugar Bowl. Heath spiced that triumph, the Sooners' 21st consecutive victory, with an 86-yard touchdown romp. "With the kind of blocking I got, almost anybody could have done it," Heath said of his long jaunt.

Heath's approach to the game of football delighted Wilkinson.

Discussing the Oklahoma coaching staff's grading system for Sooner players, Wilkinson noted that an outstanding performance was worth one point and then proceeded to tell how Heath had once merited a score of plus-two. "In a game against Nebraska, Heath was supposed to block the end," Wilkinson said. "He went out to block the end, and the end was so far across the line of scrimmage that Heath shouldered him out of the play. Then the ballcarrier, Billy Vessels, cut inside. Vessels avoided the tackle and while maneuvering, slowed up enough to let Heath move back in front of him and block the linebacker.

"This block broke Vessels clean past the line of scrimmage. He ran about 30 yards and appeared to be hemmed in against the sidelines by the defensive halfback on the Nebraska 16-yard line when Heath, once again, with an amazing burst of speed, cut across the field at the proper angle and blocked the remaining Nebraska defender.

"Heath's assignment, for which he would have gotten a zero (because of its routine nature), was to block the end out. In addition, he blocked the line-

backer and the defensive halfback and, what is most amazing, ran a total distance of approximately 85 yards between the blocks."

Heath, reflecting on that play four decades after it had occurred, deflected any glory, instead choosing to single out Vessels' running skill—"he made it possible by reversing his field"—as the key factor.

Oklahoma, paced by the passing of Claude Arnold, the running of Heath and Vessels and the ferocious line play of tackle Jim Weatherall, marched to a 10-0 record in regular-season play in 1950. A 49-35 conquest of Nebraska in the next-to-last game of the regular season—Vessels ran for 205 yards against the Cornhuskers—pushed the Sooners' winning streak to 30 games. The string reached 31 the next week in a 41-14 rout of Oklahoma A&M.

Oklahoma's magnificent season, punctuated by a scoring average of 41 points per game over the last four contests, resulted in a national championship as decreed by the wire-service polls in the days of pre-bowls final balloting. As it turned out, Wilkinson and company were fortunate that the voting was history long before the postseason rolled around.

In the January 1, 1951, Sugar Bowl, Coach Paul (Bear) Bryant's Kentucky Wildcats jolted the Sooners with bone-jarring defensive play and a pinpoint passing performance by Babe Parilli. The Wildcats' defense, led by tackles Walt Yowarsky and Bob

Nothing quite stirs Sooner passions like a victory over archrival Texas, as Wilkinson and halfback Ed Lisak (45) demonstrated in 1949.

Gain, came away with five Oklahoma fumbles and Kentucky came away a 13-7 victory.

"The mood was pretty bad," said Heath, recalling the effects of the long afternoon in New Orleans, a day that marked the end of his productive and colorful career at Oklahoma. Heath had been a standout blocker and runner, and even won a place in Sooner lore with his "Mule Train" nickname.

"One time, Bruce Drake, our basketball coach, was handling the loudspeaker at a football game when I broke loose," said Heath, remembering that Drake, caught up in the excitement of the moment, blurted, "There goes 'Mule Train.'" At the time, "Mule Train" was a hit record on the national charts. "It stuck," Heath said of the appellation.

Wilkinson, while disappointed over the end of the winning streak, wasn't making any excuses for Oklahoma's propensity for coughing up the ball. "Never were our backs hit so hard," the Sooners' mentor admitted.

The Sugar Bowl defeat aside, Oklahoma had turned a question-mark season into a memorable one. Arnold had thrown 13 touchdown passes, which still stood as a school record nearly 40 years later, while yielding only one interception. Halfback Vessels had amassed 870 yards on the ground and scored 15 touchdowns, while fullback Heath rushed for 606 yards and notched six TDs. Heath and Weatherall were consensus All-America selections. And, of course, there was that national championship, which, with the passing of time, Wilkin-

son downplayed a bit by saying the 1950 Sooners "weren't a dominant team. The first really good team we played that season was Kentucky."

By mid-1951, Wilkinson, a head coach for only four seasons and just 35 years old, was an acknowledged master of his craft. His peers had made that official in '49, when the American Football Coaches Association named him Coach of the Year.

Merrill Green, who scored Oklahoma's only touchdown in the '51 Sugar Bowl loss to Kentucky, later reflected on how Wilkinson got his troops ready for a game. Not just a big game; *any* game.

"During the regular season, practice follows a regular schedule, day in and day out," Green said. "On Sunday, you hear the scouting report and go over the previous day's game. Monday, the game films. Tuesday is the defensive meeting, Wednesday the offensive one. Thursday is a polishing day, and on Friday and Saturday there is a meeting each day.

"The coach has a favorite phrase which he brings out on Wednesday night. 'The hay's in the barn,' he says, and he feels that the Saturday game is won or lost by Wednesday."

Two of the first three Wednesdays of the 1951 season presumably were downers in the Sooners' camp, although there were extenuating circumstances in week three. After blitzing William & Mary in the '51 opener by a 49-7 score, Oklahoma dropped a 14-7 decision to Texas A&M and then fell to Texas, 9-7. The narrow loss to the archrival Longhorns was made particularly painful because of a season-ending injury in that game to the gifted Vessels, who suffered a leg fracture.

Confronted with a 1-2 record and the loss of Vessels, Oklahoma did what any first-rate team would do: It regrouped, and how. With Eddie Crowder showing a deft touch at quarterback, fullback Buck McPhail running with authority (215 yards in one game and 865 overall), freshman scatback Buddy Leake showing a nose for the end zone (13 touchdowns) and linebackers Tom Catlin and Bert Clark sparking a dogged defense, the Sooners were victorious in their last seven games of the season. They won five of those games by 27 or more points.

McPhail, who averaged an eye-popping 8.6 yards per carry in '51, got off a one-for-the-books run against Kansas State, shaking free for 96 yards. Two things made the run a memorable carry: 1. It established a record for the longest rushing play in Oklahoma history. 2. McPhail did not score on the cross-country tour.

"They had punted out of bounds," Wilkinson reminisced in the spring of 1989. "It was a counter play, and McPhail broke it clean. However, there was a 'northeaster' blowing, and McPhail was running into the wind, about 15 yards ahead of everyone. Despite the fact he was so far out in front, a Kansas State player kept pursuing him—a very good mark—and caught him from behind."

Vintage Wilkinson. His player goes 96 yards, but the football purist in him can't help but applaud the effort of the guy who caught McPhail. The diligent Kansas State defender was Carvel Oldham.

Asked if McPhail might have been a bit on the slow side, Wilkinson shot back: "He had good speed or he wouldn't have been playing."

Leake, meanwhile, came out of nowhere to make his mark in 1951.

"Coach Wilkinson gave me a try at the open position (Vessels' spot) and I wanted to do my very best," said newcomer Leake, who benefited in '51 from a reinstituted freshman-eligible rule (adopted in response to Korean War manpower shortages, just as a similar measure was implemented in the 1940s because of World War II's impact on player availability). Not only did Leake make repeated visits to the end zone—he dashed for four touchdowns in the season finale against Oklahoma A&M—but he also rushed for 646 yards overall.

Vessels was back in tiptop shape in 1952, and he and McPhail rewrote the collegiate record book with their ball-toting escapades. Vessels rushed for 1,072 yards and McPhail gained 1,018, making the Oklahoma duo the first major-college teammates to run for 1,000 yards in the same season.

Vessels had a marvelous year. He averaged 6.7 yards per rushing attempt, scored 18 touchdowns and was merely sensational in Oklahoma's lone defeat of the season. In the Sooners' first-ever meeting with Notre Dame, Vessels netted 195 yards on the ground and made three TDs, but the Fighting Irish prevailed by a 27-21 score. The only other blemish on Oklahoma's record in '52 was a season-opening

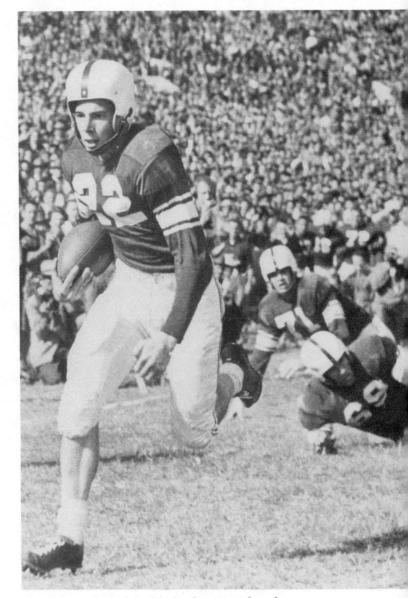

Touchdown-bound Buddy Leake stepped to the forefront in 1951 after Billy Vessels went down with an injury. Leake, a freshman, scored 13 TDs in '51.

tie against Colorado.

Oklahoma's defense suffered a letdown of sorts, allowing 20 or more points in each of the first four games of the season and later yielding four touchdowns in that loss to Notre Dame. But the offense went full throttle almost from the start. After scoring 21 points against Colorado, the Sooners tore loose for 41 or more points in their next five games and wound up with a 40.7 scoring average.

Vessels joined the list of Oklahoma's consensus All-Americas in '52, giving the Sooners five such selections in a five-season span. More important, though, in terms of awards, he became the first Sooner to cop college football's biggest individual prize—the Heisman Trophy.

Vessels, Wilkinson said, was both Oklahoma's fastest and toughest man—an "extremely rare combination."

Vessels (top, right), bolting across the 50-yard line, boosted his Heisman Trophy hopes in 1952 with a three-touchdown performance against Notre Dame.

The Sooners—and all of college football—faced a major change in the approach to the game in 1953 when rules-makers voted to do away with any semblance of two-platoon football. Oklahoma also was confronted by another battle of the numbers, this one involving heavy losses among its key personnel. Among those finishing their eligibility in '52 were Vessels, McPhail, Crowder, Catlin and linemen Ed Rowland and Jim Davis, all of whom were All-Big Seven choices. The only all-league players returning were guard J.D. Roberts and end Max Boydston—but they were extremely talented players.

In time, Wilkinson's team adjusted beautifully. But before the Sooners began to play with the precision that had become their trademark, they suffered a season-opening 28-21 loss to Notre Dame and were played to a 7-7 tie by Pittsburgh. In the latter fray, Leake, converted from halfback to quarterback before the start of the season, teamed with Larry Grigg on an 80-yard pass that accounted for the Sooners' only touchdown of the game and then added the conversion kick.

While Wilkinson had viewed Leake as potentially "the greatest runner/passer quarterback I have ever developed at Oklahoma," a shoulder injury to Leake and the emergence of Gene Calame at quarterback contributed to a reshuffling of the backfield corps. With Calame expertly guiding the club beginning with the Texas game in the third week of the season, Roberts on the way to giving the Sooners their second Outland Trophy winner in three seasons (Weatherall was the previous recipient of the best-interior-lineman-in-the-nation honor) and

the running game en route to a nation-leading average of 306.9 yards per game behind Grigg and Bob Burris, Oklahoma caught fire.

Wilkinson's Sooners ran off eight consecutive victories, achieved a No. 4 ranking in one wire-service poll and earned a date with No. 1-rated Maryland in the January 1, 1954, Orange Bowl. The Sooners capped the surge with a 7-0 triumph over the Terrapins, who played virtually all of the Miami classic without hobbled quarterback Bernie Faloney. Faloney or no Faloney, it was evident that something very special was in the making in Soonerland.

For Calame, it was heady stuff. Like many an Oklahoma youngster, he had dreamed of playing for the Sooners. Unlike most prospects, though, he didn't wait for the recruiters to come knocking. That would have been too risky.

"During that period of time, you just hoped you'd get a scholarship from Oklahoma," said Calame, who was from the small town of Sulphur. "I didn't wait—I wrote a letter and asked for a scholarship . . . and they said they'd be glad to give me one."

Calame, a heady player who excelled at reading defenses but lacked sheer physical skills, was counted upon to direct the Sooners to continued success in 1954. Oklahoma whipped California, 27-13, in the first game of the season, but trouble loomed in game two when Calame went down with a shoulder injury in a fierce contest against Texas Christian. Into the breach stepped Jimmy Harris.

A sophomore from Terrell, Tex., Harris got the

Sooners on the scoreboard against TCU with a 68-yard punt return and later rallied his team from a 16-7 fourth-quarter deficit to a 21-16 triumph. Passing infrequently but skillfully, he then led Oklahoma past Texas, 14-7. The next week, in a 65-0 blowout of Kansas, Harris bolted to a 91-yard TD run.

"I watch Gene (Calame) all the time," Harris said. "I try to do like he does. This summer, when we were in (a Minnesota boys) camp, he helped me with my faking and showed me the finer points."

By the time Harris himself was felled by an injury in the Colorado game in '54, Oklahoma had extended its two-year winning streak to 14 games. A 13-6 victory over the Buffaloes would make it 15 in a row and, by season's end, with Calame back at the controls, the string would be at 19. The Sooners' perfect record in 1954 and their impressive winning streak didn't turn Wilkinson giddy.

"Frankly, I'm not interested in records," Wilkinson said before the 1955 season. "The thing I'm proudest of is the type of boy (typically, an in-state product who would earn a college degree) represented at Oklahoma in football. When people say to me, 'Coach, what kind of team will we have this year?' I say, 'I think we'll have a good college team,' but they aren't concerned about that. All they want to know is, 'How many games are we going to win and how many are we going to lose?'

"...What takes place is that both teams are well-conditioned, smartly coached. They're both made up of fine young men. The winning or losing is in that intangible factor of mental toughness...If you're going to be a champion, you must be willing to pay a greater price than your opponent will ever pay."

Still, Wilkinson was resolute in his belief that football should provide a good time for a participant. "There must be the fun angle—not frivolity," he said, "but fun through awareness of the relationship between the end he knows can be achieved and enjoyed in Saturday's game and the sacrifice necessary to that end. Willingness to make that sacrifice demands mental toughness. When mental toughness has been rewarded by victory enough times, it adds up to a winning attitude or tradition, which is more important than personnel and coaching."

The Sooners, obviously, were mentally tough. Their opponents often were not. "We didn't think we could lose," Calame said. "Other teams didn't think they could win," Wilkinson observed.

Oklahoma's now-flourishing tradition had been further enhanced in '54 by the placing of two more Sooners on the consensus All-America team. Honored were center Kurt Burris and end Boydston. Kurt became the second Burris brother to win All-America honors at Norman—Buddy was a 1948 selection—and he was one of five siblings from a Muskogee, Okla., family to play varsity football for Oklahoma (Bob would make the all-conference team in 1955, while twins Lynn and Lyle would be on the roster the next two seasons).

As for the Sooners' winning attitude, that facet of

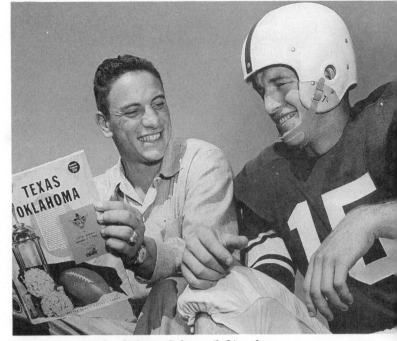

Sooners quarterback Gene Calame (left), who missed the 1954 Texas game because of an injury, talks over strategy with able replacement Jimmy Harris.

the Oklahoma program would be in grand evidence in 1955. Boasting a marvelous blend of offensive and defensive talent, Oklahoma won almost at will. After opening the season with seven- and 12-point victories over North Carolina and Pittsburgh, the Sooners beat usually troublesome Texas, 20-0, and then pummeled Kansas, 44-6. Colorado, which had come within seven points of Oklahoma in each of the previous two seasons following a tie with the Sooners in 1952, went down to a 56-21 setback. Then, after Kansas State became a 40-7 victim, Missouri, Iowa State, Nebraska and Oklahoma A&M fell to the Sooners by a combined 166-0 score. A second straight 10-0 regular season, a year in which statistics did not lie.

The 1955 Sooners led the nation in total offense and scoring, averaging 410.7 rushing/passing yards and 36.5 points per game. Additionally, they ranked second in scoring defense, allowing only 5.4

Oklahoma vs. Most Frequent Opponents

1948-1957
(5 or More Games)

Opponent	W	L	T	Pct.	Avg. Score Okla.-Opp.
Iowa State	10	0	0	1.000	39-4
Kansas	10	0	0	1.000	45-11
Kansas State	10	0	0	1.000	40-1
Missouri	10	0	0	1.000	36-10
Nebraska	10	0	0	1.000	41-9
Oklahoma A&M*	10	0	0	1.000	41-6
Colorado	7	0	1	.938	30-17
Texas	9	1	0	.900	23-10

*Now known as Oklahoma State.

points per contest.

Paced by fleet Tommy McDonald, a junior from Albuquerque, N.M., who gained 702 yards rushing, Oklahoma averaged a nation-best 328.9 yards on the ground in its 10 games. When the year drew to a close, the impact of the Sooners' running game during the Wilkinson era was abundantly clear: Oklahoma had averaged 301.1 yards rushing in its 90 regular-season games under Wilkinson, a higher mark than any team in the country (other than the Sooners) had achieved in '55 alone.

Of all the numbers that Oklahoma posted in '55, however, the most important was No. 1—the Sooners' ranking in the final national polls. The second national-championship season in six years would be capped, Oklahomans hoped, by a better postseason showing than that turned in by Wilkinson's previous kingpins, the 1950 Sooners, who not only lost in bowl competition, but also saw the school's 31-game winning streak come to a halt.

The Sooners, now boasting 29 consecutive victories in their second long winning streak under Wilkinson, were paired against No. 3 Maryland in the January 2, 1956, Orange Bowl. The game was more than a matchup of great teams; it also pitted two esteemed coaches against one another, with Bud Wilkinson going against Jim Tatum, the man whose departure as Oklahoma coach almost a decade earlier had opened the door for assistant Wilkinson to move into the Sooners' top job.

Tatum went into the game with a turnabout-is-fair-play objective. Two years earlier in the Orange Bowl, his Terrapins had been ranked No. 1 when they were stung by Wilkinson's Sooners. Now, Tatum and his players had an opportunity to do unto Oklahoma what the Sooners had done unto them.

Wilkinson was always leery of bowl games, the main reason being that there was a total change in the preparation timetable. Rather than having the usual five-day work plan, he and his staff had to allow for 3½ weeks of pre-bowl goings-on. That span of time was just long enough, Wilkinson reasoned, for an underdog to get to believing in itself. Plus, the lengthy period played havoc with the Sooners' time-tested schedule. And, sure enough, Maryland led, 6-0, at the intermission of the '56 Orange Bowl.

The Sooners got a few well-chosen words of wisdom from Wilkinson during halftime, though, and they rebounded to beat the weary Terrapins, 20-6. Words of wisdom? Weary Terrapins?

Wilkinson "told us we had been stopping ourselves by our own mistakes," quarterback Harris said. "He told us to come out fast and drive and never let up. He said we would beat Maryland if we would just stick to our bread-and-butter inside plays. He wound up saying, 'If you're men, you'll snap out of it and play the way you know how.'"

The Sooners snapped out of it, all right, with McDonald helping set up his own four-yard touchdown burst in the third quarter with a 33-yard

Center Kurt Burris, an All-America selection, was one of five brothers from a Muskogee, Okla., family to play varsity football at Oklahoma.

punt return. Second-team quarterback Jay O'Neal scored later in the period on a one-yard burst, and Carl Dodd's 82-yard interception return for a TD in the fourth quarter was the coup de grace.

By the time Dodd made his big play, the Terps were really dragging—thanks to the Sooners' game-long "hurry up" offense. Throughout the game, the Oklahoma players scrambled to their feet once a play ended, held a quick huddle and then raced back to the line of scrimmage to put the ball into play.

"Get up, Bob. Here they come again!" Maryland defender Mike Sandusky told teammate Bob Pellegrini, an All-America lineman, during one point of the afternoon.

Explaining the use of the quick sequence, Wilkinson said one objective "was to avoid letting the defense get settled and look at our line splits."

The rapid-fire running of plays also took aim at the growing defensive ploy of what Wilkinson called "jitterbugging," or the jumping around of defensive players before the ball is snapped. "They can't very well 'jitterbug' if you go quickly," the coach explained.

Perhaps most important was the fact that the strategy provided more opportunities to win the football game. "If we're hopefully as good as they are and we can run 20 more plays than they do over 30 minutes, we figure to win," Wilkinson said.

Sooner adversaries became very familiar—but

not at all comfortable—with Wilkinson's run-don't-walk style. However, opponents never quite knew what else would be sprung on them.

"The unexpected has great dividends," said Wilkinson, who at the beginning of a game often would align his players—offensively and/or defensively—in a manner that would take the opposition by surprise. "We did this," Wilkinson said, "so our opponents would not be confident that they were well-prepared. If we were successful (with the new look), we would stay with it. If not, we would go back to what we did best."

Oklahoma retained most of its top-drawer personnel—All-America guard Bo Bolinger was a notable exception—for 1956, and the Sooners were expected to ride roughshod over the opposition. Wilkinson's charges didn't disappoint. In the first three games of the season, they recorded crunching shutouts. North Carolina lost by 36 points, Kansas State absorbed a 66-point pounding and Texas succumbed by 45. Sooner opponents had been held scoreless in seven straight regular-season contests.

Defense was always close to Wilkinson's heart. The Sooners' coach used to tell his players that a team would get 13 or 14 first-and-10 opportunities per game, and that it was imperative not to blow even one of those chances on either side of the ball. "One time, against Texas," Wilkinson remembered, "our defense came off the field after the first successful stop and was yelling, 'Just 12 more (possessions) to go.' Another stop and it was '11 to go.' Then '10 to go'. . . ."

After a 34-12 victory over Kansas stretched Oklahoma's winning streak to 34 games, five short of equaling the major-college record established by the 1908-1914 Washington Huskies, the Sooners prepared for a get-together in South Bend, Ind., against Notre Dame. The Fighting Irish, off to a 1-3 start, had won the only two games ever played between the Sooners and the Irish—and those Notre Dame triumphs denied Wilkinson's team undefeated seasons in 1952 and 1953.

History would not repeat. Notre Dame, despite the presence of Heisman Trophy-winner-to-be Paul Hornung, was playing out of its league this time around. McDonald and junior Clendon Thomas, who would combine for 1,670 yards rushing before the season was over, showed their defensive prowess in this game with 55- and 35-yard interception returns for touchdowns. A blocked punt led to another Oklahoma score, and the Sooners frolicked, 40-0, on a day in which their offense was a tad sluggish (235 yards overall) but their defense played at the top of its game.

Oklahoma's next contest, in Boulder, Colo., was enough to give Wilkinson heartburn. The Sooners, extended once more by the Colorado Buffaloes, found themselves on the short end of a 19-6 score at halftime. But given a tremendous lift by a successful fourth-down gamble early in the third quarter—the Sooners went for a first down from their own 28-yard line and got three yards when they needed

Oklahoma's Larry Grigg, getting a key block from Outland Trophy winner J.D. Roberts (64), heads for the lone TD scored in the 1954 Orange Bowl.

two—Oklahoma roared back for three second-half touchdowns and a 27-19 victory.

Asked about the fourth-down call many years afterward, Wilkinson couldn't recall whether he or quarterback Harris had made the risky decision—but he emphasized that it didn't make any difference. "I was always confident that the quarterback would be prepared enough to think like the coach," Wilkinson said. "Whatever was done, we were in agreement."

The remainder of the 1956 season was a romp for the Sooners, who manhandled Iowa State by 44 points, Missouri by 53 and Nebraska by 48 before setting a major-college mark with their 40th straight victory, a 53-0 pasting of Oklahoma A&M.

Once again, the Sooners were voted No. 1 in the land by both major wire services (but there would be no bowl game, because of a no-repeat rule in

While assistant coach Gomer Jones (wearing hat) appears overcome by the Sooners' continued success, Wilkinson and his players engage in some revelry.

existence at the time). Once again, they put up eye-popping numbers, as evidenced by their nation-leading figures of 481.7 yards per game in total offense and 391 yards per outing on the ground (increases of more than 70 and 60 yards, respectively, over their 1955 averages). Also, Oklahoma's 46.6 scoring average was a little more than 10 points higher than its '55 mark.

Clendon Thomas, who averaged 7.9 yards per carry and rushed for 817 yards, wound up as the nation's leading scorer with 108 points. McDonald was fourth, behind Syracuse's Jim Brown and Utah State's Jack Hill, with 102 points. All-America honors went to McDonald, who paced the team in rushing with 853 yards, and center Jerry Tubbs.

While the Sooners obviously lived by the run, Harris demonstrated he could pass with considerable proficiency. The get-it-done senior quarterback put the ball into the air only 37 times all season, but finished with eight touchdown passes.

Before the start of the 1957 season, Wilkinson surveyed his losses and made this assessment: "Our main problem is to replace all the experience lost last year. We must find a left half who can play like

McDonald, a center who can 'lineback' like Tubbs, a fullback who can block like (Billy) Pricer, tackles who can succeed (Ed) Gray and (Tom) Emerson." Plus, Harris was gone.

As usual, the Sooners' mastermind came up with able replacements. Additionally, he had superstar holdovers in halfback Thomas and guard Bill Krisher, players who would win All-America recognition by season's end. There was another newsworthy member of the 1957 team: Prentice Gautt, the first black player ever to wear an Oklahoma football uniform.

Thirty years after Gautt had completed his collegiate career, Wilkinson, a man whose steadying influence affected so many lives, said, "If I had any contribution to the spirit of athletics and football, it was Prentice Gautt playing for Oklahoma."

Gautt considered Wilkinson's presence uplifting, to be sure.

"I remember the many negative letters he got for playing me," said Gautt, who was used sparingly in '57 but then ran for a total of 1,301 yards in 1958 and 1959. "But knowing he was back there supporting me made it seem like everything would be all right."

Oklahoma would stress quickness, as usual, in 1957. "We didn't lift weights, and we didn't have nutritional guidelines," said Krisher, alluding to Oklahoma's ongoing quest for team speed. "We kept our weight down and were encouraged to do so." Indeed, at 213 pounds, Krisher was one of the heaviest players on the squad.

The '57 season would mark the first in which Wilkinson would go head-to-head on the coaching sidelines against one of his favorite Sooner players, Darrell Royal. After two seasons as head coach at Mississippi State and one at Washington, Royal was now the top man at Texas.

Wilkinson appreciated Royal's all-around talents —he called him the "best kicker I've ever known or seen"—but he particularly liked his work ethic.

"It was maybe the second practice in '46 (when Wilkinson was an Oklahoma assistant) that I noticed Darrell practicing his punting after almost everyone had left," Wilkinson said. "Kickers usually work out before practice. He'd get the dummies set up and try to place the ball (into a specific area). He'd move 90 degrees, try it again, move another 90 degrees and try it again. I watched him another day, and I went to him and asked him about it. He said, 'When I'm called upon to punt after an offensive effort, I want to be able to punch the ball in there when I'm tired.'"

Royal, who would compile an outstanding record at Texas, said his first-ever coaching confrontation with Wilkinson "felt a little strange—but football is played in the spirit of sportsmanship, and there's nothing wrong with competing against your friends."

The '57 Sooners, setting their sights on the school's fourth straight perfect season, belted Pittsburgh and Iowa State, beat Royal's Longhorns by two touchdowns and walloped Kansas preceding an October 26 date with Colorado at Norman. Oklahoma had trouble with the Buffaloes, and that difficulty—while not exactly a surprise in view of the teams' past stem-winders—perhaps told a story. The Sooners might be slipping just a bit—and even if they weren't, their dominance had reached a point where fans' expectations just couldn't be met.

Oklahoma won, yes, increasing its winning streak to 45 games, but Coach Dal Ward's Buffaloes made Wilkinson and company squirm. The final score was 14-13, and only Krisher's blocking of an extra-point kick (actually, he shoved a Colorado player into the path of the ball) kept Oklahoma's string of victories intact. Sooner partisans were not pleased.

"They just don't realize we're human beings like everybody else," Oklahoma fullback Dennit Morris said in response to fans' discontent over the close call.

Colorado's knack for giving Oklahoma fits wasn't just happenstance.

"Dal understood my mental sets more than most coaches," Wilkinson said of the man who had served as freshman coach at Minnesota when Bud

Tommy McDonald lacked Oklahoma roots, but the talented halfback was a typical Sooner football player in that he possessed speed and quickness.

was a senior standout for the Gophers.

"Also, they were running the single wing when most teams weren't. It was hard to prepare for them."

The Sooners then defeated Kansas State, 13-0. A year earlier, Oklahoma had dispatched the Wildcats by a 66-0 score. Up next was Missouri, and Wilkinson voiced pessimism as his team prepared for the trip to Columbia. Missouri boasted a 5-1-1 record; furthermore, Coach Frank Broyles' Tigers would have a boisterous home crowd in their favor.

Oklahoma 39, Missouri 14. *Forty-seven* consecutive victories.

Notre Dame, still smarting from that 40-point thumping it had received at the Sooners' hands a year earlier, was eager for revenge and the Fighting

The Sooners' Clendon Thomas, the nation's leading scorer in 1956, is pursued by that season's Heisman Trophy recipient, Notre Dame's Paul Hornung (5).

Irish would get a chance to exact it on November 16 at Owen Field in Norman. While no one expected the Irish to prevail, this Notre Dame team, 4-2, was vastly superior to the '56 unit, which wound up with a 2-8 record. As formidable as the Irish seemed, though, they were coming off consecutive losses to Navy and Michigan State; Oklahoma, meanwhile, was 7-0 and an 18-point favorite.

In a monumental struggle, the teams battled through three scoreless quarters before Notre Dame slipped across the goal line in the final period on a three-yard run by Dick Lynch. The Sooners drove deep into Irish territory late in the game, only to have a pass intercepted in the end zone with 22 seconds remaining. The incredible winning streak was over. Notre Dame 7, Oklahoma 0.

"It was unique to feel a loss," Krisher recalled.

While the score didn't suggest it, the Fighting Irish dominated the action. They topped the Sooners in first downs, 17 to nine; rushing yards, 169 to 98, and passing yards, 79 to 47.

It was a shocking upset. Or was it?

"I don't feel the Notre Dame game was an upset at all," Wilkinson said in the ensuing months. "They were a better football team. It's my considered opinion that if we'd played Notre Dame 10 times, they would have won the majority of the games. A number of people would like to think that

it just happened because the law of averages caught up with us, but I don't feel that way at all.

"Our team. . .was, I think, a fine college football team, but we lacked offensive striking power. We had to rely on our opponent making some errors which would give us opportunities for touchdowns. . .Notre Dame played an errorless game, at least from the standpoint of giving us any big break."

Oklahoma went back to the business of winning the very next week, routing Nebraska, 32-7. In the regular-season finale of 1957, the Sooners went on a 53-6 tear against Oklahoma State, which had entered the league (now the Big Eight) over the summer, changed its name (from Oklahoma A&M) and awaited official entry into league competition (it first would be eligible for the conference title in 1960).

In the January 1, 1958, Orange Bowl, the final chapter in 10 seasons of storybook football would be written. Oklahoma crushed Duke, 48-21, with the Sooners' defense forcing the Blue Devils into repeated errors. A 94-yard interception return by David Baker for a touchdown got Oklahoma rolling early in the game, then the Sooners hit Duke with a 27-point final-quarter flurry. Wilkinson's bowl record was now 5-1, not bad for a guy who had warned about postseason pitfalls.

Jones (left, foreground), Wilkinson and a jubilant band of Sooners celebrate a come-from-behind 20-6 victory over Maryland in the 1956 Orange Bowl.

Winning 97 of 106 games, with two ties, in a 10-season stretch was a mind-boggling accomplishment. Wilkinson, when reflecting on Oklahoma football from 1948 through 1957, talked of many factors that he thought contributed to the dynasty.

Foremost, it seemed, was Oklahoma's ability to attract highly disciplined players. "It was a different game back then," said Wilkinson, focusing on the days of one-platoon football. "No specialists. A player ran a long pattern and, catch the ball or not, he was still in there for the next play. He might then run another long pattern and catch a touchdown pass. But he didn't come out of the game. He lined up for kick-return coverage. It took discipline."

Such nose-to-the-grindstone effort was evident in practice. "Everybody has the will to win on game day," Wilkinson said. "What you need is the will to prepare before that. You need the will to win when there are no marching bands around and no fans in the stands."

The Oklahoma players exhibited just such an attitude. The fact that much of their zeal no doubt was instilled by Wilkinson was something the Sooners' coach was reluctant to talk about over the years. Others weren't.

"Coach Wilkinson had the ability to get you to excel over and above what you normally could be expected to do," Krisher said. "He had a great pride in his players. He could generate enthusiasm, keep you motivated and get the most out of his players."

"He had a way of talking to the team that made it seem almost like he was talking to each player individually," Gautt recalled. "It wasn't one of those tear-jerkers. It was matter-of-fact. He wanted you to reach down inside of yourself and see what you could pull out."

Clendon Thomas called Wilkinson "the best motivator that I was ever around."

"He makes you want to win for yourself," Green said while serving as a Missouri assistant under Broyles. "He doesn't try to get you to do it for him, or for the school, or for the state of Oklahoma...And when he tells you that a club which has lost all its games can still beat you, he means it. He believes what he says."

Green, zeroing in on Wilkinson's be-prepared motto, added: "The biggest secret of his success is the fact that he is one of the hardest-working people I've ever seen."

In Harris' opinion, the mid-'50s Sooners "were great athletes for our time, but the spark was that Bud was so well-organized."

Calame lauded the Oklahoma coaching staff, saying it was far ahead of its time. "We would break into small groups at practice," Calame recalled, "and work five minutes on this and five minutes on that. Special instruction. Other schools were scrimmaging all the time, and they usually left their game on the practice field."

Calame, praised by Wilkinson for his on-field awareness (the quarterback's "sensitivity to what was going on was the greatest I've ever seen"), credited the Oklahoma coach for developing such a trait.

"The players spent hours and hours with Coach Wilkinson," Calame said. "He was very thorough

Oklahoma's dynasty was winding down when Wilkinson got together with the co-captains of the 1957 Sooners, Thomas (left) and Don Stiller.

about various and sundry things he wanted the offense to do. And doing those things just became automatic."

Heath called Wilkinson "one of the greatest. He was a great leader, got the most he could out of his talent...As for the beginning (of Oklahoma's dynasty), it was the coaching, plus the combination of young players and the more-developed players who were back from the war."

McDonald, a rare Sooner in that he was from neither Oklahoma nor Texas (which supplied some key Sooners during this era), said that "the minute I met Bud Wilkinson, I knew that's where I wanted to go to school." The New Mexican added: "He is so down-to-earth, and there is not a phony bone in his body...You were so overwhelmed by his personality and his honesty and his coaching record that you didn't want to go anywhere else."

An often-overlooked element in the Sooners' winning ways, according to Wilkinson, was the commitment to excellence of the state's high school athletes.

"There wasn't an awful lot to do in Oklahoma in those days, really, other than athletics," Wilkinson observed. "Kids wanted to play, and they wanted to be good. There was a numerical distortion, population-wise (in the state's ability to turn out exceptional prep players)." The coach proceeded to point out how Hollis, Okla., a town of about 3,000 in the late 1940s, had four players—Heath, Royal, Leon Manley and J.W. Cole—on the Sooners' unbeaten 1949 team.

"It was an outstanding coaching staff," Royal said of Wilkinson and company. "Any such streaks (31 and 47 games) tell you that."

The staff was so successful and influential that many Oklahoma players wound up as coaches in their own right—including the likes of Royal, Jim Owens, Eddie Crowder, Jack Mitchell, Wade Walker, Bert Clark, Dee Andros and J.D. Roberts.

"Their experience at Oklahoma was very important," Wilkinson allowed in a rare moment of self-tribute. "Enough felt that maybe they could teach habits of living and conduct, too. Being part of a winning tradition, they thought that 'I also can win.'"

Royal acknowledged that while many Oklahoma players were attracted to coaching once they were under the Wilkinson spell, he saw it as a career objective all along. "I'd go from coach to coach on the sidelines," Royal explained, "and ask why they were doing this or that. I wanted to coach."

The Sooners lost only one game in 1958, a one-point decision to Royal's Texas team, and then compiled a 7-3 record in 1959, a year in which they suffered their first conference loss in 75 games. It was about at this juncture that Wilkinson said he made a fundamental mistake. As other programs were showing considerable improvement and expanding their horizons in the search for talent, Oklahoma continued to limit itself to regional recruiting. "I just did not realize we had the reputa-

The telltale scoreboard and the triumphant ride of Notre Dame Coach Terry Brennan signaled the end of Oklahoma's 47-game winning streak.

tion to really recruit nationally," said Wilkinson, whose program suffered a sizable decline in quality athletes.

The bottom dropped out in 1960 when the team plummeted to a 3-6-1 record, but a 5-5 mark in 1961 was followed by 8-3 and 8-2 ledgers the next two seasons. By now, Wilkinson had taken on a new challenge. In addition to his duties in Norman, he was serving as President John F. Kennedy's chief consultant in the national physical-fitness program.

When the 1963 season concluded, Bud Wilkinson's record in 17 seasons at Oklahoma stood at 145-29-4. And there it would remain. Ready for a yet another kind of challenge, Wilkinson resigned first as football coach and soon thereafter as athletic director to seek a seat in the U.S. Senate. Running in 1964 as a Republican, Wilkinson lost a tight race in Oklahoma in what was a nationwide landslide year for Democrats (with President Lyndon B. Johnson's electoral thrashing of Barry Goldwater setting the tone).

There were more challenges to come, including a consultant position in the Nixon Administration, broadcast duties, business ventures and, after being away from the sidelines for 15 years, a surprising stint as coach of the St. Louis Cardinals of the National Football League. Never one to dwell on the past, Wilkinson, more than 25 years after leaving the Oklahoma campus as a football legend, reflected on the major occurrences in his life—the high points, the higher yet and even the not-so-high—and viewed each in the measured terms of "that's something I've done." And then this man, still active in the business world at age 73, prepared to look ahead.

Always preparing, that's Bud Wilkinson. Always prepared, that's the legacy of his Oklahoma football teams.

The Authors

Mike Bauman (Green Bay Packers) is a sports columnist for the Milwaukee Journal. After receiving a master's degree in journalism from the University of Wisconsin in 1972, he began his newspaper career with the Wisconsin State Journal before moving to the Milwaukee Journal in 1977 as a political and investigative reporter. Bauman, a native of Green Bay, moved into sports in 1982, covering the Packers and Brewers, and became a full-time columnist in '85.

Tim Burke (Montreal Canadiens) is a sports columnist for the Montreal Daily News. He began his newspaper career in 1954 for the Montreal Herald as a city reporter and moved into sports 18 years later as a hockey writer. The St. Patrick's (Ottawa) graduate also worked for the Ottawa Journal, the Montreal Star and the Montreal Gazette in a career that has spanned 35 years.

Pat Calabria (New York Islanders) is a sportswriter for Long Island-based Newsday. He began his newspaper career in 1972 covering high school and college sports before moving to the Islander beat in '75. The Hofstra University graduate covered the Islanders through their championship years before moving on to tennis and other sports in 1986.

Jack Etkin (New York Yankees), a sportswriter with the Kansas City Star and Times, has written extensively about baseball. As a beat writer, he covered the Kansas City Royals in 1986 and 1987. He is the author of "Innings Ago: Recollections by Kansas City Ballplayers of Their Days in the Game." Etkin received an economics degree from Union College in Schenectady, N.Y., in 1968 and a master's degree in business from the University of Pennsylvania three years later. He joined the Star and Times in 1978.

Chuck Finder (Pittsburgh Steelers) has dabbled in a little bit of everything during his six-year sportswriting career. The 1983 Missouri graduate has covered football, basketball, baseball and other sports for the Atlanta Journal-Constitution, the Birmingham News and, since 1985, the Pittsburgh Post-Gazette. He was born and raised outside Pittsburgh in Washington, Pa.

Joe Gergen (Brooklyn Dodgers) is a sports columnist for Long Island-based Newsday. The Brooklyn native and Boston College graduate has concentrated on baseball and pro football in his 20 years at Newsday, with side trips into just about every other sport imaginable. Gergen, who began his journalism career 26 years ago with United Press International in New York, has written four books, the most recent of which, "The Final Four," was published in 1987 by The Sporting News.

Joe Hoppel (Oklahoma Sooners) is an associate editor of The Sporting News. A University of Montana journalism graduate, he was with the Billings (Mont.) Gazette in 1966 and then worked as a copy editor at the Denver Post for 11 years before becoming a member of the sports staff of the Kansas City Star in 1979. Hoppel joined the book department of The Sporting News in 1982. In 1975, he wrote "Bronco Bible," a narrative and statistical history of the Denver Broncos.

Roland Lazenby (Boston Celtics) is a free-lance writer based in Roanoke, Va. He has written 16 books, including three with college basketball analyst Billy Packer. His latest title with Packer, "College Basketball's 25 Greatest Teams," was just released by The Sporting News. Lazenby, author of "The Boston Celtics Greenbook" and "The Detroit Pistons," is a former newspaper reporter who has written for numerous sports publications.

Bill Moor (Notre Dame) is the sports editor and columnist for the South Bend Tribune. The 1971 Indiana graduate began working at the Tribune as a sportswriter and was promoted to assistant sports editor three years later. He has held the title of sports editor for the last eight years. Moor has been associated with Notre Dame football for 15 years, either covering the Irish beat or writing columns.

Dave Newhouse (Cleveland Browns) is an author, a sports columnist for the Oakland Tribune and a sports talk-show host for a radio station in San Francisco. The San Jose State graduate has written three books, including "Heismen, After the Glory" for The Sporting News in 1985. Newhouse has covered a variety of sports as well as California and Southern Cal football during his 25-year sportswriting career.

Nick Peters (UCLA Bruins) covered Pacific-10 Conference sports for more than 20 years. He has been covering the San Francisco Giants for the Sacramento Bee since coming to the publication in 1988 and covers college basketball during the winter months. He spent nine years with the Oakland Tribune before moving to Sacramento.

Steve Springer (Los Angeles Lakers) is a sportswriter for the Los Angeles Times. The Cal State Northridge graduate began his newspaper career with the Thousand Oaks News Chronicle and then covered the Lakers for the Orange County Register for 3½ years. He has been covering professional football and boxing for the Times for the last five years. Springer is co-author of "Winnin' Times," a book about the Lakers, with Times columnist Scott Ostler.